D1234894

THE PRACTICE OF EVERYDAY LIFE

THE PRACTICE OF
EVERYDAY LIFE

Michel de Certeau

Translated by Steven Rendall

UNIVERSITY OF CALIFORNIA PRESS

Berkeley   Los Angeles   London

UNIVERSITY OF CALIFORNIA PRESS
Berkeley and Los Angeles, California

UNIVERSITY OF CALIFORNIA PRESS, LTD.
London, England

First Paperback Printing 1988

Library of Congress Cataloging in Publication Data

Certeau, Michel de.
  The practice of everyday life.

  Translation of: Arts de faire.
  1. Social history—Addresses, essays, lectures.
1. Title.
HN8.C4313   1984   909   83-18070
ISBN 0-520-06168-3

Printed in the United States of America

08 07 06 05 04 03 02 01 00
12 11 10 9 8

The paper used in this publication is both acid-free and totally
chlorine-free (TCF). It meets the minimum requirements of
ANSI/NISO Z39.48-1992 (R 1997) (*Permanence of Paper*). ∞

To the ordinary man.

To a common hero, an ubiquitous character, walking in countless thousands on the streets. In invoking here at the outset of my narratives the absent figure who provides both their beginning and their necessity, I inquire into the desire whose impossible object he represents. What are we asking this oracle whose voice is almost indistinguishable from the rumble of history to license us, to authorize us to say, when we dedicate to him the writing that one formerly offered in praise of the gods or the inspiring muses?

This anonymous hero is very ancient. He is the murmuring voice of societies. In all ages, he comes before texts. He does not expect representations. He squats now at the center of our scientific stages. The floodlights have moved away from the actors who possess proper names and social blazons, turning first toward the chorus of secondary characters, then settling on the mass of the audience. The increasingly sociological and anthropological perspective of inquiry privileges the anonymous and the everyday in which zoom lenses cut out metonymic details—parts taken for the whole. Slowly the representatives that formerly symbolized families, groups, and orders disappear from the stage they dominated during the epoch of the name. We witness the advent of the number. It comes along with democracy, the large city, administrations, cybernetics. It is a flexible and continuous mass, woven tight like a fabric with neither rips nor darned patches, a multitude of quantified heroes who lose names and faces as they become the ciphered river of the streets, a mobile language of computations and rationalities that belong to no one.

Contents

Contents

Preface to the English Translation

In translation, analyses that an author would fain believe universal are traced back to nothing more than the expression of local or—as it almost begins to seem—exotic experience. And yet in highlighting that which is specifically French in the daily practices that are the basis and the object of this study, publication in English only reinforces my thesis. For what I really wish to work out is *a science of singularity*; that is to say, a science of the relationship that links everyday pursuits to particular circumstances. And only in the *local* network of labor and recreation can one grasp how, within a grid of socio-economic constraints, these pursuits unfailingly establish relational tactics (a struggle for life), artistic creations (an aesthetic), and autonomous initiatives (an ethic). The characteristically subtle logic of these "ordinary" activities comes to light only in the details. And hence it seems to me that this analysis, as its bond to another culture is rendered more explicit, will only be assisted in leading readers to uncover for themselves, in their own situation, their own tactics, their own creations, and their own initiatives.

This translation represents just one part of a series of investigations directed by the author. Another part—*L'invention du quotidien, 2. Habiter, cuisiner* by Luce Giard and Pierre Mayol—has already been published in French (Paris, 1980). It deals with the fundamental practices of a "fine art of dwelling," in which places are organized in a network of history and relationship, and a "fine art of cooking," in which everyday skill turns nourishment into a language of the body and the body's memories. We have here two ways to "make a world." Other, still-to-be-published parts of *The Practice of Everyday Life* deal principally with "the fine art of talk" in the everyday practices of language.

The first two parts of the present volume are the more theoretic. They envision the definition and the situation, in the context of current research, of the problematic common to this set of investigations. The opening chapters, therefore, can be read separately, after the ensuing more concrete analyses, as outlined in Chapter Three.

Steven Rendall has succeeded in the long and painstaking enterprise of leading this population of French experiences and expressions on its migration into the English language. He has my warm thanks, as do Luce Giard, who was "a guide for the perplexed" in the revision of the translation, and John Miles, who has kindly attended to so many details along the route. For the rest, the work may symbolize the object of my study: within the bounds imposed by another language and another culture, the art of translation smuggles in a thousand inventions which, before the author's dazzled eyes, transform his book into a new creation.

La Jolla, California
26 February 1984

General Introduction

T HIS ESSAY IS part of a continuing investigation of the ways in which users—commonly assumed to be passive and guided by established rules—operate. The point is not so much to discuss this elusive yet fundamental subject as to make such a discussion possible; that is, by means of inquiries and hypotheses, to indicate pathways for further research. This goal will be achieved if everyday practices, "ways of operating" or doing things, no longer appear as merely the obscure background of social activity, and if a body of theoretical questions, methods, categories, and perspectives, by penetrating this obscurity, make it possible to articulate them.

The examination of such practices does not imply a return to individuality. The social atomism which over the past three centuries has served as the historical axiom of social analysis posits an elementary unit—the individual—on the basis of which groups are supposed to be formed and to which they are supposed to be always reducible. This axiom, which has been challenged by more than a century of sociological, economic, anthropological, and psychoanalytic research, (although in history that is perhaps no argument) plays no part in this study. Analysis shows that a relation (always social) determines its terms, and not the reverse, and that each individual is a locus in which an incoherent (and often contradictory) plurality of such relational determinations interact. Moreover, the question at hand concerns modes of operation or schemata of action, and not directly the subjects (or persons) who are their authors or vehicles. It concerns an operational logic whose models may go as far back as the age-old ruses of fishes and insects that disguise or transform themselves in order to survive, and which has in any case been concealed by the form of rationality currently dominant in Western culture. The purpose of this work is to make explicit the systems of operational combination (*les combinatoires d'opérations*) which also compose a "culture," and to bring to light the models of action characteristic of users whose status as the dominated

xi

element in society (a status that does not mean that they are either passive or docile) is concealed by the euphemistic term "consumers." Everyday life invents itself by *poaching* in countless ways on the property of others.

1. Consumer production

Since this work grew out of studies of "popular culture" or marginal groups,[1] the investigation of everyday practices was first delimited negatively by the necessity of not locating cultural *difference* in groups associated with the "counter-culture"—groups that were already singled out, often privileged, and already partly absorbed into folklore—and that were no more than symptoms or indexes. Three further, positive determinations were particularly important in articulating our research.

Usage, or consumption

Many, often remarkable, works have sought to study the representations of a society, on the one hand, and its modes of behavior, on the other. Building on our knowledge of these social phenomena, it seems both possible and necessary to determine the *use* to which they are put by groups or individuals. For example, the analysis of the images broadcast by television (representation) and of the time spent watching television (behavior) should be complemented by a study of what the cultural consumer "makes" or "does" during this time and with these images. The same goes for the use of urban space, the products purchased in the supermarket, the stories and legends distributed by the newspapers, and so on.

The "making" in question is a production, a *poiēsis*[2]—but a hidden one, because it is scattered over areas defined and occupied by systems of "production" (television, urban development, commerce, etc.), and because the steadily increasing expansion of these systems no longer leaves "consumers" any *place* in which they can indicate what they *make* or *do* with the products of these systems. To a rationalized, expansionist and at the same time centralized, clamorous, and spectacular production corresponds *another* production, called "consumption." The latter is devious, it is dispersed, but it insinuates itself everywhere, silently and almost invisibly, because it does not manifest itself through its own products, but rather through its *ways of using* the products imposed by a dominant economic order.

For instance, the ambiguity that subverted from within the Spanish colonizers' "success" in imposing their own culture on the indigenous Indians is well known. Submissive, and even consenting to their subjection, the Indians nevertheless often *made of* the rituals, representations, and laws imposed on them something quite different from what their conquerors had in mind; they subverted them not by rejecting or altering them, but by using them with respect to ends and references foreign to the system they had no choice but to accept. They were *other* within the very colonization that outwardly assimilated them; their use of the dominant social order deflected its power, which they lacked the means to challenge; they escaped it without leaving it. The strength of their difference lay in procedures of "consumption." To a lesser degree, a similar ambiguity creeps into our societies through the use made by the "common people" of the culture disseminated and imposed by the "elites" producing the language.

The presence and circulation of a representation (taught by preachers, educators, and popularizers as the key to socioeconomic advancement) tells us nothing about what it is for its users. We must first analyze its manipulation by users who are not its makers. Only then can we gauge the difference or similarity between the production of the image and the secondary production hidden in the process of its utilization.

Our investigation is concerned with this difference. It can use as its theoretical model the *construction* of individual sentences with an *established* vocabulary and syntax. In linguistics, "performance" and "competence" are different: the act of speaking (with all the enunciative strategies that implies) is not reducible to a knowledge of the language. By adopting the point of view of enunciation—which is the subject of our study—we privilege the act of speaking; according to that point of view, speaking operates within the field of a linguistic system; it effects an appropriation, or reappropriation, of language by its speakers; it establishes a *present* relative to a time and place; and it posits a *contract with the other* (the interlocutor) in a network of places and relations. These four characteristics of the speech act[3] can be found in many other practices (walking, cooking, etc.). An objective is at least adumbrated by this parallel, which is, as we shall see, only partly valid. Such an objective assumes that (like the Indians mentioned above) users make (*bricolent*)

innumerable and infinitesimal transformations of and within the dominant cultural economy in order to adapt it to their own interests and
their own rules. We must determine the procedures, bases, effects, and
possibilities of this collective activity.

The procedures of everyday creativity

A second orientation of our investigation can be explained by reference
to Michel Foucault's *Discipline and Punish*. In this work, instead of
analyzing the apparatus exercising power (i.e., the localizable, expansionist, repressive, and legal institutions), Foucault analyzes the mechanisms (*dispositifs*) that have sapped the strength of these institutions and
surreptitiously reorganized the functioning of power: "miniscule" technical procedures acting on and with details, redistributing a discursive
space in order to make it the means of a generalized "discipline" (*surveillance*).[4] This approach raises a new and different set of problems to
be investigated. Once again, however, this "microphysics of power"
privileges the productive apparatus (which produces the "discipline"),
even though it discerns in "education" a system of "repression" and
shows how, from the wings as it were, silent technologies determine or
short-circuit institutional stage directions. If it is true that the grid of
"discipline" is everywhere becoming clearer and more extensive, it is all
the more urgent to discover how an entire society resists being reduced
to it, what popular procedures (also "miniscule" and quotidian) manipulate the mechanisms of discipline and conform to them only in order to
evade them, and finally, what "ways of operating" form the counterpart,
on the consumer's (or "dominee's"?) side, of the mute processes that
organize the establishment of socioeconomic order.

   These "ways of operating" constitute the innumerable practices by
means of which users reappropriate the space organized by techniques of
sociocultural production. They pose questions at once analogous and
contrary to those dealt with in Foucault's book: analogous, in that the
goal is to perceive and analyze the microbe-like operations proliferating
within technocratic structures and deflecting their functioning by means
of a multitude of "tactics" articulated in the details of everyday life;
contrary, in that the goal is not to make clearer how the violence of
order is transmuted into a disciplinary technology, but rather to bring to
light the clandestine forms taken by the dispersed, tactical, and makeshift creativity of groups or individuals already caught in the nets of

"discipline." Pushed to their ideal limits, these procedures and ruses of consumers compose the network of an antidiscipline[5] which is the subject of this book.

The formal structure of practice

It may be supposed that these operations—multiform and fragmentary, relative to situations and details, insinuated into and concealed within devices whose mode of usage they constitute, and thus lacking their own ideologies or institutions—conform to certain rules. In other words, there must be a logic of these practices. We are thus confronted once again by the ancient problem: What is an *art* or "way of making"? From the Greeks to Durkheim, a long tradition has sought to describe with precision the complex (and not at all simple or "impoverished") rules that could account for these operations.[6] From this point of view, "popular culture," as well as a whole literature called "popular,"[7] take on a different aspect: they present themselves essentially as "arts of making" this or that, i.e., as combinatory or utilizing modes of consumption. These practices bring into play a "popular" *ratio*, a way of thinking invested in a way of acting, an art of combination which cannot be dissociated from an art of using.

In order to grasp the formal structure of these practices, I have carried out two sorts of investigations. The first, more descriptive in nature, has concerned certain ways of making that were selected according to their value for the strategy of the analysis, and with a view to obtaining fairly differentiated variants: readers' practices, practices related to urban spaces, utilizations of everyday rituals, re-uses and functions of the memory through the "authorities" that make possible (or permit) everyday practices, etc. In addition, two related investigations have tried to trace the intricate forms of the operations proper to the recompositon of a space (the Croix-Rousse quarter in Lyons) by familial practices, on the one hand, and on the other, to the tactics of the art of cooking, which simultaneously organizes a network of relations, poetic ways of "making do" (*bricolage*), and a re-use of marketing structures.[8]

The second series of investigations has concerned the scientific literature that might furnish hypotheses allowing the logic of unselfconscious thought to be taken seriously. Three areas are of special interest. First, sociologists, anthropologists, and indeed historians (from E. Goffman to P. Bourdieu, from Mauss to M. Détienne, from J. Boissevain to E. O.

Laumann) have elaborated a theory of such practices, mixtures of rituals and makeshifts (*bricolages*), manipulations of spaces, operators of networks.[9] Second, in the wake of J. Fishman's work, the ethnomethodological and sociolinguistic investigations of H. Garfinkel, W. Labov, H. Sachs, E. A. Schegloff, and others have described the procedures of everyday interactions relative to structures of expectation, negotiation, and improvisation proper to ordinary language.[10]

Finally, in addition to the semiotics and philosophies of "convention" (from O. Ducrot to D. Lewis),[11] we must look into the ponderous formal logics and their extension, in the field of analytical philosophy, into the domains of action (G. H. von Wright, A. C. Danto, R. J. Bernstein),[12] time (A. N. Prior, N. Rescher and J. Urquhart),[13] and modalisation (G. E. Hughes and M. J. Cresswell, A. R. White).[14] These extensions yield a weighty apparatus seeking to grasp the delicate layering and plasticity of ordinary language, with its almost orchestral combinations of logical elements (temporalization, modalization, injunctions, predicates of action, etc.) whose dominants are determined in turn by circumstances and conjunctural demands. An investigation analogous to Chomsky's study of the oral uses of language must seek to restore to everyday practices their logical and cultural legitimacy, at least in the sectors—still very limited—in which we have at our disposal the instruments necessary to account for them.[15] This kind of research is complicated by the fact that these practices themselves alternately exacerbate and disrupt our logics. Its regrets are like those of the poet, and like him, it struggles against oblivion: "And I forgot the element of chance introduced by circumstances, calm or haste, sun or cold, dawn or dusk, the taste of strawberries or abandonment, the half-understood message, the front page of newspapers, the voice on the telephone, the most anodyne conversation, the most anonymous man or woman, everything that speaks, makes noise, passes by, touches us lightly, meets us head on."[16]

The marginality of a majority

These three determinations make possible an exploration of the cultural field, an exploration defined by an investigative problematics and punctuated by more detailed inquiries located by reference to hypotheses that remain to be verified. Such an exploration will seek to situate the types of *operations* characterizing consumption in the framework of an economy, and to discern in these practices of appropriation indexes of the creativity that flourishes at the very point where practice ceases to have its own language.

Marginality is today no longer limited to minority groups, but is rather massive and pervasive; this cultural activity of the non-producers of culture, an activity that is unsigned, unreadable, and unsymbolized, remains the only one possible for all those who nevertheless buy and pay for the showy products through which a productivist economy articulates itself. Marginality is becoming universal. A marginal group has now become a silent majority.

That does not mean the group is homogeneous. The procedures allowing the re-use of products are linked together in a kind of obligatory language, and their functioning is related to social situations and power relationships. Confronted by images on television, the immigrant worker does not have the same critical or creative elbow-room as the average citizen. On the same terrain, his inferior access to information, financial means, and compensations of all kinds elicits an increased deviousness, fantasy, or laughter. Similar strategic deployments, when acting on different relationships of force, do not produce identical effects. Hence the necessity of differentiating both the "actions" or "engagements" (in the military sense) that the system of products effects within the consumer grid, *and* the various kinds of room to maneuver left for consumers by the situations in which they exercise their "art."

The relation of procedures to the fields of force in which they act must therefore lead to a *polemological* analysis of culture. Like law (one of its models), culture articulates conflicts and alternately legitimizes, displaces, or controls the superior force. It develops in an atmosphere of tensions, and often of violence, for which it provides symbolic balances, contracts of compatibility and compromises, all more or less temporary. The tactics of consumption, the ingenious ways in which the weak make use of the strong, thus lend a political dimension to everyday practices.

2. The tactics of practice

In the course of our research, the scheme, rather too neatly dichotomized, of the relations between consumers and the mechanisms of production has been diversified in relation to three kinds of concerns: the search for a problematics that could articulate the material collected; the description of a limited number of practices (reading, talking, walking, dwelling, cooking, etc.) considered to be particularly significant; and the extension of the analysis of these everyday operations to scientific fields apparently governed by another kind of logic. Through the presentation of our investigation along these three lines, the overly schematic character of the general statement can be somewhat nuanced.

Trajectories, tactics, and rhetorics

As unrecognized producers, poets of their own acts, silent discoverers of their own paths in the jungle of functionalist rationality, consumers produce through their signifying practices something that might be considered similar to the "wandering lines" ("*lignes d'erre*") drawn by the autistic children studied by F. Deligny (17): "indirect" or "errant" trajectories obeying their own logic. In the technocratically constructed, written, and functionalized space in which the consumers move about, their trajectories form unforeseeable sentences, partly unreadable paths across a space. Although they are composed with the vocabularies of established languages (those of television, newspapers, supermarkets, or museum sequences) and although they remain subordinated to the prescribed syntactical forms (temporal modes of schedules, paradigmatic orders of spaces, etc.), the trajectories trace out the ruses of other interests and desires that are neither determined nor captured by the systems in which they develop.[18]

Even statistical investigation remains virtually ignorant of these trajectories, since it is satisfied with classifying, calculating, and putting into tables the "lexical" units which compose them but to which they cannot be reduced, and with doing this in reference to its own categories and taxonomies. Statistical investigation grasps the material of these practices, but not their *form*; it determines the elements used, but not the "phrasing" produced by the *bricolage* (the artisan-like inventiveness) and the discursiveness that combine these elements, which are all in general circulation and rather drab. Statistical inquiry, in breaking down these "efficacious meanderings" into units that it defines itself, in reorganizing the results of its analyses according to its own codes, "finds" only the homogenous. The power of its calculations lies in its ability to divide, but it is precisely through this ana-lytic fragmentation that it loses sight of what it claims to seek and to represent.[19]

"Trajectory" suggests a movement, but it also involves a plane projection, a flattening out. It is a transcription. A graph (which the eye can master) is substituted for an operation; a line which can be reversed (i.e., read in both directions) does duty for an irreversible temporal series, a tracing for acts. To avoid this reduction, I resort to a distinction between *tactics* and *strategies.*

I call a "strategy" the calculus of force-relationships which becomes possible when a subject of will and power (a proprietor, an enterprise, a city, a scientific institution) can be isolated from an "environment." A strategy assumes a place that can be circumscribed as *proper* (*propre*) and thus serve as the basis for generating relations with an exterior distinct from it (competitors, adversaries, "clientèles," "targets," or "objects" of research). Political, economic, and scientific rationality has been constructed on this strategic model.

I call a "tactic," on the other hand, a calculus which cannot count on a "proper" (a spatial or institutional localization), nor thus on a border-line distinguishing the other as a visible totality. The place of a tactic belongs to the other.[20] A tactic insinuates itself into the other's place, fragmentarily, without taking it over in its entirety, without being able to keep it at a distance. It has at its disposal no base where it can capitalize on its advantages, prepare its expansions, and secure independence with respect to circumstances. The "proper" is a victory of space over time. On the contrary, because it does not have a place, a tactic depends on time—it is always on the watch for opportunities that must be seized "on the wing." Whatever it wins, it does not keep. It must constantly manipulate events in order to turn them into "opportunities." The weak must continually turn to their own ends forces alien to them. This is achieved in the propitious moments when they are able to combine heterogeneous elements (thus, in the supermarket, the housewife confronts heterogeneous and mobile data—what she has in the refrigerator, the tastes, appetites, and moods of her guests, the best buys and their possible combinations with what she already has on hand at home, etc.); the intellectual synthesis of these given elements takes the form, however, not of a discourse, but of the decision itself, the act and manner in which the opportunity is "seized."

Many everyday practices (talking, reading, moving about, shopping, cooking, etc.) are tactical in character. And so are, more generally, many "ways of operating": victories of the "weak" over the "strong" (whether the strength be that of powerful people or the violence of things or of an imposed order, etc.), clever tricks, knowing how to get away with things, "hunter's cunning," maneuvers, polymorphic simulations, joyful discoveries, poetic as well as warlike. The Greeks called these "ways of operating" *mētis.*[21] But they go much further back, to the immemorial intelligence displayed in the tricks and imitations of plants and fishes. From the depths of the ocean to the streets of modern megalopolises, there is a continuity and permanence in these tactics.

In our societies, as local stabilities break down, it is as if, no longer fixed by a circumscribed community, tactics wander out of orbit, making consumers into immigrants in a system too vast to be their own, too tightly woven for them to escape from it. But these tactics introduce a Brownian movement into the system. They also show the extent to which intelligence is inseparable from the everyday struggles and plea-sures that it articulates. Strategies, in contrast, conceal beneath objective calculations their connection with the power that sustains them from within the stronghold of its own "proper" place or institution.

The discipline of rhetoric offers models for differentiating among the types of tactics. This is not surprising, since, on the one hand, it describes the "turns" or tropes of which language can be both the site and the object, and, on the other hand, these manipulations are related to the ways of changing (seducing, persuading, making use of) the will of another (the audience).[22] For these two reasons, rhetoric, the science of the "ways of speaking," offers an array of figure-types for the analysis of everyday ways of acting even though such analysis is in theory excluded from scientific discourse. Two logics of action (the one tactical, the other strategic) arise from these two facets of practicing language. In the space of a language (as in that of games), a society makes more explicit the formal rules of action and the operations that differentiate them.

In the enormous rhetorical corpus devoted to the art of speaking or operating, the Sophists have a privileged place, from the point of view of tactics. Their principle was, according to the Greek rhetorician Corax, to make the weaker position seem the stronger, and they claimed to have the power of turning the tables on the powerful by the way in which they made use of the opportunities offered by the particular situation.[23] Moreover, their theories inscribe tactics in a long tradition of reflection on the relationships between reason and particular actions and situations. Passing by way of *The Art of War* by the Chinese author Sun Tzu[24] or the Arabic anthology, *The Book of Tricks*,[25] this tradition of a logic articulated on situations and the will of others continues into contemporary sociolinguistics.

Reading, talking, dwelling, cooking, etc.

To describe these everyday practices that produce without capitalizing, that is, without taking control over time, one starting point seemed inevitable because it is the "exorbitant" focus of contemporary culture and its consumption: *reading*. From TV to newspapers, from advertising to all sorts of mercantile epiphanies, our society is characterized by a cancerous growth of vision, measuring everything by its ability to show or be shown and transmuting communication into a visual journey. It is a sort of *epic* of the eye and of the impulse to read. The economy itself, transformed into a "semeiocracy" (26), encourages a hypertrophic development of reading. Thus, for the binary set production-consumption, one would substitute its more general equivalent: writing-reading. Reading (an image or a text), moreover, seems to constitute the maximal development of the passivity assumed to characterize the consumer, who is conceived of as a voyeur (whether troglodytic or itinerant) in a "show biz society."[27]

In reality, the activity of reading has on the contrary all the characteristics of a silent production: the drift across the page, the metamorphosis of the text effected by the wandering eyes of the reader, the improvisation and expectation of meanings inferred from a few words, leaps over written spaces in an ephemeral dance. But since he is incapable of stockpiling (unless he writes or records), the reader cannot protect himself against the erosion of time (while reading, he forgets himself and he forgets what he has read) unless he buys the object (book, image) which is no more than a substitute (the spoor or promise) of moments "lost" in reading. He insinuates into another person's text the ruses of pleasure and appropriation: he poaches on it, is transported into it, pluralizes himself in it like the internal rumblings of one's body. Ruse, metaphor, arrangement, this production is also an "invention" of the memory. Words become the outlet or product of silent histories. The readable transforms itself into the memorable: Barthes reads Proust in Stendhal's text;[28] the viewer reads the landscape of his childhood in the evening news. The thin film of writing becomes a movement of strata, a play of spaces. A different world (the reader's) slips into the author's place.

This mutation makes the text habitable, like a rented apartment. It transforms another person's property into a space borrowed for a moment by a transient. Renters make comparable changes in an apartment they furnish with their acts and memories; as do speakers, in the language into which they insert both the messages of their native tongue and, through their accent, through their own "turns of phrase," etc., their own history; as do pedestrians, in the streets they fill with the forests of their desires and goals. In the same way the users of social codes turn them into metaphors and ellipses of their own quests. The ruling order serves as a support for innumerable productive activities, while at the same time blinding its proprietors to this creativity (like those "bosses" who simply *can't* see what is being created within their own enterprises).[29] Carried to its limit, this order would be the equivalent of the rules of meter and rhyme for poets of earlier times: a body of constraints stimulating new discoveries, a set of rules with which improvisation plays.

Reading thus introduces an "art" which is anything but passive. It resembles rather that art whose theory was developed by medieval poets and romancers: an innovation infiltrated into the text and even into the terms of a tradition. Imbricated within the strategies of modernity (which identify creation with the invention of a personal language, whether cultural or scientific), the procedures of contemporary consumption appear to constitute a subtle art of "renters" who know how to insinuate their countless differences into the dominant text. In the Middle Ages, the text was framed by the four, or seven, interpretations of which it was held to be susceptible. And it was a book. Today, this text no longer comes from a tradition. It is imposed by the generation of a productivist technocracy. It is no longer a referential book, but a whole society made into a book, into the writing of the anonymous law of production.

It is useful to compare other arts with this art of readers. For example, the art of conversationalists: the rhetoric of ordinary conversation consists of practices which transform "speech situations," verbal productions in which the interlacing of speaking positions weaves an oral fabric without individual owners, creations of a communication that belongs to no one. Conversation is a provisional and collective effect of competence in the art of manipulating "commonplaces" and the inevitability of events in such a way as to make them "habitable."[30]

But our research has concentrated above all on the uses of space,[31] on the ways of frequenting or dwelling in a place, on the complex processes of the art of cooking, and on the many ways of establishing a kind of reliability within the situations imposed on an individual, that is, of making it possible to live in them by reintroducing into them the plural mobility of goals and desires—an art of manipulating and enjoying.[32]

Extensions: prospects and politics

The analysis of these tactics was extended to two areas marked out for study, although our approach to them changed as the research proceeded: the first concerns prospects, or futurology, and the second, the individual subject in political life.

The "scientific" character of futurology poses a problem from the very start. If the objective of such research is ultimately to establish the intelligibility of present reality, and its rules as they reflect a concern for coherence, we must recognize, on the one hand, the nonfunctional status of an increasing number of concepts, and on the other, the inadequacy of procedures for thinking about, in our case, space. Chosen here as an object of study, space is not really accessible through the usual political and economic determinations; besides, futurology provides no theory of space.[33] The metaphorization of the concepts employed, the gap between the atomization characteristic of research and the generalization required in reporting it, etc., suggest that we take as a definition of futurological discourse the "simulation" that characterizes its method.

Thus in futurology we must consider: (1) the relations between a certain kind of *rationality* and an imagination (which is in discourse the mark of the locus of its production); (2) the difference between, on the one hand, the tentative moves, pragmatic ruses, and successive *tactics* that mark the stages of practical investigation and, on the other hand, the *strategic* representations offered to the public as the product of these operations.[34]

In current discussions, one can discern the surreptitious return of a rhetoric that metaphorizes the fields "proper" to scientific analysis, while, in research laboratories, one finds an increasing distance between actual everyday practices (practices of the same order as the art of cooking) and the "scenarios" that punctuate with utopian images the hum of operations in every laboratory: on the one hand, mixtures of science and fiction; on the other, a disparity between the spectacle of overall strategies and the opaque reality of local tactics. We are thus led to inquire into the "underside" of scientific activity and to ask whether it does not function as a collage—juxtaposing, but linking less and less effectively, the theoretical ambitions of the discourse with the stubborn persistence of ancient tricks in the everyday work of agencies and laboratories. In any event, this split structure, observable in so many administrations and companies, requires us to rethink all the tactics which have so far been neglected by the epistemology of science.

The question bears on more than the procedures of production: in a different form, it concerns as well the *status of the individual* in technical systems, since the involvement of the subject diminishes in proportion to the technocratic expansion of these systems. Increasingly constrained, yet less and less concerned with these vast frameworks, the individual detaches himself from them without being able to escape them and can henceforth only try to outwit them, to pull tricks on them, to rediscover, within an electronicized and computerized megalopolis, the "art" of the hunters and rural folk of earlier days. The fragmentation of the social fabric today lends a *political* dimension to the problem of the subject. In support of this claim can be adduced the symptoms represented by individual conflicts and local operations, and even by ecological organizations, though these are preoccupied primarily with the effort to control relations with the environment collectively. These ways of reappropriating the product-system, ways created by consumers, have as their goal a *therapeutics for deteriorating social relations* and make use of techniques of re-employment in which we can recognize the procedures of everyday practices. A politics of such ploys should be developed. In the perspective opened up by Freud's *Civilization and Its Discontents*, such a politics should also inquire into the public ("democratic") image of the microscopic, multiform, and innumerable connections between *manipulating* and *enjoying*, the fleeting and massive reality of a social activity at play with the order that contains it.

Witold Gombrowicz, an acute visionary, gave this politics its hero—the anti-hero who haunts our research—when he gave a voice to the small-time official (Musil's "man without qualities" or that ordinary man to whom Freud dedicated *Civilization and Its Discontents*) whose refrain is "When one does not have what one wants, one must want what one has": "I have had, you see, to resort more and more to very small, almost invisible pleasures, little extras. . . . You've no idea how great one becomes with these little details, it's incredible how one grows."[35]

Part I
A Very Ordinary Culture

Chapter I A Common Place: Ordinary Language

T HE EROSION AND DENIGRATION of the singular or the extraordinary was announced by *The Man Without Qualities*: "Perhaps it is precisely the petit-bourgeois who has the presentiment of the dawn of a new heroism, a heroism both enormous and collective, on the model of ants."[1] And indeed, the advent of this anthill society began with the masses, who were the first to be subjected to the framework of levelling rationalities. The tide rose. Next it reached the managers who were in charge of the apparatus, managers and technicians absorbed into the system they administered; and finally it invaded the liberal professions that thought themselves protected against it, including even men of letters and artists. The tide tumbles and disperses in its waters works formerly isolated but today transformed into drops of water in the sea, or into metaphors of a linguistic dissemination which no longer has an author but becomes the discourse or indefinite citation of the other.

"Everyman" and "nobody"

There are, of course, antecedents, but they are organized by a community in "common" madness and death, and not yet by the levelling of a technical rationality. Thus at the dawn of the modern age, in the sixteenth century, the ordinary man appears with the insignia of a general misfortune of which he makes sport. As he appears in an ironical literature proper to the northern countries and already democratic in inspiration, he has "embarked" in the crowded human ship of fools and mortals,

1

a sort of inverse Noah's Ark, since it leads to madness and loss. In this vessel he is trapped in the *common* fate. Called *Everyman* (a name that betrays the absence of a name), this anti-hero is thus also *Nobody*, *Nemo*, just as the French *Chacun* becomes *Personne*, or the German *Jedermann Niemand*.[2] He is always the other, without his own responsibilities ("It's not my fault, it's the other: destiny") or particular properties which limit a home (death effaces all differences). Nevertheless, on this humanist stage, he still laughs. In this respect he is wise and mad, lucid and ridiculous, in the destiny which all must undergo and which reduces to *nothing* the exemption which *every man* claims.

In fact, by producing a certain kind of anonymous laugher a literature defines its own status: because it is only a simulacrum, it is the truth of a world of honors and glamor destined to die. The "anyone" or "everyone" is a common place, a philosophical *topos*. The role of this general character (everyman and nobody) is to formulate a universal connection between illusory and frivolous scriptural productions and death, the law of the other. He plays out on the stage the very definition of literature as a world and of the world as literature. Rather than being merely represented in it, the ordinary man acts out the text itself, in and by the text, and in addition he makes plausible the universal character of the particular place in which the mad discourse of a knowing wisdom is pronounced. He is both the nightmare or philosophical dream of humanist irony and an apparent referentiality (a common history) that make credible a writing that turns "everyone" into the teller of his ridiculous misfortune. But when elitist writing uses the "vulgar" speaker as a disguise for a metalanguage about itself, it also allows us to see what dislodges it from its privilege and draws it outside of itself: an Other who is no longer God or the Muse, but the anonymous. The straying of writing outside of its own place is traced by this ordinary man, the metaphor and drift of the doubt which haunts writing, the phantom of its "vanity," the enigmatic figure of the relation that writing entertains with all people, with the loss of its exemption, and with its death.

Freud and the ordinary man

Our contemporary references offer examples of this "philosophical" character that are no doubt even more pregnant. When Freud takes *der gemeine Mann* (the ordinary man) as the starting point and subject of his analyses of civilization (in *Civilization and Its Discontents*) and religion (in *The Future of an Illusion*),[3] those two forms of culture, he remains faithful to the Enlightenment and does not limit himself to opposing the illumination of psychoanalysis ("a method of investigation, an impartial instrument, that one could consider similar to the [infinitesimal] calculus"[4]) to the obscurantism of "the large majority" and to articulating common beliefs in a new knowledge. He not only adopts the old schema that inevitably combines the "illusion" of the mind and social misfortune with "the common man" (such is the theme of *Civilization and Its Discontents*, but in Freud, contrary to the tradition, the ordinary man no longer laughs); he wants to link his pioneering "elucidation" (*Aufklärung*) with this "infantile" majority.[5] Leaving aside the "small number" of "thinkers" and "artists" capable of transforming work into pleasure through sublimation, thus excluding that "rare elect" who nevertheless designate the place in which his text is elaborated, he signs a contract with "the ordinary man" and weds his discourse to the masses whose *common* destiny is to be duped, frustrated, forced to labor, and who are thus subject to the law of deceit and to the pain of death. It seems that this contract, analogous to the contract linking Michelet's history to "the People"—who, however, never speak in it—[6] ought to allow the theory to be universalized and to be based on the reality of history. It provides the theory with a secure place.

It is true that the ordinary man is accused of yielding—thanks to the God of religion—to the illusion of being able to "solve all the riddles of this world" and of being "assured that a Providence watches over his life."[7] In this way, he confers on himself at small expense a knowledge of the totality and a guarantee of his status (by guaranteeing his future). But is it not also true that Freudian theory derives an analogous advantage from the general experience it invokes? As the representative of an abstract universal, the ordinary man in Freudian theory still plays the role of a god who is recognizable in his effects, even if he has humbled himself and merged with superstitious common people: he furnishes Freud's discourse with the means of *generalizing* a particular knowledge and of *guaranteeing* its validity by the whole of history. He authorizes it to transcend its limits—those of a psychoanalytic competence circumscribed within a few cures, and also those of language itself as a whole, deprived of the reality which, as referential, it posits. He assures it of both its difference ("enlightened" discourse remains distinct from "common" discourse) and of its universality (enlightened discourse expresses and explains common experience). Despite Freud's personal opinion of "the mob"[8] (the opposite opinion is to be found in Michelet's optimistic views about the People), the ordinary man renders a service to Freud's discourse, that of figuring in it as a principle of totalization and as a principle of plausibility. This principle permits Freud to say, "It is true of *all*" and "It is the *reality* of history." The ordinary man functions here in the same way as the God of former times.

But Freud himself suspected as much in his old age. He ironically describes *Civilization and Its Discontents* and *The Future of an Illusion* as the result of "a completely superfluous" leisure activity ("One can't smoke and play cards all day long"), a "pastime" concerned with "elevated subjects" which cause him "to rediscover the most commonplace truths."[9] He distinguishes it from his "earlier works," which were organized in accord with the rules of a method and constructed on the basis of particular cases. Here we are no longer concerned with Little Hans, Dora, or Schreber. The ordinary man represents first of all Freud's temptation to be a moralist, the return of ethical generalizations into the professional field, an excess or a falling-short with respect to psychoanalytic procedures. In that way, he makes explicit an overturning of knowledge. In fact, if Freud mocks this introduction to a future "pathology of civilized societies," it is because he is *himself* the ordinary man of whom he speaks, with a few "commonplace" and bitter truths in his hands. He ends his reflections with a pirouette. "The complaint that I offer no consolation is justified,"[10] he writes, for he has none. He is in the same boat as everyone else and begins to laugh. An ironic and wise madness is linked to the fact that he has lost the singularity of a competence and found himself, anyone or no one, in the common history. In the philosophical tale that is *Civilization and Its Discontents*, the ordinary man is the speaker. He is the point in the discourse where the scientist and the common man come together—the return of the other (everyone and no one) into the place which had been so carefully set apart from him. Freud once again traces the way in which banality overflows speciality and brings knowledge back to its general presupposition: I don't have solid knowledge of anything. I'm like everyone else.

"Privation," "repression," "Eros," "Thanatos," etc.: these tools of technical work mark the stages of the movement in *Civilization and Its Discontents* from a triumphant "Aufklärung" to commonplaces, but the Freudian analysis of culture is characterized first of all by the trajectory of this overturning movement. An apparently minor and yet fundamental difference distinguishes its result from the trivialities retailed by cultural specialists, for their trivialities no longer designate the *object* of discourse, but rather its *place*. In Freud the trivial is no longer the other (which is supposed to ground the exemption of the one who dramatizes it); it is the productive experience of the text. The approach to culture begins when the ordinary man *becomes* the narrator, when it is he who defines the (common) place of discourse and the (anonymous) space of its development.

This place is no more given to the speaker of the discourse than to anyone else. It is the endpoint of a trajectory. It is not a state, an initial flaw or grace, but something which *comes into being*, the product of a process of deviation from rule-governed and falsifiable practices, an overflowing (*débordement*) of the common in a particular position. Such is the case for Freud, when at the end of the investigation he finishes off (as one "finishes off" a condemned man) with his last stories concerning the ordinary man: he performs a work of mourning by putting knowledge into the realm of fiction.[11]

The important thing here is the fact that the *work* of overflowing operates by the insinuation of the ordinary into established scientific fields. Far from arbitrarily assuming the privilege of speaking in the name of the ordinary (it cannot be spoken), or claiming to be in that general place (that would be a false "mysticism"), or, worse, offering up a hagiographic everydayness for its edifying value, it is a matter of restoring historicity to the movement which leads analytical procedures back to their frontiers, to the point where they are changed, indeed disturbed, by the ironic and mad banality that speaks in "Everyman" in the sixteenth century and that has returned in the final stages of Freud's knowledge. I shall try to describe the erosion that lays bare the ordinary in a body of analytical techniques, to reveal the openings that mark its trace on the borders where a science is mobilized, to indicate the displacements that lead toward the *common place* where "anyone" is finally silent, except for repeating (but in a different way) banalities. Even if it is drawn into the oceanic rumble of the ordinary, the task consists not in substituting a representation for the ordinary or covering it up with mere words, but in showing how it introduces itself into our techniques— in the way in which the sea flows back into pockets and crevices in beaches—and how it can reorganize the place from which discourse is produced.

The expert and the philosopher

The technical path to be followed consists, in a first approximation, in bringing scientific practices and languages back toward their native land, everyday life. This return, which is today more and more insistent, has the paradoxical character of also being a going into exile with respect to the disciplines whose rigor is measured by the strict definition of its own limits. Ever since scientific work (*scientificité*) has given itself its own proper and appropriable places through rational projects capable of determining their procedures, with formal objects and specified conditions under which they are falsifiable, ever since it was founded as a plurality of limited and distinct fields, in short ever since it stopped being theological, it has constituted the *whole* as its *remainder*; this remainder has become what we call culture.

This cleavage organizes modernity. It cuts it up into scientific and dominant islands set off against the background of practical "resistances" and symbolizations that cannot be reduced to thought. Even if the ambition of "Science" is to conquer this remainder by starting out from the areas where the powers of our knowledge can be exercised, even if, in order to prepare the full realization of this empire, reconnaissance missions are already exploring the frontier regions and linking the light to the darkness (there are the gray discourses of mixed sciences called "human," accounts of expeditions that tend to make assimilable—if not thinkable—and determine the frontiers of the dark regions of violence, superstition, and otherness: history, anthropology, pathology, etc.), the gap scientific institutions have opened between the artificial languages of a regulated operativity and the modes of speech of social groups has always been the scene of battles and compromises. This line of demarcation, which is, moreover, unstable and changing, remains strategic in the struggles to increase or contest the influence of artificial techniques on social practices. It separates artificial languages, articulating the procedures of a specific kind of knowledge, from natural languages, organizing common signifying activity.

A few of these debates (which concern precisely the relation of each science to culture) can be made more explicit, and their possible outcomes indicated, by examining two figures, curiously similar and contrasting, who are facing them: the Expert and the Philosopher. Both have the task of mediating between society and a body of knowledge, the first insofar as he introduces his speciality into the wider and more complex arena of socio-political decisions, the second insofar as he re-establishes the relevance of general questions to a particular technique (mathematics, logic, psychiatry, history, etc.). In the Expert, competence is transmuted into social authority; in the Philosopher, ordinary questions become a skeptical principle in a technical field. The Philosopher's ambiguous relation to the Expert (sometimes one of fascination, sometimes one of rejection) often seems to subtend his procedures: sometimes philosophical enterprises aim enviously at the Expert's realization of their ancient utopia (to maintain access to general problems in the name of a specific kind of scientific knowledge); sometimes, defeated by history but still rebellious, these enterprises turn their backs on what has been taken away from them by science in order to accompany the Subject, the king of yesteryear, today driven out of a technocratic society into its exile (O memories! O symbolic transgressions! O unconscious kingdoms!).

It is true that the Expert is growing more common in this society, to the point of becoming its generalized figure, distended between the exigency of a growing specialization and that of a communication that has become all the more necessary. He blots out (and in a certain way replaces) the Philosopher, formerly the specialist of the universal. But his success is not so terribly spectacular. In him, the productivist law that requires a specific assignment (the condition of efficiency) and the social law that requires circulation (the form of exchange) enter into contradiction. To be sure, a specialist is more and more often driven to *also* be an Expert, that is, an interpreter and translator of his competence for other fields. That is obvious even within the laboratories themselves: as soon as decisions regarding objectives, promotions, or financing are to be made, the Experts intervene "in the name of"—but outside of—their particular experience. How do they succeed in moving from their technique—a language they have mastered and which regulates their discourse—to the more common language of another situation? They do it through a curious operation which "converts" competence into authority. Competence is exchanged for authority. Ultimately, the more authority the Expert has, the less competence he has, up to the point where his fund of competence is exhausted, like the energy necessary to put a mobile into movement. During the process of conversion, he is not without some competence (he either has to have some or make people think he has), but he abandons the competence he possesses as his authority is extended further and further, drawn out of its orbit by social demands and/or political responsibilities. That is the (general?) paradox of authority: a knowledge is ascribed to it and this knowledge is precisely what it lacks where it is exercised. Authority is indissociable from an "abuse of knowledge"[12]—and in this fact we ought perhaps to recognize the effect of the social law that divests the individual of his competence in order to establish (or re-establish) the capital of a collective competence, that is, of a common verisimilitude.

Since he cannot limit himself to talking about what he knows, the Expert pronounces on the basis of the *place* that his specialty has won for him. In that way he inscribes himself and is inscribed in a *common* order where specialization, as the *rule* and hierarchically ordering *practice* of the productivist economy, has the value of *initiation*. Because he has successfully submitted himself to this initiatory practice, he can, on questions foreign to his technical competence but not to the power he has acquired through it, pronounce with authority a discourse which is no longer a function of knowledge, but rather a function of the socioeconomic order. He speaks as an ordinary man, who can receive authority in exchange for knowledge just as one receives a paycheck in exchange for work. He inscribes himself in the common language of practices, where an overproduction of authority leads to the devaluation of authority, since one always gets more in exchange for an equal or inferior amount of competence. But when he continues to believe, or make others believe, that he is acting as a scientist, he confuses social *place* with technical *discourse*. He takes one for the other: it is a simple case of mistaken identity. He misunderstands the order which he represents. He no longer knows *what* he is saying. A few individuals, after having long considered themselves experts speaking a scientific language, have finally awoken from their slumbers and suddenly realized that for the last few moments they have been walking on air, like Felix the Cat in the old cartoons, far from the scientific ground. Though legitimized by scientific knowledge, their discourse is seen to have been no more than the ordinary language of tactical games between economic powers and symbolic authorities.

The Wittgensteinian model of ordinary language

For all that, the "universal" discourse of earlier philosophy does not recover its rights. Insofar as it concerns language, the philosophical question in our technical societies has to do with the distinction between discursivities regulating specialization (they maintain a social *reason* by means of an operative partitioning) and the narrativities of exchange on a massive scale (they multiply the ruses permitting or restraining a *circulation* within a power network). Independently of the analyses that have brought both of these under the common rubric of linguistic *practices*[13], or of research which reveals *either* the insinuation of beliefs, of the verisimilar, of metaphors, that is, of the "common," into scientific discourse, *or* the complex logics implied by ordinary language[14]—efforts to rejoin pieces of language which were disconnected and abusively hierarchized—it is also possible to turn to a philosophy which furnishes a "model" and which undertakes to carry out a rigorous examination of ordinary language: that of Wittgenstein. From the perspective in which I place myself, it can be considered as a radical critique of the Expert. The corollary: it is also a critique of the Philosopher as Expert.

If Wittgenstein intends "to bring words back from their metaphysical to their everyday use,[15] a project which he developed especially during his later period, he does not allow himself, or any philosopher, a metaphysical overflow beyond what speech *can* say. This is his constant program: "To say nothing except what can be said . . . and then, whenever someone else wanted to say something metaphysical, to demonstrate to him that he had failed to give a meaning to certain signs in his propositions".[16] Wittgenstein set himself the task of being the scientist of the activity of signifying in the common language. Anything else can be considered as language only by analogy or comparison with "the apparatus of our ordinary language."[17] But the problem is to treat it in such a way as not to state anything that exceeds the competence of this language and thus never to become an expert, or an interpreter, in another linguistic field (for example, metaphysics or ethics), never to speak *elsewhere* "in its name." In that way the conversion of competence into authority is to be rendered impossible.

What is fascinating in the enterprise of this Hercules who set out to clean the Augean stables of contemporary intellectual life is not so much his restrictive procedures, which are the effects of the passion for exactitude that he puts at the service of a certain reserve in the analysis of "everyday" language (this "everyday" replaces, in the linguistic approach, the *Everyman* of Renaissance ethics, but bears the same question); but rather, more fundamentally, the way in which Wittgenstein draws *"from the inside" of this language* (to use his expression) the limits of that which, whether ethical or mystical, exceeds it.[18] It is exclusively from the inside that he recognizes an outside which itself remains ineffable. His work thus operates a double erosion: one which, from the interior of ordinary language, makes these limits appear; another which reveals the unacceptable character (the nonsense) of any proposition that attempts to escape toward "that which cannot be said." The analysis locates the empty places that sap language, and it destroys the statements that claim to fill them in. It works with what language shows without being able to *say* it. Wittgenstein examines a play of regional and combined syntaxes whose foundations, coherence, and overall significance depend on questions that are pertinent, and even essential, but cannot be treated in their "proper" place because language cannot become the object of a discourse. "We do not *command a clear view* of the use of our words."[19] Rarely has the reality of language—that is, the *fact* that it defines our historicity, that it dominates and envelops us in the mode of the ordinary, that no discourse can therefore "escape from it," put itself at the distance from it in order to observe it and tell us its meaning—been taken seriously with so much rigor.

In this way, Wittgenstein maintains himself in the present of his historicity without having recourse to the "past" of the historian. He would reject even historiography because, by separating a past from the present, it privileges in effect a *proper* and productive place from which it claims to "command a clear view" of linguistic facts (or "documents") and to distinguish itself from the *given*, a *product* which is alone supposed to be subject to common rules. Wittgenstein recognizes that he is "caught" in *common* linguistic historicity. Accordingly, he will not allow this dependence to be *localized* in the ob-ject (designated as "past") whose historiographic operation is fictively detached (through a fiction that is moreover the very space where the scientific challenge of mastering history is produced).[20] In reality, his position is not risked there, but rather in a double combat whose articulation furnishes us with a formal landmark for the study of culture. On the one hand, he combats the professionalization of philosophy, that is, its reduction to the technical (i.e., positivist) discourse of a specialty. More generally, he rejects the purifying process that, by eliminating the ordinary use of language (everyday language), makes it possible for science to produce and master an artificial language. On the other hand, he combats the rashness of metaphysics and the impatience of ethics, which are always led to subsume the rules of correct use and to pay with the meaninglessness of some statements for the authority of their discourse on the language of common experiences. He attacks the presumption that leads philosophy to proceed "as if" it gave meaning to ordinary use, and to suppose that it has its own place from which it can reflect on the everyday.

We are subject to, but not identified with, ordinary language. As in the ship of fools, we are embarked, without the possibility of an aerial view or any sort of totalization. That is the "prose of the world" Merleau-Ponty spoke of. It encompasses every discourse, even if human experiences cannot be reduced to what it can say about them. In order to constitute themselves, scientific methods allow themselves to *forget* this fact and philosophers *think they dominate it* so that they can authorize themselves to deal with it. In this respect, neither touches the philosophical question, endlessly reopened by that "urge" that "pushes man to run up against the limits of language" ("*an die Grenze der Sprache anzurennen*").[21] Wittgenstein reintroduces this language *both* into philosophy, which has indeed taken it for a formal object while according itself a fictional mastery over it, *and* into the sciences, which have excluded it in order to accord themselves an actual mastery.

He thus changes the *place* of analysis, henceforth defined by a *universality* identical with *submission* to ordinary use. This change of place modifies the status of the discourse. By being "caught" within ordinary language, the philosopher no longer has his own (*propre*) appropriable place. Any position of mastery is denied him. The analyzing discourse and the analyzed "object" are in the same situation: both are organized by the practical activity with which they are concerned, both are determined by rules they neither establish nor see clearly, equally scattered in differentiated ways of working (Wittgenstein wanted his work itself to be composed only of fragments), inscribed in a texture in which each can by turns "appeal" to the other, cite it and refer to it. There is a continual exchange of distinct places. Philosophical or scientific privilege disappears into the ordinary. This disappearance has as its corollary the invalidation of truths. From what privileged place could they be signified? There will thus be *facts* that are no longer *truths*. The inflation of the latter is controlled, if not shut off, by criticism of the places of authority in which facts are converted into truths. Detecting them by their mixture of meaninglessness and power, Wittgenstein attempts to reduce these truths to linguistic facts and to that which, *in* these facts, refers to an ineffable or "mystical" exteriority of language.

This position can be connected to the increasing importance in Wittgenstein's work of linguistic behaviors and uses. To discuss language "within" ordinary language, without being able "to command a clear

view" of it, without being able to see it from a distance, is to grasp it as
an ensemble of practices in which one is implicated and through which
the prose of the world is at work. The analysis will therefore be a
"looking into the workings of our language" ("*eine Einsicht in das
Arbeiten unserer Sprache*").[22] It thus cannot avoid reproducing the dissemination which fragments every system. But by trying to "determine
the morphology of use" of expressions, that is, to examine their "domains
of use" and to "describe the forms,"[23] it can "recognize" different modes
of everyday functioning, governed by "pragmatic rules," themselves
dependent on "forms of life" (*Lebensformen*).[24]

A contemporary historicity

Wittgenstein's elaboration of this analysis, to whose sociolinguistic or
"ethnomethodological" developments we shall return later, owes a great
deal to the philosophical tradition he came to know at Cambridge.
From Cook Wilson to G. E. Moore and J. L. Austin, it had concentrated
on the "ways of speaking" of ordinary or everyday language, to the
point that Austin's program was "to track the minutiae of ordinary
language" and his reputation that of being "the evangelist of ordinary
language" (*TLS*, 16 November 1973). Several reasons were advanced in
support of this approach, and they concern us as well: 1. the usual ways
of speaking do not have *any equivalent* in philosophical discourse and
they cannot be translated into it because they are richer and more varied
than it is; 2. they constitute a *reserve* of "distinctions" and "connections" accumulated by historical experience and stored up in everyday
speech;[25] 3. as linguistic *practices*, they manifest *logical complexities*
unnoticed by scientific formalizations.[26]

But these more or less professional exchanges cannot erase the primary
historical context of Wittgenstein's thought. Three aspects of this context
are particularly indicative of its importance. First, parallel to the reaction that inspired the architect Adolf Loos to write *Ornament and Crime*,
a book defending a functionalist austerity against the decorative degen-
eracy of Vienna,[27] or that which elicits the clinical irony of Musil's
observations in Cacania,[28] there is in Wittgenstein's work an almost
puritanical "execration" of the "fallacious" charm and the "journalistic"
brilliance of a "rotting culture" and of the "drivel" that resembles them.[29]
"Purity"[30] and reserve mark the style of an engagement in contemporary

history, a philosophical politics of culture. The critical return of the ordinary, as Wittgenstein understands it, must destroy all the varieties of rhetorical brilliance associated with powers that hierarchize and with nonsense that enjoys authority.

Another, equally striking, analogy: through his experience as a superior technician, then as a mathematician, Wittgenstein had, like Musil's Ulrich, the man without qualities, a "second try" and a third try, "the most important." He, too, possessed "fragments of a new way of thinking and feeling" and saw "the spectacle of novelty, at first so intense," dissolve "into the multiplication of details." For him, too, "there remained only philosophy to which he could dedicate himself."[31] But, like Ulrich, in the area of the "good use of his [linguistic] abilities" he retained the "marvelous clarity"[32] which the scientific method had sharpened— thus combining technical rigor with respect for its "object." Unlike the Expert's discourse, Wittgenstein's does not profit from knowledge by exchanging it against the right to speak in its name; he retains its exactingness but not its mastery.

Finally, this science of the ordinary is defined by a threefold foreignness: the foreignness of the specialist (and of the wealthy bourgeois) to common life, of the scientist to philosophy, and, until the very end, of the German to the everyday English language (in which he never settled down). This situation is comparable to those of the ethnologist and the historian, but more radical. In the accidental ways of being a foreigner *away from home* (like any traveler or keeper of records) Wittgenstein sees the metaphors of *foreign* analytical procedures *inside* the very language that circumscribes them. "When we do philosophy [that is, when we are working in the place which is the only "philosophical" one, the prose of the world] we are like savages, primitive people, who hear the expressions of civilized men, put a false interpretation on them, and then draw the queerest conclusions from it."[33] This is no longer the position of professionals, supposed to be civilized men among savages; it is rather the position which consists in being a foreigner *at home*, a "savage" in the midst of ordinary culture, lost in the complexity of the common agreement and what goes without saying. And since one does not "leave" this language, since one cannot find another place from which to interpret it, since there are therefore no separate groups of false interpretations and true interpretations, but only illusory interpretations, since in short there is no *way out*, the fact remains that we are *foreigners* on the inside—*but there is no outside*. Thus we must constantly "run up against the limits" of ordinary language—a situation close to the Freudian position except that Wittgenstein does not allow himself an unconscious referent to name this foreignness-at-home.

By these characteristics, Wittgenstein's fragmented and rigorous body of work seems to provide a philosophical blueprint for a contemporary science of the ordinary. Without going into the details of its theses, we must compare this model, taken as a theoretical hypothesis, with positive contributions of the "human sciences" (sociology, ethnology, history, etc.) to the knowledge of ordinary culture.

Chapter II Popular Cultures: Ordinary Language

T O LEAVE VIENNA or Cambridge, to leave theoretical texts, is not to leave Wittgenstein behind (he was a teacher in a village elementary school between 1920 and 1926) but rather to set out toward the open sea of common experience that surrounds, penetrates, and finally carries away every discourse—if one is not satisfied with substituting a political mastery for scientific appropriation. Memories come back to me, the places of these mute silences of memory. For instance, as an introduction to a seminar on the popular culture of Northeast Brazil, a walk through the night, alive with sound, in the town of Salvador towards the Igreja do Passo. Contrasting with the subtle theatricality of the Misericórdia, the church's dark facade lifts up into its dignity all the dust and sweat of the city. Standing above the old parts of town full of vague murmurings and human voices, it presents their monumental, silent secret. It dominates the narrow Ladeira do Passo. It does not yield itself to researches who nevertheless have it there before them, just as popular language escapes them, when they approach it, for it comes from too far away and too high. Very different from the Church do Rosário, which is all blue and openness, this dark stone raises the nocturnal face of Bahian irony. An unconquerable rock even though (or because) it is familiar, totally without solemnity, similar to the songs of the Brazilian *saudade*. Returning from this pilgrimage, the passing faces in the streets seem, in spite of their vivacious mobility, to multiply the indecipherable and nearby secret of the monument.

A Brazilian "art"

Our investigation moves on, groping its way, as we did, in interdisciplinary local teams, in Rio, in Salvador, and in Recife (Brazil), or again in Santiago and Concepción (Chile), in Posadas (Argentina), etc. For example, one of these analyses concerned the language used by the

15

peasants of the Pernambuco (in Crato, Juazeiro, Itapetim, etc.) in talking about their situation in 1974 and about the great deeds of Frei Damião, the charismatic hero of the region.[1] The discourse parted space in such a way as to stratify it on two levels. On the one hand, a socio-economic space, organized by an immemorial struggle between "the powerful" and "the poor," presented itself as the field of constant victories by the rich and the police, but also as the reign of mendacity (there no truth is said, except in whispers and among peasants: "*Agora a gente sabe, mas não pode dizar alto*"). In this space, the strong always win and words always deceive—an experience in accord with that of a Maghrebian syndicalist in Billancourt:* "They always fuck us over." On the other hand, distinct from this *polemological* space which perspicacious country people saw as a network of innumerable conflicts covered up with words, there was also a *utopian* space in which a possibility, by definition miraculous in nature, was affirmed by religious stories. Frei Damião was the almost immobile center of this space, constantly qualified by the successive accounts of the celestial punishments visited upon his enemies.

As far as the actual power relationships were concerned, we can say that a lucid discourse cunningly turned up fake words and prohibitions on speaking in order to reveal an ubiquitous injustice—not simply the injustice of the established powers, but, more profoundly, that of history. It recognized in that injustice an order of things that seemed immutable: it is always so; people see it every day. But no legitimacy whatever was accorded this state of affairs. On the contrary, just because it was a constantly repeated fact, this relationship of forces did not become any more acceptable. The *fact* was not accepted as a *law*, even if it remained inescapably a fact. Trapped in dependency, forced to submit to the facts, this conviction is nevertheless opposed to the *statutory* fact of an order presenting itself as natural, a goal of non-acceptance, and to its fatality, an *ethical* protest (if science can permit itself different options concerning the relation between facts and laws, it is above all because it can escape from that dependence). But in order to affirm the non-coincidence of fact and meaning, another scene was required, the religious scene that reintroduces, in the mode of supernatural events, the historical contingency of this "nature" and, by means of celestial landmarks, creates a place for this protest. The unacceptability of an order which is nevertheless established was articulated, appropriately enough, as a miracle.

---

* The Renault automobile factory in Billancourt (on the outskirts of Paris) employs many immigrants from North Africa. (Tr.)

There, in a language necessarily foreign to the analysis of socioeconomic relationships, the hope could be *maintained* that the vanquished of history—the body on which the victories of the rich or their allies are continually inscribed—might, in the "person" of the humiliated "saint" Damião, rise again as a result of the blows rained on its adversaries from on high.

Without diminishing in any way what one sees every day, the stories of miracles respond to it "from aside" with irrelevance and impertinence in a different discourse, a discourse one can only *believe*—just as an ethical reaction must believe that life cannot be reduced to what one sees of it. In the same way, in J.-L. Comolli's film *La Cecilia*, the anarchist songs form the counterpoint to the events that gradually destroy, as it develops, the socialist commune founded in Brazil by Tito Rossi: the songs remain intact and, in the end, from the very ruins of a history restored to order, these songs rise again, escaping from the battlefield of defeat, lifting up a voice that will bring to life, elsewhere, other movements:

Un' idea l'amante mia	An idea is my darling,
A cui detti braccio e cuor . . .[2]	I gave it grip and heart
Deh t'affretta a sorgere	Ah, hurry to rise
O sol dell'avvenir	You sun of the future
Vivere vogliam liberi	It's free we would live
Non vogliam più servir.[3]	We would serve no more.

In the same way as the voodoo *Loas*, the "spirits" and voices from another realm,[4] the stories of miracles are also songs, but serious ones, relating not to uprisings but to the recognition of the permanent repression. In spite of everything, they provide the possible with a site that is impregnable, because it is a nowhere, a utopia. They create another space, which coexists with that of an experience deprived of illusions. They tell a truth (the miraculous) which is not reducible to the particular beliefs that serve it as metaphors or symbols. They exist *alongside* the analysis of facts, as the equivalent of what a political ideology introduces *into* that analysis.

The rural "believers" thus subvert the fatality of the established order. And they do it by using a frame of reference which also proceeds from an external power (the religion imposed by Christian missions). They re-employ a system that, far from being their own, has been constructed and spread by others, and they mark this re-employment by "super-stitions," excrescences of this belief in miracles which civil and religious authorities have always correctly suspected of putting in question the "reason" behind power and knowledge hierarchies. A ("popular") use of religion modifies its functioning. A way of speaking this received language transforms it into a song of resistance, but this internal metamorphosis does not in any way compromise the sincerity with which it may be believed nor the lucidity with which, from another point of view, the struggles and inequalities hidden under the established order may be perceived.

More generally, *a way of using* imposed systems constitutes the resistance to the historical law of a state of affairs and its dogmatic legitimations. A practice of the order constructed by others redistributes its space; it creates at least a certain play in that order, a space for maneuvers of unequal forces and for utopian points of reference. That is where the opacity of a "popular" culture could be said to manifest itself—a dark rock that resists all assimilation. What is there called "wisdom" (*sabedoria*) may be defined as a stratagem (*trampolinagem*, which a play on words associates with the acrobatics of the mountebank and his art of jumping on the trampoline, *trampolim*) and as "trickery" (*trapaçaria*, ruse, deception, in the way one uses or cheats with the terms of social contracts).[5] Innumerable ways of playing and foiling the other's game (*jouer/déjouer le jeu de l'autre*), that is, the space instituted by others, characterize the subtle, stubborn, resistant activity of groups which, since they lack their own space, have to get along in a network of already established forces and representations. People have to make do with what they have. In these combatants' stratagems, there is a certain art of placing one's blows, a pleasure in getting around the rules of a constraining space. We see the tactical and joyful dexterity of the mastery of a technique. Scapin and Figaro are only literary echoes of this art. Like the skill of a driver in the streets of Rome or Naples, there is a skill that has its connoisseurs and its esthetics exercised in any labyrinth of powers, a skill ceaselessly recreating opacities and ambiguities—spaces of darkness and trickery—in the universe of technocratic transparency, a skill that disappears into them and reappears again, taking no responsibility for the administration of a totality. Even the field of misfortune is refashioned by this combination of manipulation and enjoyment.

The proverbial enunciation

Is this too hasty a generalization? It is a hypothesis for research, to be sure, but it is based on the examinations of other terrains[6] and situated, naturally, in an ensemble of precedents and neighboring inquiries, for example, the recent research on the "practical intelligence" (*mētis*) of the Greeks[7] or on the "practical sense" and the "strategies" of the peoples of Béarn (in Southern France) and Kabylia (in North Africa).[8]

This approach to popular culture takes its inspiration from a problematics of enunciation, in the triple sense due to Austin's analysis of performative utterances, to A. J. Greimas' semiotics of manipulation, and to the semiology of the Prague School. Although it was initially concerned with the *speech act* through which a speaker actualizes and appropriates his mother tongue in a particular situation of exchange or "contract,"[9] this problematics can be extended to culture as a whole on the basis of the resemblance between the ("enunciative") *procedures* which articulate actions in both the field of language and the network of social practices. It differs from more traditional studies concerned with legendary, proverbial (etc.) statements, or, more generally, with the objective form of rites or behaviors in that it constitutes a corpus *peculiar* to popular culture and analyzes the variable terms of invariable functions within finite *systems*. The postulates and methods of the two perspectives are divergent: whereas the one seeks to discern the types of *operations* for which historical conjunctures provide the space, the other prefers to identify the *structural* equilibria whose constancy each society manifests in differing ways.

The differences are of course neither so simple nor so antithetical. Thus Pierre Bourdieu combines both in a "theory of practice" to which we shall have to return. But one can clarify what is at stake in these alternatives by reference to a particular case, that of the *proverb*.

One method consists in first isolating proverbs and then collecting them, as Aarne or Propp did for folktales. Once the material has been collected, one can treat either the content, divided by labels or semantic units (actions, themes, agents), whose relationships are analyzable in terms of structures and whose aggregates indicate the mental geography peculiar to a given group;[10] or one can study the modes of production, for example the way in which proverbs (generally distichs: "Out of sight, out of mind," "When the cat's away, the mice will play," "Red sky in morning, sailor take warning," etc.) reinforce the impact of the meaning by diminishing differences in sound (through rhyme, alliteration, etc.).[11] On the one hand, one is concerned with systems of signification, on the other, with systems of fabrication. Through a twofold control of the corpus they circumscribe and of the operations they carry out on it, these methods succeed in defining their object themselves (what is a proverb?), in rationalizing its collection, in classifying the types and transforming the "given" into something reproducible (for example, if one knows the rules of the production of proverbs, one can fabricate series of them). These techniques thus provide, by explaining them, the ability to *construct* social phenomena, just as biology synthesizes insulin.

Because the analysis of myths has been further developed than that of proverbs, such analysis, from Aarne to Lévi-Strauss, has shown how a science of these discourses, by isolating and sifting them, by refining and formalizing the minimum units it treats,[12] can classify a literature that is supposed to be heterogenous, can reveal a "savage mind" (*pensée sauvage*) and a logic in bodies of material constituted as "foreign," and, in this way, can renew the interpretation and production of our own discourse.

The drawback of this method, which is at the same time the condition of its success, is that it extracts the documents from their *historical* context and eliminates the *operations* of speakers in particular situations of time, place, and competition. Everyday linguistic practices (as well as the space of their tactics) have to be ignored in order for the scientific practices to be able to operate in their own field. The innumerable tricks of bringing in a proverb at just the right moment and with a particular interlocutor are thus not taken into account. This art and its practitioners are excluded from the laboratory, not only because the scientific method requires a delimitation and simplification of its objects, but also because there corresponds to the constitution of a scientific space, as the precondition of any analysis, the necessity of being able to *transfer* the objects of study into it. Only what can be transported can be treated. What cannot be uprooted remains by definition outside the field of research. Hence the privilege that these studies accord to *discourses*, the data that can most easily be grasped, recorded, transported, and examined in secure places; in contrast, the speech *act* cannot be parted from its circumstances. Of the practices themselves, science will retain only movable elements (tools and products to be put in display cases) or descriptive schemas (quantifiable behaviors, stereotypes of the staging of social intercourse, ritual structures), leaving aside the aspects of a society that cannot be so uprooted and transferred to another space: ways of using things or words according to circumstances. Something essential is at work in this everyday *historicity*, which cannot be dissociated from the *existence* of the subjects who are the agents and authors of conjunctural operations. Indeed, like Schreber's God, who "communicates only with cadavers,"[13] our knowledge seems to consider and tolerate in a social body only inert objects.

Was it fate? I remember the marvelous Shelburne Museum in Vermont where, in thirty-five houses of a reconstructed village, all the signs, tools, and products of nineteenth-century everyday life teem; everything, from cooking utensils and pharmaceutical goods to weaving instruments, toilet articles, and children's toys can be found in profusion. The display includes innumerable familiar objects, polished, deformed, or made more beautiful by long use; everywhere there are as well the marks of the active hands and laboring or patient bodies for which these things composed the daily circuits, the fascinating presence of absences whose traces were everywhere. At least this village full of abandoned and salvaged objects drew one's attention, through them, to the ordered murmurs of a hundred past or possible villages, and by means of these imbricated traces one began to dream of countless combinations of existences. Like tools, proverbs (and other discourses) are *marked by* uses; they offer to analysis the *imprints of acts* or of processes of enunciation;[14] they signify the *operations* whose object they have been, operations which are relative to situations and which can be thought of as the conjunctural *modalizations* of statements or of practices;[15] more generally, they thus indicate a social *historicity* in which systems of representations or processes of fabrication no longer appear only as normative frameworks but also as *tools manipulated by users*.

Logics: games, tales, and the arts of speaking

From these imprints on language, we are already returning toward operators' ways of operating. But it is not enough to describe individual ruses and devices. In order to think them, one must suppose that to these ways of operating correspond a finite number of procedures (invention is not unlimited and, like improvisations on the piano or on the guitar, it presupposes the knowledge and application of codes), and that they imply a *logic of the operation of actions relative to types of situations*. This logic, which turns on *circumstances*, has as its precondition, contrary to the procedures of Western science, the non-autonomy of its field of action. A rich elucidation of this logic can be found in Chinese thought, in the canonical *I Ching* (or *Book of Changes*) or in Sun Tzu's *Art of War*,[16] or in the Arab tradition of the *Book of Tricks*.[17] But need we seek our models so far abroad? Every society always

manifests somewhere the formal rules which its practices obey. But
where should we look for them in the West, since our scientific method,
by substituting its "own" places for the complex geography of social
ruses and its "artificial" languages for ordinary language,[18] has allowed
and even required reason to adopt a logic of mastery and transparency?
Like Poe's "purloined letter," the inscriptions of these various logics are
written in places so obvious that one does not see them. Without referring again to ordinary language, we can already suggest three places in
which, hidden only by their very evidence, the formal rules of these
circumstantial ways of making are already visible.

First of all, in the specific *games* of each society: games, which as
operations are disjunctive, because they produce differentiating events,[19]
give rise to spaces where *moves* are proportional to *situations*. From the
game of chess, an aristocratic form of the "art of war" which came from
China and was brought by the Arabs into medieval Western culture
where it constituted a very important part of manorial culture, to
pinochle, Lotto, and Scrabble, games formulate (and already formalize)
rules organizing moves and constitute as well *a memory* (a storage and a
classification) of schemas of actions articulating replies with respect to
circumstances. They exercise that function precisely because they are
detached from those everyday combats which forbid one to "show his
hand" and whose stakes, rules, and moves are too complex. The ex-
plicitness of the rules is always inversely proportional to the practical
engagement involved. If we observe a formalization of tactics in these
games (as has been done with respect to the game of *go*),[20] or compare
to games the technique of divination, whose formal framework has the
purpose of adjusting a decision to concrete situations,[21] we gain a preliminary body of material concerning the kinds of rationality proper to
the practice of spaces—spaces that are closed and "historicized" by the
variability of the events to be treated.

To these games correspond *accounts* of particular games: people tell
each other about the hand they had to play the night before, or the slam
they made the previous week. These stories represent a succession of
combinations among all those that the synchronic organization of a
space, of rules, of deals, etc., make possible. They are paradigmatic
projections of a choice among these possibilities—a choice corresponding to a particular actualization (or enunciation). Like the bridge or
chess articles in *The New York Times*, the stories could be formulated in
a special code, thus making it clear that every event is a particular

application of the formal framework. But in replaying the games, in telling about them, these accounts record the rules and the moves simultaneously. To be memorized as well as memorable, they are *repertories of schemas of action* between partners. With the attraction that the element of surprise introduces, these mementos teach the tactics possible within a given (social) system.

Tales and legends seem to have the same role.[22] They are deployed, like games, in a space outside of and isolated from daily competition, that of the past, the marvelous, the original. In that space can thus be revealed, dressed as gods or heroes, the models of good or bad ruses that can be used every day. Moves, not truths, are recounted. One can already find an example of these panoplies of strategies in the work of Propp, a pioneer whose work became a rigidified model for "formalist" research on folktales.[23] The four hundred fabulous tales he had examined were reduced to a "fundamental series"[24] of *functions*, the "function" being "the action of a character, defined from the point of view of its signification in the development of the plot."[25] It is not certain, as A. Régnier noted, that the homologizing of these functions is coherent, nor, as both Lévi-Strauss and Greimas have shown, that the units Propp delimited are stable; but the novelty of Propp's work, which remains important today, lies in the analysis of the tactics for which the tales offer both an inventory and a repertory of combinations, on the basis of elementary units which are not significations or beings, but actions relative to conflictual situations. With others that have since appeared, Propp's reading would allow us to recognize in the tales the strategic discourses of the people. Hence the privilege that these tales accord to simulation/dissimulation.[26] The formality of everyday practices is indicated in these tales, which frequently reverse the relationships of power and, like the stories of miracles, ensure the victory of the unfortunate in a fabulous, utopian space. This space protects the weapons of the weak against the reality of the established order. It also hides them from the social categories which "make history" because they dominate it. And whereas historiography recounts in the past tense the strategies of instituted powers, these "fabulous" stories offer their audience a repertory of tactics for future use.

Finally, in these tales themselves, the stylistic effects—devices and "figures," alliterations, inversions and plays on words—also participate in the collation of these tactics. They are also, more discreetly, living museums of these tactics, the benchmarks of an apprenticeship. Both rhetoric and everyday practices can be defined as internal manipulations of a system—that of language or that of an established order. "Turns" (or "tropes") inscribe in ordinary language the ruses, displacements, ellipses, etc., that scientific reason has eliminated from operational discourses in order to constitute "proper" meanings. But the practice of these ruses, the memory of a culture, remains in these "literary" zones into which they have been repressed (as in dreams, where Freud rediscovered them). These tricks characterize a popular *art of speaking.* So quick, so perspicacious in recognizing them in the discourse of the raconteur and the peddler, the ear of the peasant or worker can discern in a way of speaking a way of treating the received language. His amused or artistic appreciation also concerns an art of living in the other's field. It distinguishes in these linguistic turns a style of thought and action— that is, models of practice.[27]

A diversionary practice: "la perruque"

With these examples of terrains on which one can locate the specific modalities of "enunciative" practices (manipulations of imposed spaces, tactics relative to particular situations), the possibility is opened up of analyzing the immense field of an "art of practice" differing from the models that (in theory) reign from top to bottom in a culture certified by education (from the universities to the elementary schools), models that all postulate the constitution of a space of their own (a scientific space or a blank page to be written on), independent of speakers and circumstances, in which they can construct a system based on rules ensuring the system's production, repetition, and verification. Two questions burden this inquiry. They concern, moreover, the two sides of a single political problem. First, on what grounds can we call this "art" *different*? Second, *from what position* (from what distinct place) can we set out to analyze it? Perhaps by resorting to the very procedures of this art, we can revise our views on both its definition as "popular" and our position as observers.

To be sure, there remain social, economic, historical differences between the practitioners (peasants, workers, etc.) of these ruses and ourselves as analysts. It is no accident that their culture is elaborated in terms of the conflictual or competitive relations between the stronger and the weaker, leaving no room for a legendary or ritual space that would be merely neutral. This difference can moreover be seen within the study itself, in the gap that separates the time of solidarity (marked by docility and gratitude toward one's hosts) from the time of writing; the latter reveals the institutional affiliations (scientific, social) and the profit (intellectual, professional, financial, etc.) for which this hospitality is objectively the means. The Bororos of Brazil sink slowly into their collective death, and Lévi-Strauss takes his seat in the French Academy. Even if this injustice disturbs him, the facts remain unchanged. This story is ours as much as his. In this one respect (which is an index of others that are more important), the intellectuals are still borne on the backs of the common people.

We need not stress here either the socioeconomic implications or the *locus* of ethnological or historical research,[28] or the political situation that, from the very beginning of contemporary research, has inscribed the concept *popular* in a problematics of repression.[29] But one pressing question must be confronted here: if one does not expect a revolution to transform the laws of history, how is it possible to foil here and now the social hierarchization which organizes scientific work on popular cultures and repeats itself in that work? The resurgence of "popular" practices within industrial and scientific modernity indicates the paths that might be taken by a transformation of the object of our study and the place from which we study it.

The operational models of popular culture cannot be confined to the past, the countryside, or primitive peoples. They exist in the heart of the strongholds of the contemporary economy. Take, for example, what in France is called *la perruque*, "the wig." *La perruque* is the worker's own work disguised as work for his employer. It differs from pilfering in that nothing of material value is stolen. It differs from absenteeism in that the worker is officially on the job. *La perruque* may be as simple a matter as a secretary's writing a love letter on "company time" or as complex as a cabinetmaker's "borrowing" a lathe to make a piece of furniture for his living room. Under different names in different countries this phenomenon is becoming more and more general, even if managers penalize it or "turn a blind eye" on it in order not to know about it.[30] Accused of stealing or turning material to his own ends and using the machines for his own profit, the worker who indulges in *la perruque* actually diverts time (not goods, since he uses only scraps) from the factory for work that is free, creative, and precisely not directed toward profit. In the very place where the machine he must serve reigns supreme, he cunningly takes pleasure in finding a way to create gratuitous products whose sole purpose is to signify his own capabilities through his *work* and to confirm his solidarity with other workers or his family through *spending* his time in this way. With the complicity of other workers (who thus defeat the competition the factory tries to instill among them), he succeeds in "putting one over" on the established order on its home ground. Far from being a regression toward a mode of production organized around artisans or individuals, *la perruque* re-introduces "popular" techniques of other times and other places into the industrial space (that is, into the Present order).

Many other examples would show the constant presence of these practices in the most ordered spheres of modern life. With variations, practices analogous to *la perruque* are proliferating in governmental and commercial offices as well as in factories. No doubt they are just as widespread as formerly (though they ought still to be studied), just as widely suspected, repressed, or ignored. Not only workshops and offices, but also museums and learned journals penalize such practices or ignore them. The authority of ethnological or folklore studies permits some of the material or linguistic objects of these practices to be collected, labelled according to place of origin and theme, put in display cases, offered for inspection and interpretation, and thus that authority conceals, as rural "treasures" serving to edify or satisfy the curiosity of city folk, the legitimization of an order supposed by its conservators to be immemorial and "natural." Or else they use the tools and products taken from a language of social operations to set off a display of technical gadgets and thus arrange them, inert, on the margins of a system that itself remains intact.

The actual order of things is precisely what "popular" tactics turn to their own ends, without any illusion that it will change any time soon. Though elsewhere it is exploited by a dominant power or simply denied by an ideological discourse, here order is *tricked* by an art. Into the institution to be served are thus insinuated styles of social exchange, technical invention, and moral resistance, that is, an economy of the *"gift"* (generosities for which one expects a return), an esthetics of *"tricks"* (artists' operations) and an ethics of *tenacity* (countless ways of refusing to accord the established order the status of a law, a meaning, or a fatality). "Popular" culture is precisely that; it is not a corpus considered as foreign, fragmented in order to be displayed, studied and "quoted" by a system which does to objects what it does to living beings.

The progressive partitioning of times and places, the disjunctive logic of specialization through and for work, no longer has an adequate counterpart in the conjunctive rituals of mass communications. This *fact* cannot become our *law*. It can be gotten around through departments that, "competing" with the gifts of our benefactors, offer them products at the expense of the institution that divides and pays the workers. This practice of economic *diversion* is in reality the return of a sociopolitical ethics into an economic system. It is no doubt related to the *potlatch* described by Mauss, an interplay of voluntary allowances that counts on reciprocity and organizes a social network articulated by the "obligation to give."[31] In our societies, the market economy is no longer determined by such an "emulation": taking the abstract individual as a basic unit, it regulates all exchanges among these units according to the code of generalized equivalence constituted by money. This individualistic axiom is, of course, now surfacing as the question that disturbs the free market system as a whole. The a priori assumption of an historical Western option is becoming its point of implosion. However that may be, the *potlatch* seems to persist within it as the mark of another type of economy. It survives in our economy, though on its margins or in its interstices. It is even developing, although held to be illegitimate, within modern market economy. Because of this, the politics of the "gift" *also* becomes a diversionary tactic. In the same way, the loss that was voluntary in a gift economy is transformed into a transgression in a profit economy: it appears as an excess (a waste), a challenge (a rejection of profit), or a crime (an attack on property).

This path, relative to our economy, derives from another; it compensates for the first even though it is illegal and (from this point of view) marginal. The same pathway allows investigations to take up a position that is no longer defined only by an acquired power and an observational knowledge, with the addition of a pinch of nostalgia. Melancholy is not enough. Certainly, with respect to the sort of writing that separates domains in the name of the division of labor and reveals class affiliations, it would be "fabulous" if, as in the stories of miracles, the groups that formerly gave us our masters and that are currently lodged in our corpus were to rise up and themselves mark their comings and goings in the texts that honor and bury them at the same time. This hope has disappeared, along with the beliefs which have long since vanished from our cities. There are no longer any ghosts who can remind the living of reciprocity. But in the order organized by the power of knowledge (ours), as in the order of the countryside or the factories, a diversionary practice remains possible.

Let us try to make a *perruque* in the economic system whose rules and hierarchies are repeated, as always, in scientific institutions. In the area of scientific research (which defines the current order of knowledge), working with its machines and making use of its scraps, we can divert the time owed to the institution; we can make textual objects that signify an art and solidarities; we can play the game of free exchange, even if it is penalized by bosses and colleagues when they are not willing to "turn a blind eye" on it; we can create networks of connivances and sleights of hand; we can exchange gifts; and in these ways we can subvert the law that, in the scientific factory, puts work at the service of the machine and, by a similar logic, progressively destroys the requirement of creation and the "obligation to give." I know of investigators experienced in this art of diversion, which is a return of the ethical, of pleasure and of invention within the scientific institution. Realizing no profit (profit is produced by work done for the factory), and often at a loss, they take something from the order of knowledge in order to inscribe "artistic achievements" on it and to carve on it the graffiti of their debts of honor. To deal with everyday tactics in this way would be to practice an "ordinary" art, to find oneself in the common situation, and to make a kind of *perruque* of writing itself.

Chapter III "Making Do":
Uses and Tactics

I N SPITE OF MEASURES taken to repress or conceal it, *la perruque* (or its equivalent) is infiltrating itself everywhere and becoming more and more common. It is only one case among all the practices which introduce *artistic* tricks and competitions of *accomplices* into a system that reproduces and partitions through work or leisure. Sly as a fox and twice as quick: there are countless ways of "making do."

From this point of view, the dividing line no longer falls between work and leisure. These two areas of activity flow together. They repeat and reinforce each other. Cultural techniques that camouflage economic reproduction with fictions of surprise ("the event"), of truth ("information") or communication ("promotion") spread through the workplace. Reciprocally, cultural production offers an area of expansion for rational operations that permit work to be managed by dividing it (analysis), tabulating it (synthesis) and aggregating it (generalization). A distinction is required other than the one that distributes behaviors according to their *place* (of work or leisure) and qualifies them thus by the fact that they are located on one or another square of the social checkerboard — in the office, in the workshop, or at the movies. There are differences of another type. They refer to the *modalities* of action, to the *formalities* of practices. They traverse the frontiers dividing time, place, and type of action into one part assigned for work and another for leisure. For example, *la perruque* grafts itself onto the system of the industrial assembly line (its counterpoint, in the same place), as a variant of the activity which, outside the factory (in another place), takes the form of *bricolage*.

Although they remain dependent upon the possibilities offered by circumstances, these transverse *tactics* do not obey the law of the place, for they are not defined or identified by it. In this respect, they are not any more localizable than the technocratic (and scriptural) *strategies* that seek to create places in conformity with abstract models. But what

distinguishes them at the same time concerns the *types of operations* and
the role of spaces: strategies are able to produce, tabulate, and impose
these spaces, when those operations take place, whereas tactics can only
use, manipulate, and divert these spaces.

We must therefore specify the operational schemas. Just as in literature one differentiates "styles" or ways of writing, one can distinguish
"ways of operating"—ways of walking, reading, producing, speaking,
etc. These styles of action intervene in a field which regulates them at a
first level (for example, at the level of the factory system), but they
introduce into it a way of turning it to their advantage that obeys other
rules and constitutes something like a second level interwoven into the
first (for instance, *la perruque*). These "ways of operating" are similar
to "instructions for use," and they create a certain play in the machine
through a stratification of different and interfering kinds of functioning.
Thus a North African living in Paris or Roubaix (France) insinuates
into the system imposed on him by the construction of a low-income
housing development or of the French language the ways of "dwelling"
(in a house or a language) peculiar to his native Kabylia. He super-
imposes them and, by that combination, creates for himself a space in
which he can find *ways of using* the constraining order of the place or of
the language. Without leaving the place where he has no choice but to
live and which lays down its law for him, he establishes within it a
degree of *plurality* and creativity. By an art of being in between, he
draws unexpected results from his situation.

These modes of use—or rather re-use—multiply with the extension of
acculturation phenomena, that is, with the displacements that substitute
manners or "methods" of transiting toward an identification of a person
by the place in which he lives or works. That does not prevent them
from corresponding to a very ancient art of "making do." I give them
the name of uses, even though the word most often designates stereo-
typed procedures accepted and reproduced by a group, its "ways and
customs." The problem lies in the ambiguity of the word, since it is
precisely a matter of recognizing in these "uses" "actions" (in the military
sense of the word) that have their own formality and inventiveness and
that discreetly organize the multiform labor of consumption.

Use, or consumption

In the wake of the many remarkable works that have analyzed "cultural products," the system of their production,[1] the geography of their

distribution and the situation of consumers in that geography,[2] it seems possible to consider these products no longer merely as data on the basis of which statistical tabulations of their circulation can be drawn up or the economic functioning of their diffusion understood, but also as parts of the repertory with which users carry out operations of their own. Henceforth, these facts are no longer the data of our calculations, but rather the lexicon of users' practices. Thus, once the images broadcast by television and the time spent in front of the TV set have been analyzed, it remains to be asked what the consumer *makes* of these images and during these hours. The thousands of people who buy a health magazine, the customers in a supermarket, the practitioners of urban space, the consumers of newspaper stories and legends—what do they make of what they "absorb," receive, and pay for? What do they do with it?

The enigma of the consumer-sphinx. His products are scattered in the graphs of televised, urbanistic, and commercial production. They are all the less visible because the networks framing them are becoming more and more tightly woven, flexible, and totalitarian. They are thus protean in form, blending in with their surroundings, and liable to disappear into the colonizing organizations whose products leave no room where the consumers can mark their activity. The child still scrawls and daubs on his schoolbooks; even if he is punished for this crime, he has made a space for himself and signs his existence as an author on it. The television viewer cannot write anything on the screen of his set. He has been dislodged from the product; he plays no role in its apparition. He loses his author's rights and becomes, or so it seems, a pure receiver, the mirror of a multiform and narcissistic actor. Pushed to the limit, he would be the image of appliances that no longer need him in order to produce themselves, the reproduction of a "celibate machine."[3]

In reality, a rationalized, expansionist, centralized, spectacular and clamorous production is confronted by an entirely different kind of production, called "consumption" and characterized by its ruses, its fragmentation (the result of the circumstances), its poaching, its clandestine nature, its tireless but quiet activity, in short by its quasi-invisibility, since it shows itself not in its own products (where would it place them?) but in an art of using those imposed on it.

The cautious yet fundamental inversions brought about by consumption in other societies have long been studied. Thus the spectacular victory of Spanish colonization over the indigenous Indian cultures was diverted from its intended aims by the use made of it: even when they were subjected, indeed even when they accepted their subjection, the Indians often used the laws, practices, and representations that were imposed on them by force or by fascination to ends other than those of their conquerors; they made something else out of them; they subverted them from within—not by rejecting them or by transforming them (though that occurred as well), but by many different ways of using them in the service of rules, customs or convictions foreign to the colonization which they could not escape.[4] They metaphorized the dominant order: they made it function in another register. They remained other within the system which they assimilated and which assimilated them externally. They diverted it without leaving it. Procedures of consumption maintained their difference in the very space that the occupier was organizing.

Is this an extreme example? No, even if the resistance of the Indians was founded on a memory tattooed by oppression, a past inscribed on their body.[5] To a lesser degree, the same process can be found in the use made in "popular" milieus of the cultures diffused by the "elites" that produce language. The imposed knowledge and symbolisms become objects manipulated by practitioners who have not produced them. The language produced by a certain social category has the power to extend its conquests into vast areas surrounding it, "deserts" where nothing equally articulated seems to exist, but in doing so it is caught in the trap of its assimilation by a jungle of procedures rendered invisible to the conqueror by the very victories he seems to have won. However spectacular it may be, his privilege is likely to be only apparent if it merely serves as a framework for the stubborn, guileful, everyday practices that make use of it. What is called "popularization" or "degradation" of a culture is from this point of view a partial and caricatural aspect of the revenge that utilizing tactics take on the power that dominates production. In any case, the consumer cannot be identified or qualified by the newspapers or commercial products he assimilates: between the person (who uses them) and these products (indexes of the "order" which is imposed on him), there is a gap of varying proportions opened by the use that he makes of them.

Use must thus be analyzed in itself. There is no lack of models, especially so far as language is concerned; language is indeed the privileged terrain on which to discern the formal rules proper to such practices. Gilbert Ryle, borrowing Saussure's distinction between "*langue*" (a system) and "*parole*" (an act), compared the former to a fund of *capital* and the latter to the *operations* it makes possible: on the one hand, a stock of materials, on the other, transactions and uses.[6] In the case of consumption, one could almost say that production furnishes the capital and that users, like renters, acquire the right to operate on and with this fund without owning it. But the comparison is valid only for the relation between the knowledge of a language and "speech acts." From this alone can be derived a series of questions and categories which have permitted us, especially since Bar-Hillel's work, to open up within the study of language (*semiosis* or *semiotics*) a particular area (called *pragmatics*) devoted to use, notably to *indexical expressions*, that is, "words and sentences of which the reference cannot be determined without knowledge of the context of use."[7]

We shall return later to these inquiries which have illuminated a whole region of everyday practices (the use of language); at this point, it suffices to note that they are based on a problematics of enunciation.[8] By situating the act in relation to its circumstances, "contexts of use" draw attention to the traits that specify the act of speaking (or practice of language) and are its effects. Enunciation furnishes a model of these characteristics, but they can also be discovered in the relation that other practices (walking, residing, etc.) entertain with non-linguistic systems. Enunciation presupposes: (1) a *realization* of the linguistic system through a speech act that actualizes some of its potential (language is real only in the act of speaking); (2) an *appropriation* of language by the speaker who uses it; (3) the postulation of an interlocutor (real or fictive) and thus the constitution of a relational *contract* or allocution (one speaks to someone); (4) the establishment of a *present* through the act of the "I" who speaks, and conjointly, since "the present is properly the source of time," the organization of a temporality (the present creates a before and an after) and the existence of a "now" which is the presence to the world.[9]

These elements (realizing, appropriating, being inscribed in relations, being situated in time) make of enunciation, and secondarily of use, a nexus of circumstances, a nexus adherent to the "context" from which it can be distinguished only by abstraction. Indissociable from the present *instant*, from particular circumstances and from a *faire* (a peculiar way of doing things, of producing language and of modifying the dynamics of a relation), the speech act is at the same time a use *of* language and an operation performed *on* it. We can attempt to apply this model to many non-linguistic operations by taking as our hypothesis that all these uses concern consumption.

We must, however, clarify the nature of these operations from another angle, not on the basis of the relation they entertain with a system or an order, but insofar as *power relationships* define the networks in which they are inscribed and delimit the circumstances from which they can profit. In order to do so, we must pass from a linguistic frame of reference to a polemological one. We are concerned with battles or games between the strong and the weak, and with the "actions" which remain possible for the latter.

Strategies and tactics

Unrecognized producers, poets of their own affairs, trailblazers in the jungles of functionalist rationality, consumers produce something resembling the *"lignes d'erre"* described by Deligny.[10] They trace "indeterminate trajectories"[11] that are apparently meaningless, since they do not cohere with the constructed, written, and prefabricated space through which they move. They are sentences that remain unpredictable within the space ordered by the organizing techniques of systems. Although they use as their *material* the *vocabularies* of established languages (those of television, newspapers, the supermarket or city planning), although they remain within the framework of prescribed *syntaxes* (the temporal modes of schedules, paradigmatic organizations of places, etc.), these "traverses" remain heterogeneous to the systems they infiltrate and in which they sketch out the guileful ruses of *different* interests and desires. They circulate, come and go, overflow and drift over an imposed terrain, like the snowy waves of the sea slipping in among the rocks and defiles of an established order.

Statistics can tell us virtually nothing about the currents in this sea theoretically governed by the institutional frameworks that it in fact gradually erodes and displaces. Indeed, it is less a matter of a liquid circulating in the interstices of a solid than of different *movements* making use of the elements of the terrain. Statistical study is satisfied with classifying, calculating and tabulating these elements—"lexical" units, advertising words, television images, manufactured products, constructed places, etc.—and they do it with categories and taxonomies that conform to those of industrial or administrative production. Hence such study can grasp only the material used by consumer practices—a material which is obviously that imposed on everyone by production—and not the *formality* proper to these practices, their surreptitious and guileful "movement," that is, the very activity of "making do." The strength of these computations lies in their ability to divide, but this ana-lytical ability eliminates the possibility of representing the tactical trajectories which, according to their own criteria, select fragments taken from the vast ensembles of production in order to compose new stories with them.

What is counted is *what* is used, not the *ways* of using. Paradoxically, the latter become invisible in the universe of codification and generalized transparency. Only the effects (the quantity and locus of the consumed products) of these waves that flow in everywhere remain perceptible. They circulate without being seen, discernible only through the objects that they move about and erode. The practices of consumption are the ghosts of the society that carries their name. Like the "spirits" of former times, they constitute the multiform and occult postulate of productive activity.

In order to give an account of these practices, I have resorted to the category of "trajectory."[12] It was intended to suggest a temporal movement through space, that is, the unity of a diachronic *succession* of points through which it passes, and not the *figure* that these points form on a space that is supposed to be synchronic or achronic. Indeed, this "representation" is insufficient, precisely because a trajectory is drawn, and time and movement are thus reduced to a line that can be seized as a whole by the eye and read in a single moment, as one projects onto a map the path taken by someone walking through a city. However useful this "flattening out" may be, it transforms the *temporal* articulation of places into a *spatial* sequence of points. A graph takes the place of an operation. A reversible sign (one that can be read in both directions, once it is projected onto a map) is substituted for a practice indissociable from particular moments and "opportunities," and thus irreversible (one cannot go backward in time, or have another chance at missed opportunities). It is thus a mark *in place of* acts, a relic in place of performances: it is only their remainder, the sign of their erasure. Such a projection postulates that it is possible to take the one (the mark) for the other (operations articulated on occasions). This is a *quid pro quo* typical of the reductions which a functionalist administration of space must make in order to be effective.

A distinction between *strategies* and *tactics* appears to provide a more adequate initial schema. I call a *strategy* the calculation (or manipulation) of power relationships that becomes possible as soon as a subject with will and power (a business, an army, a city, a scientific institution) can be isolated. It postulates a *place* that can be delimited as its *own* and serve as the base from which relations with an *exteriority* composed of targets or threats (customers or competitors, enemies, the country surrounding the city, objectives and objects of research, etc.) can be managed. As in management, every "strategic" rationalization seeks first of all to distinguish its "own" place, that is, the place of its own power and will, from an "environment." A Cartesian attitude, if you wish: it is an effort to delimit one's own place in a world bewitched by the invisible powers of the Other. It is also the typical attitude of modern science, politics, and military strategy.

The establishment of a break between a place appropriated as one's own and its other is accompanied by important effects, some of which we must immediately note:

(1) The "proper" is *a triumph of place over time*. It allows one to capitalize acquired advantages, to prepare future expansions, and thus to give oneself a certain independence with respect to the variability of circumstances. It is a mastery of time through the foundation of an autonomous place.

(2) It is also a mastery of places through sight. The division of space makes possible a *panoptic practice* proceeding from a place whence the eye can transform foreign forces into objects that can be observed and measured, and thus control and "include" them within its scope of vision.[13] To be able to see (far into the distance) is also to be able to predict, to run ahead of time by reading a space.

(3) It would be legitimate to define the *power of knowledge* by this ability to transform the uncertainties of history into readable spaces. But it would be more correct to recognize in these "strategies" a specific type of knowledge, one sustained and determined by the power to provide oneself with one's own place. Thus military or scientific strategies have always been inaugurated through the constitution of their "own" areas (autonomous cities, "neutral" or "independent" institutions, laboratories pursuing "disinterested" research, etc.). In other words, *a certain power is the precondition of this knowledge* and not merely its effect or its attribute. It makes this knowledge possible and at the same time determines its characteristics. It produces itself in and through this knowledge.

By contrast with a strategy (whose successive shapes introduce a certain play into this formal schema and whose link with a particular historical configuration of rationality should also be clarified), a *tactic* is a calculated action determined by the absence of a proper locus. No delimitation of an exteriority, then, provides it with the condition necessary for autonomy. The space of a tactic is the space of the other. Thus it must play on and with a terrain imposed on it and organized by the law of a foreign power. It does not have the means to *keep to itself*, at a distance, in a position of withdrawal, foresight, and self-collection: it is a maneuver "within the enemy's field of vision," as von Bülow put it,[14] and within enemy territory. It does not, therefore, have the options of planning general strategy and viewing the adversary as a whole within a district, visible, and objectifiable space. It operates in isolated actions, blow by blow. It takes advantage of "opportunities" and depends on them, being without any base where it could stockpile its winnings, build up its own position, and plan raids. What it wins it cannot keep. This nowhere gives a tactic mobility, to be sure, but a mobility that must accept the chance offerings of the moment, and seize on the wing the possibilities that offer themselves at any given moment. It must vigilantly make use of the cracks that particular conjunctions open in the surveillance of the proprietary powers. It poaches in them. It creates surprises in them. It can be where it is least expected. It is a guileful ruse.

In short, a tactic is an art of the weak. Clausewitz noted this fact in discussing deception in his treatise *On War*. The more a power grows, the less it can allow itself to mobilize part of its means in the service of deception: it is dangerous to deploy large forces for the sake of appearances; this sort of "demonstration" is generally useless and "the gravity of bitter necessity makes direct action so urgent that it leaves no room for this sort of game." One deploys his forces, one does not take chances with feints. Power is bound by its very visibility. In contrast, trickery is possible for the weak, and often it is his only possibility, as a "last resort": "The weaker the forces at the disposition of the strategist, the more the strategist will be able to use deception."[15] I translate: the more the strategy is transformed into tactics.

Clausewitz also compares trickery to wit: "Just as wit involves a certain legerdemain relative to ideas and concepts, trickery is a sort of legerdemain relative to acts."[16] This indicates the mode in which a tactic, which is indeed a form of legerdemain, takes an order by surprise. The art of "pulling tricks" involves a sense of the opportunities afforded by a particular occasion. Through procedures that Freud makes explicit with reference to wit,[17] a tactic boldly juxtaposes diverse elements in order suddenly to produce a flash shedding a different light on the language of a place and to strike the hearer. Cross-cuts, fragments, cracks and lucky hits in the framework of a system, consumers' ways of operating are the practical equivalents of wit.

Lacking its own place, lacking a view of the whole, limited by the blindness (which may lead to perspicacity) resulting from combat at close quarters, limited by the possibilities of the moment, a tactic is determined by the *absence of power* just as a strategy is organized by the postulation of power. From this point of view, the dialectic of a tactic may be illuminated by the ancient art of sophistic. As the author of a great "strategic" system, Aristotle was already very interested in the procedures of this enemy which perverted, as he saw it, the order of truth. He quotes a formula of this protean, quick, and surprising adversary that, by making explicit the basis of sophistic, can also serve finally to define a tactic as I understand the term here: it is a matter, Corax said, of "making the worse argument seem the better."[18] In its paradoxical concision, this formula delineates the relationship of forces that is the starting point for an intellectual creativity as persistent as it is subtle, tireless, ready for every opportunity, scattered over the terrain of the dominant order and foreign to the rules laid down and imposed by a rationality founded on established rights and property.

In sum, strategies are actions which, thanks to the establishment of a place of power (the property of a proper), elaborate theoretical places (systems and totalizing discourses) capable of articulating an ensemble of physical places in which forces are distributed. They combine these three types of places and seek to master each by means of the others. They thus privilege spatial relationships. At the very least they attempt to reduce temporal relations to spatial ones through the analytical attribution of a proper place to each particular element and through the combinatory organization of the movements specific to units or groups of units. The model was military before it became "scientific." Tactics are procedures that gain validity in relation to the pertinence they lend to time—to the circumstances which the precise instant of an intervention transforms into a favorable situation, to the rapidity of the movements that change the organization of a space, to the relations among successive moments in an action, to the possible intersections of durations and heterogeneous rhythms, etc. In this respect, the difference corresponds to two historical options regarding action and security (options that moreover have more to do with constraints than with possibilities): strategies pin their hopes on the resistance that the *establishment of a place* offers to the erosion of time; tactics on a clever *utilization of time*, of the opportunities it presents and also of the play that it introduces into the foundations of power. Even if the methods practiced by the everyday art of war never present themselves in such a clear form, it nevertheless remains the case that the two ways of acting can be distinguished according to whether they bet on place or on time.

The rhetorics of practice, ancient ruses

Various theoretical comparisons will allow us better to characterize the tactics or the polemology of the "weak." The "figures" and "turns" ana-lyzed by *rhetoric* are particularly illuminating in this regard. Freud already noticed this fact and used them in his studies on wit and on the forms taken by the return of the repressed within the field of an order: verbal economy and condensation, double meanings and misinterpreta-tions, displacements and alliterations, multiple uses of the same material, etc.[19] There is nothing surprising about these homologies between prac-tical ruses and rhetorical movements. In relation to the legalities of syntax and "proper" sense, that is, in relation to the general definition of a "proper" (as opposed to what is not "proper"), the good and bad tricks of rhetoric are played on the terrain that has been set aside in this way. They are manipulations of language relative to occasions and are in-tended to seduce, captivate, or invert the linguistic position of the addressee.[20] Whereas grammar watches over the "propriety" of terms, rhetorical alterations (metaphorical drifts, elliptical condensations, meto-nymic miniaturizations, etc.) point to the use of language by speakers in particular situations of ritual or actual linguistic combat. They are the indexes of consumption and of the interplay of forces. They depend on a problematics of enunciation. In addition, although (or because) they are excluded in principle from scientific discourse, these "ways of speaking" provide the analysis of "ways of operating" with a repertory of models and hypotheses. After all, they are merely variants within a general semiotics of tactics. To be sure, in order to work out that semiotics, it would be necessary to review arts of thinking and acting other than the one that the articulation of a certain rationality has founded on the delimitation of a proper: from the sixty-four hexagrams of the Chinese *I-Ching*[21] or the Greek *mētis*[22] to the Arabic *ḥīla*,[23] other "logics" can be discerned.

I am not concerned directly here with the constitution of such a semiotics, but rather with suggesting some ways of thinking about everyday practices of consumers, supposing from the start that they are of a tactical nature. Dwelling, moving about, speaking, reading, shopping, and cooking are activities that seem to correspond to the characteristics of tactical ruses and surprises: clever tricks of the "weak" within the order established by the "strong," an art of putting one over on the adversary on his own turf, hunter's tricks, maneuverable, polymorph mobilities, jubilant, poetic, and warlike discoveries.

Perhaps these practices correspond to an ageless art which has not only persisted through the institutions of successive political orders but goes back much farther than our histories and forms strange alliances preceding the frontiers of humanity. These practices present in fact a curious analogy, and a sort of immemorial link, to the simulations, tricks, and disguises that certain fishes or plants execute with extraordinary virtuosity. The procedures of this art can be found in the farthest reaches of the domain of the living, as if they managed to surmount not only the strategic distributions of historical institutions but also the break established by the very institution of consciousness. They maintain formal continuities and the permanence of a memory without language, from the depths of the oceans to the streets of our great cities.

In any event, on the scale of contemporary history, it also seems that the generalization and expansion of technocratic rationality have created, between the links of the system, a fragmentation and explosive growth of these practices which were formerly regulated by stable local units. Tactics are more and more frequently going off their tracks. Cut loose from the traditional communities that circumscribed their functioning, they have begun to wander everywhere in a space which is becoming at once more homogeneous and more extensive. Consumers are transformed into immigrants. The system in which they move about is too vast to be able to fix them in one place, but too constraining for them ever to be able to escape from it and go into exile elsewhere. There is no longer an elsewhere. Because of this, the "strategic" model is also transformed, as if defeated by its own success: it was by definition based on the definition of a "proper" distinct from everything else; but now that "proper" has become the whole. It could be that, little by little, it will exhaust its capacity to transform itself and constitute only the space (just as totalitarian as the cosmos of ancient times) in which a cybernetic society will arise, the scene of the Brownian movements of invisible and innumerable tactics. One would thus have a proliferation of aleatory and indeterminable manipulations within an immense framework of socioeconomic constraints and securities: myriads of almost invisible movements, playing on the more and more refined texture of a place that is even, continuous, and constitutes a proper place for all people. Is this already the present or the future of the great city?

Leaving aside the multimillenial archeology of ruses as well as the possibility of their anthill-like future, the study of a few current everyday tactics ought not to forget the horizon from which they proceed, nor, at the other extreme, the horizon towards which they are likely to go. The evocation of these perspectives on the distant past or future at least allows us to resist the effects of the fundamental but often exclusive and obsessive analysis that seeks to describe institutions and the mechanisms of *repression*. The privilege enjoyed by the problematics of repression in the field of research should not be surprising: scientific institutions belong to the system which they study, they conform to the well-known genre of the family story (an ideological criticism does not change its functioning in any way; the criticism merely creates the appearance of a distance for scientists who are members of the institution); they even add the disturbing charm of devils or bogey-men whose stories are told during long evenings around the family hearth. But this elucidation of the apparatus by itself has the disadvantage of *not seeing* practices which are heterogeneous to it and which it represses or thinks it represses. Nevertheless, they have every chance of surviving this apparatus *too*, and, in any case, they are *also* part of social life, and all the more resistant because they are more flexible and adjusted to perpetual mutation. When one examines this fleeting and permanent reality carefully, one has the impression of exploring the night-side of societies, a night longer than their day, a dark sea from which successive institutions emerge, a maritime immensity on which socioeconomic and political structures appear as ephemeral islands.

The imaginary landscape of an inquiry is not without value, even if it is without rigor. It restores what was earlier called "popular culture," but it does so in order to transform what was represented as a matrix-force of history into a mobile infinity of tactics. It thus keeps before our eyes the structure of a social imagination in which the problem constantly takes different forms and begins anew. It also wards off the effects of an analysis which necessarily grasps these practices only on the margins of a technical apparatus, at the point where they alter or defeat its instruments. It is the study itself which is marginal with respect to the phenomena studied. The landscape that represents these phenomena in an imaginary mode thus has an overall corrective and therapeutic value in resisting their reduction by a lateral examination. It at least assures their presence as ghosts. This return to another scene thus reminds us of the relation between the experience of these practices and what remains of them in an analysis. It is evidence, evidence which can only be fantastic and not scientific, of the disproportion between everyday tactics and a strategic elucidation. Of all the things everyone does, how much gets written down? Between the two, the image, the phantom of the expert but mute body, preserves the difference.

Part II
Theories of the Art of Practice

E VERYDAY PRACTICES depend on a vast ensemble which is difficult to delimit but which we may provisionally designate as an ensemble of *procedures*. The latter are schemas of operations and of technical manipulations. On the basis of some recent and fundamental analyses (those of Foucault, Bourdieu, Vernant and Détienne, and others) it is possible, if not to define them, at least to clarify their functioning relative to discourse (or to "ideology," as Foucault puts it), to the acquired (Bourdieu's *habitus*), and to the form of time we call an *occasion* (the *kairos* discussed by Vernant and Détienne). These are different ways of locating a technicity of a certain type and at the same time situating the study of this technicity with respect to current trends in research.

By situating this essay in a larger ensemble and at a point that has already been written on (in spite of a persistent fiction, we never write on a blank page, but always on one that has already been written on), I seek neither to present a review of the theoretical and descriptive works that have organized the question or illuminated it obliquely (a review that would in any case be illusory), nor merely to acknowledge my debts. What is at stake is the status of the analysis and its relation to its object. As in a workshop or laboratory, the objects produced by an inquiry result from its (more or less original) contribution to the field that has made it possible. They thus refer to a "state of the question"— that is, to a network of professional and textual exchanges, to the "dialectic" of an inquiry in progress (if one takes "dialectic" in the sixteenth-century sense of the movement of relations among different procedures on the same stage, and not in the sense of the power assigned to a particular place to totalize or "surmount" these differences). From this point of view, the "objects" of our research cannot be detached from the intellectual and social "commerce" that organizes their definition and their displacements.

In "forgetting" the collective inquiry in which he is inscribed, in isolating the object of his discourse from its historical genesis, an "author" in effect denies his real situation. He creates the fiction of a place of his own (*une place propre*). In spite of the contradictory ideologies that may accompany it, the setting aside of the subject-object relation or of the discourse-object relation is the abstraction that generates an illusion of "authorship." It removes the traces of belonging to a network—traces that always compromise the author's rights. It camouflages the conditions of the production of discourse and its object. For this negated genealogy is substituted a drama combining the simulacrum of an object with the simulacrum of an author. A discourse can maintain a certain scientific character, however, by making explicit the rules and conditions of its production, and first of all the relations out of which it arises.

This detour has led us back to a debt, but to a debt that is essential in any new discourse, and not merely to a borrowing that can be exorcized by homage or acknowledgment. Rabelais' Panurge, for once waxing lyrical, saw in this sort of debt the index of a universal solidarity. Every "proper" place is altered by the mark others have left on it. This fact also excludes the "objective" representation of the proximate or distant positions called "influences." They appear in a text (or in the definition of an investigation) through the effects of alteration and operation they have produced in it. Debts cannot be transformed into objects either. Every particular study is a many-faceted mirror (others reappear everywhere in this space) reflecting the exchanges, readings, and confrontations that form the conditions of its possibility, but it is a broken and anamorphic mirror (others are fragmented and altered by it).

Chapter IV Foucault and Bourdieu

1. Scattered technologies: Foucault

From the outset we face the problem of the relation of these procedures to discourse. Procedures lack the repetitive fixity of rites, customs or reflexes, kinds of knowledge which are no longer (or not yet) articulated in discourse. Their mobility constantly adjusts them to a diversity of objectives and "coups," without their being dependent on a verbal elucidation. Are they, however, completely autonomous with respect to the latter? Tactics in discourse can, as we have seen, be the formal indicator of tactics that have no discourse.[1] Moreover, the ways of thinking embedded in ways of operating constitute a strange—and massive—case of the relations between practices and theories.

In *Discipline and Punish*, his study of the organization of the "procedures" of penitential, educational, and medical control at the beginning of the nineteenth century, Foucault offers a variety of synonyms, words that dance about and successively approach an impossible proper name: "apparatuses" ("*dispositifs*"), "instrumentalities," "techniques," "mechanisms," "machineries," etc.[2] The uncertainty and the mobility of the thing in language are already significant. But the very history he narrates, that of an enormous substitution, postulates and puts in position a dichotomy between "ideologies" and "procedures" in the process of tracing their distinct evolutions and their intersections. He analyzes the process of a chiasm: the place occupied by the reformist projects of the late eighteenth century has been "colonized," "vampirized," by the disciplinary procedures that subsequently organize the social space. This detective story about a substituted body would have pleased Freud.

In Foucault's work, the drama pits against each other two forces whose relationship is reversed by the tricks of time. On the one hand, the ideology of the Enlightenment, revolutionary with regard to penal justice. For the "torture" of the Ancien Régime, a violent corporal ritual dramatizing the triumph of royal order over felons chosen for their symbolic value, the reformist projects of the eighteenth century seek to substitute punishments applicable to all, in proportion to the crimes, useful to society, edifying for the condemned. In fact, disciplinary procedures gradually perfected in the army and in schools quickly won out over the vast and complex judicial apparatus constructed by the Enlightenment. These techniques are refined and extended without recourse to an ideology. Through a cellular space of the same type for everyone (schoolboys, soldiers, workers, criminals or the ill), the techniques perfected the visibility and the gridwork of this space in order to make of it a tool capable of disciplining under control and "treating" any human group whatever. The development is a matter of technological details, miniscule and decisive procedures. The details overcome theory: through these procedures the universalization of a uniform penalty— imprisonment—is imposed, which inverts revolutionary institutions from within and establishes everywhere the "penitentiary" in the place of penal justice.

Foucault thus distinguishes two heterogeneous systems. He outlines the advantages won by a political technology of the body over the elaboration of a body of doctrine. But he is not content merely to separate two forms of power. By following the establishment and victorious multiplication of this "minor instrumentality," he tries to bring to light the springs of this opaque power that has no possessor, no privileged place, no superiors or inferiors, no repressive activity or dogmatism, that is almost autonomously effective through its technological ability to distribute, classify, analyze and spatially individualize the object dealt with. (All the while, ideology babbles on!) In a series of clincial tableaux (also marvelously "panoptic"), he tries to name and classify in turn the "general rules," "conditions of functioning," "techniques" and "procedures," distinct "operations," "mechanisms," "principles," and "elements" that compose a "microphysics of power."[3] This gallery of diagrams has the twin functions of delimiting a social stratum of practices that have no discourse and of founding a discourse on these practices.

In what then does this level of decisive practices isolated by analysis consist? By a detour that characterizes the strategy of his inquiries, Foucault discerns at this level *the move* (*le geste*) *which has organized the discursive space*. This move is not, as in his earlier book, *The History of Madness*, the epistemological and social move of isolating excluded people from normal social intercourse in order to create the space that makes possible a rational order; rather it is the miniscule and ubiquitously reproduced move of "gridding" (*quadriller*) a visible space in such a way as to make its occupants available for observation and "information." The procedures that repeat, amplify, and perfect this move organize the discourse that has taken the form of the "human sciences." In that way a *non-discursive move* is identified which, being privileged for social and historical reasons that remain to be explained, is articulated in contemporary scientific knowledge.

To the extremely novel perspectives opened up by this analysis[4]—which would, moreover, allow the development of another theory of "style" (style, a way of walking through a terrain, a non-textual move or attitude, organizes the text of a thought)—we may add a few questions relevant to our inquiry:

1. In undertaking to produce an archeology of the human sciences (his explicit goal since *The Order of Things/Les mots et les choses*) and in seeking a "common matrix," viz., a "technology of power," which would be at the origin of both criminal law (the punishment of human beings) and the human sciences (the knowledge of human beings), Foucault is led to make a *selection* from the ensemble of procedures that form the fabric of social activity in the eighteenth and nineteenth centuries. This surgical operation consists in starting out from a proliferating contemporary system—a judicial and scientific technology—and *tracing it back through history, isolating* from the whole body the cancerous growth that has invaded it, and *explaining* its current functioning *by its genesis* over the two preceding centuries. From an immense body of historical material (penal, military, educational, medical), the operation extracts the optical and panoptical procedures which increasingly multiply within it and discerns in them the at first scattered indexes of an apparatus whose elements become better defined, combine with each other, and reproduce themselves little by little throughout all the strata of society.

This remarkable historiographical "operation" raises simultaneously two questions which must nevertheless not be confused: on the one hand, the decisive role of technological procedures and apparatuses in the organization of a society; on the other, the exceptional development of a particular category of these apparatuses. It is thus still necessary to ask ourselves:

(a) How can we explain the *privileged development* of the particular series constituted by panoptic apparatuses?

(b) What is the status of so many other series which, pursuing their silent itineraries, have not given rise to a discursive configuration or to a technological systematization? They could be considered as an *immense* reserve constituting either the beginnings or traces of *different developments.*

It is in any case impossible to reduce the functioning of a society to a dominant type of procedures. Recent studies have pointed to other technological apparatuses and their interplay with ideology; these studies which have also underlined the dominant character of these apparatuses, though from different points of view—thus, for example, the work of Serge Moscovici, especially on urban organization,[5] or that of Pierre Legendre, on the apparatus of medieval law.[6] These apparatuses seem to prevail over a more or less lengthy period of time, then fall back into the stratified mass of procedures, while others replace them in the role of "informing" a system.

A society is thus composed of certain foregrounded practices organizing its normative institutions *and* of innumerable other practices that remain "minor," always there but not organizing discourses and preserving the beginnings or remains of different (institutional, scientific) hypotheses for that society or for others. It is in this multifarious and silent "reserve" of procedures that we should look for "consumer" practices having the double characteristic, pointed out by Foucault, of being able to organize both spaces and languages, whether on a minute or a vast scale.

2. The final formation (the contemporary technologies of observation and discipline) which serves as the point of departure for the regressive history practiced by Foucault explains the impressive coherence of the practices he selects and examines. But can it be assumed that the ensemble of procedures exhibits the same coherence? A priori, no. The exceptional, indeed cancerous, development of panoptic procedures seems to be indissociable from the historical role to which they have been assigned, that of being a weapon to be used in combatting and controlling heterogeneous practices. The coherence in question is the result of a particular success, and will not be characteristic of all technological practices. Beneath what one might call the "monotheistic" privilege that panoptic apparatuses have won for themselves, a *"polytheism" of scattered practices* survives, dominated but not erased by the triumphal success of one of their number.

3. What is the status of a particular apparatus when it is transformed into the organizing principle of a technology of power? What effect does foregrounding have on it? What new relationships within the dispersed

ensemble of procedures are established when one of them is institution-alized as a penitentiary-scientific system? The apparatus thus privileged might well lose the effectiveness that it owed, according to Foucault, to its miniscule and silent technical advances. By leaving the obscure stratum in which Foucault locates the determining mechanisms of a society, it would be in the position of institutions slowly "colonized" by still silent procedures. Perhaps in fact (this is, at least, one of the hypotheses of this essay), the system of discipline and control which took shape in the nineteenth century on the basis of earlier procedures, is today itself "vampirized" by other procedures.

4. Can one go even further? Is not the very fact that, as a result of their expansion, the apparatuses of control become an object of clarifi-cation and thus part of the language of the Enlightenment, proof that they ceased to determine discursive institutions? When the discourse can deal with some effects of the organizing apparatuses that means that they no longer play this determining role. One must ask what type of apparatus articulates the discourse in such a way that the discourse cannot make it its object. Unless it is the case that one discourse (that of *Discipline and Punish*), by analyzing the practices on which it itself depends, overcomes in this way the division, posited by Foucault, be-tween "ideologies" and "procedures."

These questions, to which one could at the moment give only pre-mature answers, indicate at least the transformations that Foucault has introduced into his analysis of procedures and the perspectives that have opened up since his study. By showing, in one case, the heterogeneity and equivocal relations of apparatuses and ideologies, he constituted as a treatable historical object this zone in which technological procedures have specific *effects of power*, obey their own *logical modes of function-ing*, and can produce a fundamental *diversion* within the institutions of order and knowledge. It remains to be asked how we should consider other, equally infinitesimal, procedures, which have not been "privileged" by history but are nevertheless active in innumerable ways in the open-ings of established technological networks. This is particularly the case of procedures that do not enjoy the precondition, associated with all those studied by Foucault, of having *their own place* (*un lieu propre*) on which the panoptic machinery can operate. These techniques, which are also operational, but initially deprived of what gives the others their force, are the "tactics" which I have suggested might furnish a formal index of the ordinary practices of consumption.

2. "Docta ignorantia": Bourdieu

Our "tactics" seem to be analyzable only indirectly, through another society: the France of the Ancien Régime or the nineteenth century, in the case of Foucault; Kabylia or Béarn,, in that of Bourdieu; ancient Greece, in that of Vernant and Détienne, etc. They return to us from afar, as though a different space were required in which to make visible and elucidate the tactics marginalized by the Western form of rationality. Other regions give us back what our culture has excluded from its discourse. But have tactics not been defined precisely as what we have eliminated or lost? As in *Tristes tropiques*,[7] we travel abroad to discover in distant lands something whose presence at home has become unrecognizable. The tactical and rhetorical tricks condemned as illegitimate by the scientific family into which Freud long sought to be accepted as an adopted son, he also discovered through the discovery and exploration of a *terra incognita*, the unconscious; but they came to him from a more ancient and yet nearer region—from a Jewish foreignness he long rejected, and which rises with him into scientific discourse, but disguised as dreams and slips of the tongue. Freudianism might thus be considered as a combination of the legitimate strategies that issued from the Enlightenment and the "turns" that return from further back under the mantle of the unconscious.

Two halves

In Bourdieu's work, *Esquisse d'une théorie de la pratique. Précédée de trois études d'ethnologie kabyle* (1972), Kabylia plays the role of a Trojan horse within a "theory of practice"; the three texts devoted to it (the three best that Bourdieu has written, especially "The Kabyle House or the World Reversed") serve as a multiple vanguard for a long epistemological discourse; like poems, these "three studies of Kabylian ethnology" lead into a theory (a sort of commentary in prose) and provide it with a fund of material that can be indefinitely cited in marvelous fragments; in the end, at the point when Bourdieu publishes his three "early" texts, their referential and poetic locus is erased from the title (which reverts to commentary: *a theory*); and, scattered in the effects that it produces in the authorized discourse, this Kabylian origin itself gradually disappears, a sun obscured by the speculative landscape that it still illuminates: these traits are already characteristic of the position of practice in theory.[8]

This is no accident. Bourdieu's studies since 1972 which have been concerned with "the practical sense"[9] are organized in the same way, except for "Avenir de classe et causalité du probable,"[10] with one variant, the study on "matrimonial strategies" (concerned precisely with the genealogical economy), which refers to the Béarn region of Southwestern France rather than Kabylia.[11] Thus, two points of reference. Is it possible to say which—Béarn or Kabylia—is the doublet of the other? They represent two "familiarities," the one determined—and haunted—by its distance from the native land, the other by the foreignness of its cultural difference. It nevertheless seems that Béarn, *in-fans* (not-speaking) like every origin, had first to find a doublet in the Kabylian situation (so similar to that of his native land in the analysis Bourdieu gives of it) before it could be described. Having thus become "objectifiable," it furnishes the real (and legendary: where are the Béarnians of yesteryear?) support allowing the introduction of the concept of *habitus* into the human sciences, which is the personal stamp Bourdieu has put on theory. Hence the particularity of the originary experience is lost in its power of reorganizing the general discourse.

Divided into two mutually enabling parts, the *Outline of a Theory of Practice* is first of all an interdisciplinary operation. It is thus a metaphor in the sense that there is a passage from one genre to the other: from ethnology to sociology. Things are, however, not that simple. It is difficult to situate the book. Does it depend on the interdisciplinary confrontations Bourdieu earlier urged, confrontations that, going beyond the stage of simple exchanges of "data," sought a reciprocal and explicit expression of the assumptions peculiar to each discipline?[12] These confrontations are supposed to provide a mutual epistemological elucidation; they labor to bring their implicit foundations to *light*—the ambition and the myth of knowledge. But perhaps what is at stake is different and has to do rather with the otherness introduced by the move through which a discipline turns toward the darkness that surrounds and precedes it—not in order to eliminate it, but *because* it is inexpungeable and determining? In that case theory would involve an effort on the part of a science to think through its relation to this exteriority and not be satisfied with correcting its rules of production or determining the limits of its validity. Is this the path that Bourdieu's discourse takes? In any event, practices shape the opaque reality out of which a theoretical question can arise beyond the frontiers of any discipline.

His "ethnological studies" have their own style. They are a sociologist's hobby, but like all hobbies, they are more serious than his regular work. They are executed with a rare precision. Bourdieu never operates with more care for minute detail, with more perspicacity, with more virtuosity, than in these studies. His texts even have something esthetic about them, to the extent that a "fragment," a *particular* and "isolated" form,[13] becomes the figure of a *global* relation (and not merely a general one) between the discipline and a reality that is at once alien and decisive, primitive. This fragment of a society and an analysis is first of all *the dwelling*, which is, as we know, the reference of every metaphor.[14] Or better: *a* dwelling. Through the practices that articulate its interior space, it *inverts* the strategies of public space and silently *organizes* the language (a vocabulary, proverbs, etc.).[15] The inversion of the public order and the generation of discourse: these two characteristics also make the Kabylian dwelling the inverse of the French *school*, in which Bourdieu, who made it his specialty, sees nothing but the "reproduction" of the social hierarchies and the repetition of their ideologies.[16] In relation to the society sociology deals with, the residence situated "down there" is thus, in its peculiarity, a contrary and determining place. Bourdieu considers his study itself to be illegal with respect to the socioeconomic norms of the discipline: it plays too much on the symbolic scale.[17] In short, it is a lapse.

"Theory" must thus reabsorb the distance between the legalities of sociology and ethnological particularities. The rationality of a scientific field and the practices that arise outside it are to be rearticulated. The *Outline* (and subsequent articles) effect the junction of these two elements. It is a delicate maneuver, which consists in fitting the "ethnological" exception into an empty space in the sociological system. In order to follow this operation, we must consider its working more closely: on the one hand, the analysis of these particular practices; on the other, the role they are assigned in the construction of a "theory."

Strategies

Designated as "strategies," the practices studied by Bourdieu concern, for example, the system of succession in Béarn, or the interior disposition of the Kabylian dwelling, or the distribution of tasks and periods in the course of the Kabylian year. Those are only a few genera of a species that includes "strategies" of fecundity, succession, education, hygiene, social or economic investment, marriage, etc., and also of "reconversion" when there is a gap between practices and situations.[18] In each of the cases examined, differences permit us to specify "some of the properties" of a "logic of practice."

1. Genealogical tables or "trees," surveys and geometrical plans of habitations, linear calendar cycles—these are totalizing and homogeneous productions, results of observational distance and "neutralization" with respect to the strategies themselves that constitute as "islands" family relations practiced because they are useful, places that are distinguished by the inverted and successive movements of the body, or the periods of actions carried out one after another in rhythms that are peculiar to each and mutually incommensurable.[19] In contrast, there can be a synoptic representation, as the instrument of summation and mastery through vision, that levels and classes all the collected "data"; it is practice that organizes discontinuities, nodes of heterogeneous operations. Matters of family relationships, space and time are thus *not the same* in every case.

(I would add that this difference is situated at the borderline between two ruses. With its synthetic tables, scientific method conceals the operation of withdrawal and power that makes them possible. For their part, by providing the "data" sought by the investigators, practitioners necessarily do not reveal the practical difference created among these "data" by the operations that make use of them [or do not make use of them]; thus they collaborate in the production of general tabulations which conceal their tactics from the observer. Knowledge of practices is thus the result of a twofold deception.)

2. A "strategy" (for instance, that used in marrying a child off) is the equivalent of "taking a trick" in a card game: it depends both on the deal (having a good hand) and on the way one plays the cards (being a good cardplayer).[20] "Taking a trick" involves both the *postulates* that determine a playing space and the *rules* that accord a value to the deal and certain options to the player, in short, an ability to maneuver within the different conditions in which the initial capital is committed. This complex ensemble is a fabric of qualitatively distinct modes of functioning:

a) There are "*implicit principles*" or postulates (for example, in a Béarnian marriage, the primacy of the man over the woman, or of the elder son over the younger—principles ensuring the integrity and protection of patrimony in an economy conditioned by the scarcity of money), but the fact that they are not defined (that they are not made explicit) creates margins of tolerance and the possibility of setting one against the other.

b) There are "*explicit rules*" (for example, the *adot*, "the recompense allotted to younger sons in exchange for their renunciation of their rights to the land"), but they are accompanied by a limit that inverts them (for example, the *tournadot*, the restitution of the *adot* in case of a marriage without issue). Every utilization of these rules must thus take into account the possibility of this threatening—because linked to the contingencies of life—rebound against it.

c) "Strategies," subtle "combinations" ("action is tortuous"), "navigate" among the rules, "play with all the possibilities offered by traditions," make use of one tradition rather than another, compensate for one by means of another. Taking advantage of the flexible surface which covers up the hard core, they create their own relevance within this network. More than that: like students manipulating their grade-point average, balancing a high grade in an easy course against a low grade in a difficult course, they move and slide from one function to another, short-circuiting economic, social, and symbolic divisions: for example, a small number of children (a matter of fertility) compensates for a bad marriage (a matrimonial failure); or keeping a younger son unmarried in the home as a "servant without salary" (an economic investment and a restriction on fertility) allows one to avoid having to pay him the *adot* (a matrimonial advantage). Strategies do not "apply" principles or rules; they choose among them to make up the repertory of their operations.[21]

3. Comparable to *transfers* and "metaphorizations," constant passages from one genre to another, these practices presuppose a "logic." Even more clever than usual in this case, Bourdieu, outwitting the practices themselves in order to fix them in the labyrinthine developments of his language, discerns in them several essential procedures:[22]

a) *polythetism:* the same thing has uses and properties that vary according to the arrangements into which it enters;

b) *substitutability:* a thing is always replaceable by another, because of the affinity of each with the others within the totality that the thing represents;

c) *euphemism:* one must hide the fact that actions conflict with the dichotomies and antinomies represented by the symbolic system. Ritual actions furnish the model for "euphemism" by combining contraries.

Finally, *analogy* is the foundation of all these procedures, which are transgressions of the symbolic order and the limits it sets. They are camouflaged transgressions, inserted metaphors and, precisely in that measure, they become acceptable, taken as legitimate since they respect the distinctions established by language even as they undermine them. From this point of view, to acknowledge the authority of rules is exactly the opposite of applying them. This fundamental chiasm may be return-ing today, since we have to apply laws whose authority we no longer recognize. In any event, it is not without interest that Bourdieu redis-covers, at the ultimate source of these practices, the very "use of analogy" which the scientists whose works he collected in 1968 (Duhem, Bachelard, Campbell, *et al.*) held to be the essence of theoretical creation.[23]

4. In sum, these practices are all dominated by what I shall call *an economy of the proper place* (*une économie du lieu propre*). In Bour-dieu's analysis, this economy takes two forms, equally fundamental but unarticulated: on the one hand, the maximization of the capital (material and symbolic wealth) that constitutes the essence of *patrimony*; on the other, the development of the *body*, both individual and collective, that generates duration (through its fertility) and space (through its move-ments). The proliferation of tricks, of their successes or failures, is related to the economy which works to reproduce and to make fruitful these two distinct, and yet complementary, forms of the "dwelling":[24] wealth and the body—land and heirs. A politics of this "place" is everywhere at the base of these strategies.

Hence we have the two characteristics that make these strategies prac-tices entirely peculiar to the closed space in which Bourdieu examines them and to the way in which he observes them:

a) He always presupposes a twofold link between these practices and a proper place (a patrimony), on the one hand, and a collective principle of administration (the family, the group) on the other. What happens when this double postulate does not hold? This is an interesting question, because such is the case of our technocratic societies, with respect to which the proprietary and familial insularities of earlier ages and other cultures have become utopian lost worlds, if not Robinson Crusoe-like adventures. When Bourdieu encounters the same type of practices among today's "petits bourgeois," or housewives, they are merely "short-term and short-sighted strategies," "anarchical responses" relative to "a dis-parate ensemble of semi-knowledges," to a "cultural *sabir*," a mere "bric-à-brac of decontextualized concepts."[25] A single practical logic is never-theless at work, but independently of the place that controls its function-ing in traditional societies. That is to say, in the *Outline* the problematic of the place seems to win out over the problematic of practices.

b) The use of the term "strategy" is no less limited. It is justified by the fact that practices give an adequate response to contingent situa-tions. But at the same time Bourdieu repeats that it is not a matter of strategies strictly speaking; there is no choice among several possibilities, and thus no "strategic intention"; there is no introduction of correctives due to better information, and thus not "the slightest calculation"; there is no prediction, but only an "assumed world" as the repetition of the past. In short, "it is because subjects do not know, strictly speaking, what they are doing, that what they do has more meaning than they realize."[26] "*Docta ignorantia*," therefore,[27] a cleverness that does not recognize itself as such.

With these "strategies," governed by their place, knowledgeable but unknown, the most traditionalist sort of ethnology returns. In the insular reserves in which it observed them, it considered the elements of a people and its culture as *coherent* and *unconscious*: two indissociable aspects. In order for coherence to be the postulate of ethnological knowledge, to be, that is, the place it allocated for itself *and* the episte-mological model to which it referred, it was necessary to put this knowl-edge at a distance from the objectified society, and thus to presuppose that it was foreign and superior to the knowledge the society had of itself. The unconsciousness of the group studied was the price that had to be paid (the price it had to pay) for its coherence. A society could be a system only without knowing it. Whence the corollary: an ethnologist was required to know what the society was without knowing it. Today, an ethnologist would no longer dare to say (if not to think) that. How can Bourdieu compromise himself in this way in the name of sociology?

"Theory"

Insofar as sociology defines "objective structures" on the basis of "regu-larities" provided by statistics (themselves based on empirical investi-gations), and insofar as it considers every "situation" or "objective conjuncture" as a "particular state" of one of these structures,[28] it must account for the adjustment—or non-adjustment—of practices with re-spect to the structures. Where does the harmony that one generally observes between practices and structures (the latter being present as "particular cases" constituted by conjunctures) come from? Answers to this question resort either to a reflex automatism in practices or to the subjective genius of their creators. With good reason, Bourdieu rejects both of these hypotheses. He replaces them with his "theory," which seeks to explain the adequation of practices to structures through their *genesis*.

One could point out that the terms of the problem have been somewhat rigged. Of the three groups of data under consideration—structures, situations, and practices—only the second two (which correspond to each other) are *observed*; in contrast, the structures are *inferred* from statistics and are thus *constructed models*. Before allowing oneself to be locked into this "theoretical" problem, however, two preliminary epistemological questions need to be raised: (a) concerning the presumed "objectivity" of these "structures," an objectivity based on the conviction that the real itself speaks through the discourse of the sociologist; and (b) concerning the limits of observed practices or situations, and especially of statistical representations of them, in relation to the totalities "structural" models claim to account for. But unfortunately these preliminary questions are forgotten, in the name of a supposed theoretical urgency.

In the terms in which he encounters the problem of adequation, Bourdieu has to find *something* that can adjust practices to structures and yet also explain the gaps remaining between them. He needs a supplementary category. He locates it in a process which is his forte as a specialist in the sociology of education, the *acquisition* of knowledge; this is the sought-for mediation between the structures that organize it and the "dispositions" it produces. This "genesis" implies an interiorization of structures (through learning) and an exteriorization of achievements (what Bourdieu calls the *habitus*) in practices. A temporal dimension is thus introduced: practices (expressing the experience) correspond adequately to situations (manifesting the structure) if, and only if, the structure remains stable for the duration of the process of interiorization/exteriorization; if not, practices lag behind, thus resembling the structure at the preceding point, the point at which it was interiorized by the *habitus*.

According to this analysis, structures can change and thus become a principle of social mobility (and even the only one). Achievements cannot. They have no movement of their own. They are the place in which structures are inscribed, the marble on which their history is engraved. Nothing happens in them that is not the result of their exteriority. As in the traditional image of primitive or peasant societies, nothing moves, there is no history other than that written on them by an alien order. The immobility of this memory guarantees for the theory that the socioeconomic system will be faithfully reproduced in practices. Thus it is not education or training (visible phenomena) that plays the central role here, but rather their expected result: achievements, the *habitus*.[29] The *habitus* provides the basis for explaining a society in relationship to structures. But there is a price to be paid for this explanation. In order to be able to assume that the basis has such a stability, it must be unverifiable, invisible.

What interests Bourdieu is the genesis, "the mode of generation of practices"; not, as in Foucault, what they produce, but what produces them. From the "ethnological case studies" that are to examine them to the sociology that is to develop a theory of them, there is thus a displacement, which moves the discourse in the direction of the *habitus*, whose synonyms (*exis, ethos, modus operandi*, "common sense," "second nature," etc.), definitions,[30] and justifications become more and more numerous. In the transition from ethnology to sociology, the hero changes. A passive and nocturnal actor is substituted for the sly multiplicity of strategies. This immobile stone figure is supposed to be the agent that produces the phenomena observed in a society.[31] He is an essential character, in fact, because he makes the circular movement of the theory possible: henceforth, from "structures," it passes to the *habitus* (a word Bourdieu always puts in italics); from the latter, to "strategies," which are adjusted to "conjunctures," themselves reduced to the "structures" of which they are the results and particular states.

In fact, this circle moves from a *constructed* model (the structure) to an *assumed* reality (the *habitus*), and from the latter to an interpretation of *observed* facts (strategies and conjunctures). But what is even more striking than the hetereogeneous character of the pieces the theory puts in a circle is the role it assigns to the ethnological "fragments," which are to close the gap in the sociological coherence. The *other* (Kabylian or Béarnian) furnishes the element that the theory needs in order to work and "to explain everything." This remote foreign element has all the characteristics that define the *habitus*: coherence, stability, unconsciousness, territoriality (achievements are the equivalent of patrimony). It is "represented" by the *habitus*, an invisible place where, as in the Kabylian dwelling, the structures are inverted as they are interiorized, and where the writing flips over again in exteriorizing itself in the form of practices that have the deceptive appearance of being free improvisations. It is indeed the dwelling, as a silent and determining memory, which is hidden in the theory under the metaphor of the *habitus*, and which, moreover, gives the supposition a certain referentiality, an appearance of reality. As a consequence of its theoretical metaphorization, this referentiality amounts, however, to no more than a plausibility. The dwelling gives the *habitus* its form, but not a content. In any case, Bourdieu's argument is concerned less to indicate that reality then to show its necessity and the advantages of his hypothesis for the theory. Thus the *habitus* becomes a dogmatic place, if one takes dogma to mean the affirmation of a "reality" which the discourse needs in order to be totalizing. No doubt it still has, like many dogmas, the heuristic value of displacing and renewing possibilities of research.

Bourdieu's texts are fascinating in their analyses and aggressive in their theory. In reading them, I feel myself captive to a passion that they simultaneously exacerbate and excite. They are full of contrasts. Scrupulously examining practices and their logic—in a way that surely has had no equivalent since Mauss—the texts finally reduce them to a mystical reality, the *habitus*, which is to bring them under the law of reproduction. The subtle descriptions of Béarnian or Kabylian tactics suddenly give way to violently imposed truths, as if the complexity so lucidly examined required the brutal counterpoint of a dogmatic reason. There are contrasts also in the style, twisted and labyrinthine in its pursuits, and massively repetitive in its affirmations. A strange combination of an "I know that . . . " (that crafty and transgressive proliferation) and an "All the same . . . " (there *must* be a totalizing meaning). In order to escape from this aggressive seduction, I assume (in turn) that in this contrast something essential for the analysis of tactics *must* be at stake. The blanket Bourdieu's theory throws over tactics as if to put out their fire by certifying their amenability to socioeconomic rationality or as if to mourn their death by declaring them unconscious, should teach us something about their relationship with any theory.

These tactics, through their criteria and procedures, are supposed to make use of the institutional and symbolic organization in such an autonomous way that if it were to take them seriously the scientific representation of society would become lost in them, in every sense of the word. Its postulates and ambitions could not resist them. Norms, generalizations, and segmentations would yield to the transverse and "metaphorizing" pullulation of these *differentiating* activities. Mathematics and the exact sciences constantly refine their logics in order to follow the aleatory and microscopic movements of non-human phenomena. The social sciences, whose object is still more "subtle" and whose tools are much cruder, would have to defend their models (that is, their ambition to dominate and control) by exorcizing such a proliferation. And in fact, in accord with the proven methods of exorcism, they consider such a proliferation to be singular (local), unconscious (alien in

principle) and, without realizing it, revelatory of the knowledge that
their scientific judge has of these practices. When the "observer" is sufficiently enclosed within his judicial institution, and thus sufficiently
blind, everything goes fine. The discourse he produces has every appearance of holding together.

In Bourdieu's work, there is nothing of the kind. To be sure, at a first
(only too obvious) level, he gives the impression of *departing* (of going
toward these tactics), but only in order to *return* (to confirm the professional rationality). This is only a false departure, a textual "strategy."
But isn't this hasty return an indication that he *knows* the danger, the
perhaps mortal danger, to which these all too intelligent practices expose
scientific knowledge? He reflects a (distantly Pascalian) combination of
the erosion of reason and dogmatic faith. He knows a great deal about
scientific knowledge and the power by which it is established, as well as
about these tactics whose wiles he outwits with such virtuosity in his
texts. He thus proceeds to imprison these devices behind the bars of the
unconscious and to deny, through the fetish of the *habitus*, what reason
would have to have if it is to be more than *la raison du plus fort*. He
affirms, with the concept of *habitus*, the *contrary* of what he *knows*—a
traditional popular tactic—and this protection (a tribute paid to the
authority of reason) gives him the scientific possibility of observing these
tactics in carefully circumscribed places.

If that were true (but *who* could say?), Bourdieu would teach us as
much about it through his "dogmatism" as through his "case studies."
The discourse that hides what he knows (instead of hiding what he
doesn't know) would have "theoretical" value precisely insofar as it *practices* what it *knows*. It would be the result of a *conscious* relationship
with an outside it cannot eliminate, and not merely the scene of an
elucidation. Would it thus come down to the "*docta ignorantia*" claimed
to be knowledgeable without knowing it precisely because it knows only
too well what it does not and cannot say?

Chapter V   The Arts of Theory

A PARTICULAR PROBLEM arises when, instead of being a discourse on other discourses, as is usually the case, theory has to advance over an area where there are no longer any discourses. There is a sudden unevenness of terrain: the ground on which verbal language rests begins to fail. The theorizing operation finds itself at the limits of the terrain where it normally functions, like an automobile at the edge of a cliff. Beyond and below lies the ocean.

Foucault and Bourdieu situate their enterprise on this edge by articulating a discourse on non-discursive practices. They are not the first to do so. Without going back to ancient times, we can say that since Kant every theoretical effort has had to give a more or less direct explanation of its relationship to this non-discursive activity, to this immense "remainder" constituted by the part of human experience that has not been tamed and symbolized in language. An individual science can avoid this direct confrontation. It grants itself a priori the conditions that allow it to encounter things only in its own limited field where it can "verbalize" them. It lies in wait for them in the gridwork of models and hypotheses where it can "make them talk," and this interrogatory apparatus, like a hunter's trap, transforms their wordless silence into "answers," and hence into language: this is called experimentation.[1] Theoretical questioning, on the contrary, *does not forget*, cannot forget that in addition to the relationship of these scientific discourses to one another, there is also their common relation with what they have taken care to exclude from their field in order to constitute it. It is linked to the pullulation of that which does not speak (does not yet speak?) and which takes the shape (among others) of "ordinary" practices. It is *the memory of this "remainder."* It is the Antigone of what is not acceptable within the scientific jurisdiction. It constantly brings this unforgettable element back into the scientific places where technical constraints make it "politically" (methodologically, and in theory, provisionally) necessary to forget it. How

61

does it succeed in doing this? By what brilliant strokes or through what ruses?—that is the question.

Cut-out and turn-over: a recipe for theory

We must return to the works of Foucault and Bourdieu. Although they are both important, there is an obvious difference between them, and that in itself is a reason for paying attention to them on the threshold of an essay that does not claim to be a history of theories concerning practices. These two monuments situate a field of research, standing almost at its two poles. Nevertheless, however distant they may be from each other, the two bodies of work seem to be constructed by means of the same procedures. The same operational schema can be observed in both, in spite of the difference in the materials used, the problematics involved, and the perspectives opened up. We seem to have here two variants of a "way of making" the theory of practices. Like a way of cooking, this "way" can be exercised in different circumstances and with heterogeneous interests; it has its tricks of the trade and its good or bad players; it also allows one to score points. Using the imperatives that punctuate the steps in a recipe, we could say that this theorizing operation consists of two moments: first, *cut out*; then *turn over*. First an "ethnological" isolation; then a logical inversion.

The first move *cuts out* certain practices from an undefined fabric, in such a way as to treat them as *a separate population*, forming a *coherent whole* but *foreign* to the place in which the theory is produced. Thus we have Foucault's "panoptic" procedures, isolated within a multitude, or Bourdieu's "strategies," localized among the inhabitants of Béarn or Kabylia. In that way, they receive an ethnological form. Moreover, in both cases, the *genre* (Foucault) or the place (Bourdieu) isolated is considered a metonymic figure of the whole species: a part (which is observable because it is circumscribed) is supposed to represent the totality (itself undefinable) of practices. To be sure, in Foucault's work this isolation is based on the elucidation of the dynamics proper to a technology: it is a cutting-out produced by the historiographic discourse. In Bourdieu, it is supposed to be provided by the space organized by the protection of a patrimony: it is taken as a socioeconomic and geographical datum. But it remains the case that cutting-out, ethnological or metonymic, is common to the two analyses, even if the modalities of its determination are hetereogeneous in each case.

The second move *turns over* the unit thus cut out. At first obscure, silent, and remote, the unit is inverted to become the element that illuminates theory and sustains discourse. In Foucault, the procedures hidden in the details of educational, military, or clinical control, micro-apparatuses without discursive legitimacy, techniques foreign to the Enlightenment, become the reason through which both the system of our society and that of the human sciences are illuminated. *Through* them and *in* them, nothing escapes Foucault. They allow his discourse to be itself and to be theoretically panoptical, *seeing everything*. In Bourdieu, the remote and opaque place organized by wily, polymorphic and transgressive "strategies" in relation to the order of discourse is also inverted in order to give its plausibility and its essential articulation to a theory recognizing the reproduction of the same order everywhere. Reduced to the *habitus* which exteriorizes itself in them, these strategies which do not know what it is they know provide Bourdieu with the means of explaining everything and of being conscious of everything. Granted that Foucault is interested in the effect of his procedures on a system, and Bourdieu, in the "single principle" of which his strategies are the effect, both nonetheless play the same trick when they transform practices isolated as aphasic and secret into the keystone of their theory, when they make of that nocturnal population the mirror in which the decisive element of their explanatory discourse shines forth.

Inasmuch as it makes use of this device, the theory belongs to the procedures it deals with, in spite of the fact that, by considering a single category of the species, by assuming that this isolated element has a metonymic value, and by thus passing over other practices, it forgets those that guarantee its own construction. Foucault's own analysis shows that, in the case of the human sciences, discourse is determined by procedures. But his analysis, confirmed by the mode of production it reflects, also depends on an apparatus analogous to the apparatuses whose functioning it discerns. It remains to be discovered what is the difference that introduces, in relation to the panoptic procedures whose history Foucault writes, the double move of delimiting an *alien* body of practices and *inverting* its obscure content into a luminous writing.

But we should first clarify the nature of these moves, and not limit our examination of them to two bodies of work that might be selected and praised because they support our point. In reality, the procedure from which they result is far from being exceptional. Indeed, it is an old recipe, frequently used, and therefore all the more deserving of consideration. It will suffice to recall two famous examples from the beginning of the century: Durkheim's *The Elementary Forms of Religious Life* and Freud's *Totem and Taboo*. When these authors construct a theory of practices, they situate them first in a "primitive" and closed space, ethnological with respect to our "enlightened" societies, and they recognize the theoretical formula of their analysis in that remote, obscure place. It is in the sacrificial practices of the Australian Arunta, a cultural group guaranteed to be primitive even among "primitives," that Durkheim discovers the principle of a contemporary ethics and social theory: the restriction opposed (through sacrifice) to the indefinite will of each individual makes coexistence and conventions possible among members of a group; in other words, the practice of renunciation and self-sacrifice permits plurality and contracts, that is, a society: the acceptance of a limit is the foundation of the social contract.[2] For his part, Freud deciphers the essential concepts of psychoanalysis in the practices of the primitive horde: incest, castration, the articulation of the law about the death of the father.[3] This detour is all the more striking because no direct experience justifies it. Neither of these authors has observed the practices he is dealing with. They never went to see for themselves, any more than Marx ever went to a factory.[4] Why then do they constitute these practices as a hermetic enigma in which they can read in inverted form the key word of their theories?

Today, these practices bearing the secret of our rationality no longer look so remote. With time, they are coming closer. It is pointless now to look for this ethnological reality in Australia or at the beginning of history. It resides in our own system (the panoptic procedures), or next door to it, if not inside our cities (the strategies of Béarn or Kabylia), then still nearer (the "unconscious"). But however proximate the content may be, its "ethnological" *form* remains. The form given to these practices located far away from knowledge and yet possessing its secret poses a problem from the outset. One may see in this problem a figure of modernity.

The ethnologization of the "arts"

Theoretical reflection does not elect to keep practices at a distance, so that first it has to leave its own place to analyze them and then by simply inverting them may find itself at home. The partitioning (*découpage*) that it carries out, it also repeats. This partitioning is imposed on it by history. Procedures without discourse are collected and located in an area organized by the past and giving them the role, a determining one for theory, of being constituted as wild "reserves" for enlightened knowledge.

The distinction no longer refers essentially to the traditional binominal set of "theory" and "practice," specified by a further distinction between "speculation" aimed at deciphering the book of the cosmos and concrete "applications"; rather the distinction concerns two different *operations*, the one discursive (in and through language) and the other without discourse. Since the sixteenth century, the idea of *method* has progressively overturned the relation between knowing and doing: on a base of legal and rhetorical practices, changed little by little into discursive "actions" executed on diversified terrains and thus into techniques for the transformation of a milieu, is imposed the fundamental schema of a *discourse* organizing the way of *thinking* as a way of operating, as a rational management of production and as a regulated operation on appropriate fields. That is "method," the seed of modern science. Ultimately, it systematizes the *art* that Plato had already placed under the sign of activity.[7] But it orders a know-how (*savoir-faire*) by means of discourse. The frontier thus no longer separates two hierarchized bodies of knowledge, the one speculative, the other linked to particulars, the one concerned with reading the order of the world and the other coming to terms with the details of things within the framework set up for it by the first; rather it sets off practices articulated by discourse from those that are not (yet) articulated by it.

What then will be the status of this "know-how" without a discourse, essentially without writing (it is the discourse on method that is both writing and science)? It is composed of multiple but untamed operativities. This proliferation does not obey the law of discourse, but rather that of production, the ultimate value of physiocratic and later capitalist economics. It thus challenges scientific writing's privilege of organizing production. It alternately exacerbates and stimulates the technicians of language. It claims to conquer and annex not contemptible practices, but "ingenious," "complex," and "effective" forms of knowledge. From Bacon to Christian Wolff or Jean Beckmann, a gigantic effort is made to colonize this immense reserve of "arts" and "crafts" which, although they cannot yet be articulated in a science, can already by introduced into language through a *"Description"* and, in consequence, brought to a greater *"perfection."* Through these two terms—the "description" which depends on narrativity and the "perfection" that aims at a technical optimalization—the position of the "arts" is fixed, neighboring on but outside of the field of science.[8]

The *Encyclopédie* of the late eighteenth century is the result and at the same time the banner of this labor of collation: *Dictionnaire raisonné des sciences, des arts et des métiers*. It places "sciences" and "arts" side by side, in a proximity that promises a later assimilation: the sciences are the operational languages whose grammar and syntax form constructed, regulated, and thus writeable, systems; the arts are techniques that await an enlightened knowledge they currently lack. In the article "Art," Diderot tries to clarify the relation between these heterogeneous elements. We are dealing with an "art," he writes, "if the object is executed"; with a "science," "if the object is contemplated," using a distinction more Baconian than Cartesian between execution and speculation. The distinction is repeated within "art" itself, according to whether it is represented or practiced: "Every art has its speculative and its practical aspect: its speculation, which is merely the inoperative knowledge of the rules of the art; its practice, which is merely the habitual and non-reflective use of these same rules." Art is thus a kind of knowledge that operates outside the enlightened discourse which it lacks. More importantly, this *know-how* surpasses, in its complexity, enlightened science. Thus, concerning "the geometry of the arts," Diderot notes: "It is obvious that the elements of academic geometry are not more than the simplest and least complex among those in the merchant's geometry." For example, in many problems concerning levers, friction, textile twisting, clock mechanisms, etc., the usual calculations are still insufficient. The solution will be found in a very ancient "experimental and practical, *manouvrier*) mathematics," even if its "language" remains unrefined through a "lack of the proper words" and an "abundance of synonyms."[9]

Like Girard, Diderot uses the term "*manouvrier*" to designate those arts that are satisfied with "adapting" materials by cutting, shaping, joining, and so on, without giving them a "new state" (by fusion, composition, etc.) as the *manufacturing* arts do.[10] The "everyday" arts no more "form" a new product than they have their own language. They "make do" (*bricolent*). But through the reorganization and hierarchization of knowledge according to the criterion of productivity, these arts come to represent a standard, because of their operativity, and an avant-garde, because of their "experimental and *manouvrier*" subtlety. Foreign to scientific "languages," they constitute outside of the latter an *absolute* of the power of operating (an efficiency which, unmoored from discourse, nevertheless reflects its productivist ideal) and a *reserve* of knowledge one can inventory in shops or in the countryside (a *logos* is concealed within artisanry, a *logos* in which the future of science may already be faintly heard). A problematics of lag or delay is introduced into the relation between science and the arts. A *temporal handicap* separates the various kinds of know-how from their gradual elucidation by *epistemologically superior sciences.*

"Observers" thus move quickly in the direction of these practices that remain at a distance from the sciences but in advance of them. Fontenelle suggested as early as 1699 that "artisans' shops sparkle everywhere with an intelligence and a creativity that nevertheless does not attract our attention. Spectators are lacking for these very useful and very ingeniously contrived instruments and practices...."[11] These "spectators" become collectors, describers, analysts. But at the same time that they acknowledge in these practices a kind of knowledge preceding that of the scientists, they have to release it from its "improper" language and invert into a "proper" discourse the erroneous expression of "marvels" that are already present in everyday ways of operating. Science will make princesses out of all these Cinderellas. The principle of an ethnological operation on practices is thus formulated: their *social isolation* calls for a sort of "education" which, through a *linguistic inversion,* introduces them into the field of scientific written language.

It is a notable fact that from the eighteenth to the twentieth centuries, ethnologists or historians consider these techniques intrinsically worthy of respect: they consider what these techniques *do.* No need to interpret. It suffices to describe. In contrast, these scholars consider the stories by means of which a group situates or symbolizes its activities to be "legends" that mean something other than what is said. There is strange disparity between the way of treating practices and that of treating discourses. Whereas the first way records a "truth" about operating, the second way decodes the "lies" of speech. Moreover, the brief descriptions of the first way contrast with the prolix interpretations which have made myths and legends an object privileged by the professionals of language, intellectuals long accustomed to using the hermeneutic procedures transmitted by jurists to professors and/or ethnologists to comment on, gloss, and "translate" referential documents into scientific texts.

The issues are already settled. The mute jurisdiction of practices is historically limited. A hundred and fifty years after Diderot, Durkheim accepts almost without correction this "ethnological" definition—and even reinforces it—when he takes up the problem of art (the art of operating), that is, of "pure practice without theory." The absolute of operativity is there, in its "purity." He writes: "An art is a system of ways of operating that are adjusted to special ends and the product of either a traditional experience communicated through education or the personal experience of the individual." Encysted in particularity, deprived of the generalizations proper to discourse alone, art nevertheless forms a "system" and is organized by "ends"—two postulates that permit a science and an ethics to keep *in its place* the discourse of its own which art lacks, that is, to inscribe themselves in the place and in the name of these practices.

It is also characteristic of Durkheim, the great pioneer who linked the foundation of sociology to a theory of education, that he should take such an interest in the production or acquisition of art: "One can acquire it only by putting oneself in connection with the things on which the action is to be exercised and in exercising it oneself." To the "immediacy" of operation, Durkheim no longer opposes, as Diderot did, a lagging-behind of theory in relation to the *manouvrier* knowledge of artisans. There remains only a hierarchy established by the criterion of education. "To be sure," Durkheim goes on, "it can happen that art is enlightened [the key word of the Enlightenment] through reflection, but reflection is not its essential element, since art can exist without it. But there does not exist a single art in which everything is reflective."[12]

Does any science exist in which "everything is reflective"? In any event, in a vocabulary still very close that of the *Encyclopédie* (which spoke of "contemplating"), theory is given the task of "reflecting" this "whole." More generally, for Durkheim, society is a kind of writing that only he can read. Here, knowledge is already written in practices, but not yet enlightened. Science will be the mirror that makes it readable, the discourse "reflecting" an immediate and precise operativity lacking language and consciousness, an operativity already knowledgeable but unrefined.

The tales of the unrecognized

Like sacrifice, which "is closer to us than one would think in view of its apparent brutality,"[13] art is a kind of knowledge essential in itself but unreadable without science. This is a dangerous position for science to be in because it retains only the power of expressing the knowledge which it lacks. Moreover, in the relation between science and art is envisaged not an alternative but a complementarity and, if possible, an articulating link; that is, as Wolff thought in 1740 (after Swedenborg, or before Lavoisier, Désaudray, Auguste Comte, et al.), "a *third man* who would combine in his person both science and art: he would repair the infirmity of the theoreticians, and free amateurs of the arts from the prejudice according to which the latter could perfect themselves without theory. . . ."[14] This mediator between "the man of the theorem" and "the man of experience"[15] would be the *engineer*.

The "third man" haunted enlightened discourse (whether philosophical or scientific) and continues to do so today,[16] but he has not turned out with the personality which had been hoped. The place he has been accorded (currently being slowly overtaken by that of the technocrat) is a function of the process that all through the nineteenth century on the one hand isolated artistic techniques from art itself and on the other "geometrized" and mathematicized these techniques. From this know-how, what could be *detached from human performance* was gradually cut out and "perfected" with *machines* that use regulatable combinations of forms, materials, and forces. These "technical organs" are withdrawn from manual competence (they transcend it in becoming machines) and placed in a space of their own under the jurisdiction of the engineer. They depend on a technology. Henceforth know-how (*savoir-faire*) finds itself slowly deprived of what objectively articulated it with respect to a "how-to-do" (*un faire*). As its techniques are gradually taken away from it in order to transform them into machines, it seems to withdraw into a subjective *knowledge* (*savoir*) separated from the language of its procedures (which are then reverted to it in the form imposed by technologically-produced machines). Thus know-how takes on the appearance of an "intuitive" or "reflex" ability, which is almost invisible and whose status remains unrecognized. The technical optimization of the nineteenth century, by drawing from the reservoir of the "arts" and "crafts" the models, pretexts or limits of its mechanical inventions, left to everyday practices only a space without means or products of its own; the optimization constitutes that space as a folkloric region or rather as an overly silent land, still without a verbal discourse and henceforth deprived of its *manouvrier* language as well.

A sort of "knowledge" remains there, though deprived of its technical apparatus (out of which machines have been made); the remaining ways of operating are those that have no legitimacy with respect to productivist rationality (e.g., the everyday arts of cooking, cleaning, sewing, etc.). On the other hand, what is left behind by ethnological colonization acquires the status of a "private" activity, is charged with symbolic investments concerning everyday activity, and functions under the sign of collective or individual particulars; it becomes in short the legendary and at the same time active memory of what remains on the margins or in the interstices of scientific or cultural orthopraxis. As indexes of particulars—the poetic or tragic murmurings of the everyday—ways of operating enter massively into the novel or the short story, most notably into the nineteenth-century realistic novel. They find there a new representational space, that of fiction, populated by everyday virtuosities that science doesn't know what to do with and which become the signatures, easily recognized by readers, of everyone's micro-stories. *Literature* is transformed into a repertory of these practices that have no technological copyright. They soon occupy a privileged place in the stories that patients tell in the wards of psychiatric institutions or in psychoanalysts' offices.

In other words, "stories" provide the decorative container of a *narrativity* for everyday practices. To be sure, they describe only fragments of these practices. They are no more than its metaphors. But, in spite of the ruptures separating successive configurations of knowledge, they represent a new variant in the continuous series of narrative documents which, from folktales providing a panoply of schemas for action[17] to the *Descriptions des Arts* of the classical age, set forth ways of operating in the form of *tales*. This series includes therefore the contemporary novel as well as the micro-novels often constituted by ethnological descriptions of the techniques of craftwork, cooking, etc. A similar continuity suggests a certain *theoretical* relevance of narrativity so far as everyday practices are concerned.

The "return" of these practices in narration (we shall have to examine their bearing on many other examples) is connected with a broader and historically less determined phenomenon, which one might designate as an *estheticization of the knowledge* implied by know-how. Detached from its procedures, this knowledge may pass for a kind of "taste," "tact," or even "genius." It is accorded the characteristics of an intuition that is alternately artistic and automatic. It is supposed to be a knowledge that is unaware of itself. This "cognitive operation" is supposed not to be accompanied by that self-consciousness that would give it mastery through reduplication or internal "reflection." Between practice and theory, it occupies a "third" position, no longer discursive but primitive. It is secluded, originary, like a "source" of something that will later differentiate and elucidate itself.

This *knowledge* is not *known*. In practices, it has a status analogous to that granted fables and myths as the expression of kinds of knowledge that do not know themselves. In both cases it is a knowledge that subjects do not reflect. They bear witness to it without being able to appropriate it. They are in the end the renters and not the owners of their own know-how. Concerning them it occurs to no one to ask *whether* there is knowledge; it is assumed that there *must* be, but that it is *known* only by people other than its bearers. Like that of poets and painters, the know-how of daily practices is supposed to be known only by the interpreter who illuminates it in his discursive mirror though he does not possess it either. It thus belongs to no one. It passes from the unconsciousness of its practitioners to the reflection of non-practitioners without involving any individual subject. It is an anonymous and referential knowledge, a condition of the possibility of technical or scientific practices.

Freudian psychoanalysis provides a particularly interesting version of this secluded knowledge lacking both expressive procedures (it has no language of its own) and legitimate proprietor (it has no subject of its own). Everything works on a postulate that its effects have caused to be taken for a reality: there is *knowledge*, but it is *unconscious*; reciprocally, it is the unconscious that knows.[18] Patients' stories and Freudian case histories (*Krankengeschichte*) narrate the knowledge at length. Moreover, since Freud, every psychoanalyst has learned from his experience that "people already know everything" that he, in his position of being the one who is "supposed to know," can or might be able to allow them to articulate. It is as though the "artisanal shops" Diderot spoke of had become the metaphor of the repressed and secluded place in whose depths "experimental and *manouvrier*" knowledge still precedes the discourse pronounced about it by theory or the psychoanalytic academy. About patients—and about everyone else as well—the analyst often says: "They know it somewhere." "Somewhere": but where? Their practices know it—moves, behaviors, ways of talking or walking, etc. A knowledge is there, but whose? It is so rigorous and precise that all the values of scientific method seem to have moved wholesale over to the side of this unconscious element, so that in consciousness itself there remain only fragments and effects of this knowledge, devices and tactics analogous to those that earlier characterized "art." Through this reversal, it is the rational that is not reflective and does not speak, the unrecognized and the unspoken (*l'insu et l'in-fans*), whereas "enlightened" consciousness is only the "improper" language of that knowledge.

But this reversal is aimed far more at the privilege of consciousness than at changing the distribution of knowledge and discourse. In the artisanal "workshops," as in those of the unconscious, lies a fundamental and primitive knowledge that precedes enlightened discourse but lacks its own culture. The analyst offers this knowledge of the unconscious— and that of the "arts"—the possibility of having its "own" words and a means of distinguishing between "synonyms." Theory reflects in the daylight of "scientific" language a portion of what moves about obscurely in the depths of this well of knowledge. Over three centuries, in spite of the historical avatars of consciousness or the successive definitions of knowledge, the combination of two distinct terms persists unchanged, the first being a referential and unrefined knowledge, and the second an explanatory discourse that brings forth into the light an inverted representation of its opaque source. This discourse is what we call "theory." It retains the word's ancient and classical meaning of "looking at/showing" ("*voir/faire voir*") or of "contemplating" (*theōrein*). It is "enlightened." Primitive knowledge, insofar as it has been gradually dissociated from the techniques and languages that objectified it, becomes another form of intelligence possessed by the individual subject and poorly defined except in neutral terms (to have a flair, tact, taste, judgment, instinct, etc.) that oscillate among the esthetic, cognitive, and reflex systems, as if "know-how" amounted to a principle of knowledge that nobody could capture.

An art of thinking: Kant

Characteristically, Kant treats the relation between the art of operating (*Kunst*) and science (*Wissenschaft*), or between a technique (*Technik*) and theory (*Theorie*), in the context of an investigation that has moved from earlier versions on taste toward a critique of judgment.[19] He encounters art, on the road leading from taste to judgment, as the parameter of a practical knowledge exceeding knowledge and having an esthetic form. Kant discerns in it what he calls, in a stroke of genius, a "logical tact" (*logische Takt*). Inscribed in the orbit of an esthetics, the art of operating is placed under the sign of the faculty of judgment, the "alogical" condition of thought.[20] The traditional antinomy between "operativity" and "reflection" is transcended through a point of view which, acknowledging an *art* at the root of thought, makes judgment a "middle term" (*Mittelglied*) between theory and praxis. This art of thinking constitutes a synthetic unity of the two terms.

Kant's examples concern precisely everyday practices: "The faculty of judgment exceeds the understanding. . . . The faculty of judging what clothes a chambermaid should wear. The faculty of judging by the dignity appropriate to an edifice what ornaments will not conflict with the goal in view."[21] Judgment does not bear on social conventions (the elastic equilibrium of a network of tacit contracts) alone, but more generally on the *relation* among a great number of elements, and it exists only in the act of concretely creating a new set by putting one more element into a convenient connection with this relation, just as one adds a touch of red or ochre to a painting, changing it without destroying it. The transformation of a given equilibrium into another one characterizes art.

To explain this, Kant mentions the general authority of discourse, an authority which is nevertheless never more than local and concrete: where I come from, he writes (*in meinem Gegenden*: in my region, in my "homeland"), "the ordinary man" (*der Gemeine Mann*) says (*sagt*) that charlatans and magicians (*Taschenspielers*) depend on knowledge (you can do it if you know the trick), whereas tightrope dancers (*Seiltänzers*) depend on an art.[22] Dancing on a tightrope requires that one maintain *an equilibrium* from one moment to the next by recreating it at every step by means of new adjustments; it requires one to maintain a balance that is never permanently acquired; constant readjustment renews the balance while giving the impression of "keeping" it. The art of operating is thus admirably defined, all the more so because in fact the practitioner himself is part of the equilibrium that he modifies without compromising it. In this ability to create a new set on the basis of a preexisting harmony and to maintain a formal relationship in spite of the variation of the elements, it very closely resembles artistic production. It could be considered the ceaseless creativity of a kind of taste in practical experience.

But this art also designates that which, in scientific work itself, does not depend on the (necessary) application of rules or models and so remains in the final analysis, as Freud also says, "a matter of tact" (*eine Sache des Takts*).[23] When he returns to this point, Freud has diagnosis in view, a question of judgment that, in a practical treatment, concerns precisely a relationship or an equilibrium among a multitude of elements. For Freud as for Kant, it is a matter of an autonomous faculty that can be defined but not learned: "The lack of judgment," Kant says, "is properly what one calls stupidity, and for this vice there is no remedy."[24] The scientist is no more spared this vice than anyone else.

Between the understanding that knows and the reason that desires, the faculty of judgment is thus a formal "composition," a subjective "equilibrium" of imagining and understanding. It has the form of a *pleasure*, relative not to an exteriority, but to a mode of exercise: it puts into play the *concrete* experience of a *universal* principle of harmony between the imagination and the understanding. It is a *sense* (*Sinn*), but it is "common": common sense (*Gemeinsinn*) or judgment. Without going into the details of a thesis that disqualifies the ideological divisions between kinds of knowledge, and thus also their social hierarchization, we can at least point out that this tact ties together (moral) freedom, (esthetic) creation, and a (practical) act—three elements already present in the practice of "*la perruque*," that modern-day example of an everyday tactic.[25]

The antecedents of this judgment invested in an ethical and poetic act are perhaps to be sought in the religious experience of earlier times, which was also a kind of "tact," the apprehension and creation of a "harmony" among particular practices, the ethical and poetic gesture of *religare* (tying together) or making a concordance through an indefinite series of concrete acts. Newman still sees this experience as involving a sort of "tact." But as a result of historical changes that have singularly limited the equilibria open to the religious art of "tightrope dancing," it has slowly been replaced by a practice of esthetics, itself progressively isolated from the operational and scientific method to the point that, for example, from Schleiermacher to Gadamer, it has become the marginal experience to which a "hermeneutic" tradition constantly appeals to support its critique of the objective sciences. Because of his own genius and his historical intellectual background (from the art of J. S. Bach to that of the French Revolution), Kant is situated at a crossroads where the ethical and esthetic form of the concrete religious act remains (though its dogmatic content is disappearing), and where artistic creation is still considered as a moral and technical act. This transitionary combination, which in his work already oscillates between a "Critique of taste" and a "Metaphysics of morals," furnishes a modern point of reference that is fundamental for the analysis of the esthetic, ethical, and practical nature of everyday know-how.

Kant tries to define this tact again in a piece of superior journalism published during the French Revolution in the *Berlinische Monatsschrift* (September 1793) concerning the "old saw," "That may be right in theory, but it won't work in practice."[26] This important theoretical text takes a common saying as its subject and title, and adopts newspaper language (people have spoken of Kant's "popular works"). In it Kant participates in a debate: he responds to Christian Garve's objections (1792), and articles by Friedrich Gentz (December 1793) and August Wilhelm Rehber (February 1794) continue the discussion of this saying in the same journal. This "saying" is a *Spruch*, that is, at once a proverb (a form of wisdom), a maxim (a statement), and an oracle (a verbal formula legitimizing a certain knowledge). Is it a byproduct of the Revolution that a proverb should be accorded the philosophical pertinence of a verse (*Spruch*) from Holy Scripture and have mobilized around it, as in the old editions of the Talmud, the Koran, and the Bible, the exegetical efforts of the theoreticians?[27] This philosophical debate concerning a proverb calls to mind the Gospel story of the Child (*Infans*) discoursing among the teachers in the Temple, or the popular theme of the "*enfant sage à trois ans*" ("wise three-year-old").[28] But the discussion is no longer concerned with the theme of childhood, any more than with that of old age (as Kant's translators make it appear in rendering his *Gemeinspruch* by "old saw") but rather with anyone and everyone, with the "common" and "ordinary" (*Gemein*) man, whose *saying* once again *questions* the intellectuals and makes their commentaries proliferate.

The common "saying" does not affirm a principle. It notes a fact, which Kant interprets as the sign of either the practitioner's insufficient interest in theory or an insufficient development of theory on the part of the theoretician himself. "If theory has still little (*noch wenig*) effect on practice, it is not theory's fault; it is rather that there is not enough (*nicht genug*) of the sort of theory that one should have learned from experience. . . ."[29] Regardless of the examples he gives (they involve the traditional problem of friction), Kant organizes his demonstration in a three-act drama in which the ordinary man appears alternately in the role of three characters (the business man, the politician, and the citizen of the world) that are opposed to three philosophers (Garve, Hobbes, and Mendelssohn) and allow Kant to analyze in succession questions relative to ethics, constitutional law, and international order. What is more important here than these variations is the principle of a *formal harmony* of the mental faculties in the judgment. The latter can be located neither in scientific discourse, nor in a particular technique, nor yet again in an artistic expression. It is an art of thinking on which ordinary practices as well as theory depend. Like the tightrope walker's activity, it has an ethical, esthetic, and practical character. It is then hardly surprising that there is an art that organizes discourses dealing

with practices in the name of a theory, for example, Foucault's or
Bourdieu's analyses. But to move in that direction is to open a not very
Kantian question concerning a discourse which would be the art of
talking about or constructing theory as well as the theory of that art—
that is, a discourse that would be the memory and the practice, or in
short, *the life-story of tact itself.*

Chapter VI   Story Time

A
S ONE EXPLORES the terrain of these practices, something is constantly slipping away, something that can be neither said nor
"taught" but must be "practiced." That is what Kant thought
about judgment or tact. If he places the question at a "transcendental"
level in relation to practice and theory (and not in the position of a
referential remainder in relation to the powers [*lumières*] of reason), he
does not explain what its language might be. On this subject, he resorts
to quotation: a common saw, something said by the "ordinary" man.
This still juridical (and already ethnological) procedure makes *someone
else* utter the fragment to be glossed. The popular oracle (*Spruch*) must
speak about this art; the commentary will then *explain* this "saying." To
be sure, in proceeding in this way the discourse takes this saying seriously
(and does not consider it merely a deceptive blanket thrown over practices), but it places itself outside, at the distance of an evaluating observation. It speaks about what someone else says about his art, not about
the art itself. If one maintains that this "art" can only be practiced, and
that outside of this practice it has no statement, language must also be
involved in this practice. It is an art of speaking, then, which exercises
precisely that art of operating in which Kant discerned an art of thinking. In other words, it is a narration. If the art of speaking is itself an art
of operating and an art of thinking, practice and theory can be present
in it.

An art of speaking

The preceding investigations point in this direction. I shall distinguish
between what is established and what remains hypothetical.

1) First, one *fact* is indicative. The ways of operating do not merely
designate activities that a theory might take as its objects. They also
organize its construction. Far from remaining external to theoretical

77

creation or at its threshold, Foucault's "procedures," Bourdieu's "strategies," and tactics in general form *a field of operations within which
the production of theory also takes place.* We thus return, though
on a different terrain, to Wittgenstein's position regarding "ordinary
language."[1]

2) A *possibility* offers itself for making explicit the relation of theory
to the procedures from which it results and to those which are its objects:
a discourse composed of stories. The narrativizing of practices is a
textual "way of operating" having its own procedures and tactics. Marx
and Freud (not to go any further back) provide authoritative examples.
Foucault moreover claims to write only "stories" (*"récits"*). For his part,
Bourdieu makes stories the vanguard and reference of his system. In
many works, narrativity insinuates itself into scientific discourse as its
general denomination (its title), as one of its parts ("case" studies, "life
stories," or stories of groups, etc.) or as its counterpoint (quoted
fragments, interviews, "sayings," etc.). Narrativity haunts such discourse.
Shouldn't we recognize its *scientific* legitimacy by assuming that instead
of being a remainder that cannot be, or has not yet been, eliminated
from discourse, narrativity has a necessary function in it, and that
*a theory of narration is indissociable from a theory of practices, as its
condition as well as its production*?

To do that would be to recognize the theoretical value of the novel,
which has become the zoo of everyday practices since the establishment
of modern science. It would also be to return "scientific" significance to
the traditional act which has always *recounted* practices (this act, *ce
geste*, is also *une geste*, a tale of high deeds). In this way, the folktale
provides scientific discourse with a model, and not merely with textual
objects to be dealt with. It no longer has the status of a document that
does not know what it says, cited (summoned and quoted) before and by
the analysis that knows it. On the contrary, it is a know-how-to-say
(*"savoir-dire"*) exactly adjusted to its object, and, as such, no longer the
Other of knowledge; rather it is a variant of the discourse that knows
and an authority in what concerns theory. One can then understand the
alternations and complicities, the procedural homologies and social im-
brications that link the "arts of speaking" to the "arts of operating": the
same practices appear now in a verbal field, now in a field of non-
linguistic actions; they move from one field to the other, being equally
tactical and subtle in both; they keep the ball moving between them—
from the workday to evening, from cooking to legends and gossip, from
the devices of lived history to those of history retold.

Can this narrativity be reduced to the "Description" we know from the classical age? One fundamental difference distinguishes them: in narration, it is no longer a question of approaching a "reality" (a technical operation, etc.) as closely as possible and making the text acceptable through the "real" that it exhibits. On the contrary, narrated history creates a fictional space. It moves away from the "real"—or rather it pretends to escape present circumstances: "once upon a time there was. . . ." In precisely that way, it *makes* a hit (*"coup"*) far more than it describes one. To adopt the words cited by Kant, it is itself an *act* of tightrope-walking, a balancing act in which the circumstances (place, time) and the speaker himself participate, a way of knowing how to manipulate, dispose, and "place" a saying by altering a set—in short, "a matter of tact."

Narration does indeed have a content, but it also belongs to the art of making a *coup*: it is a detour by way of a past ("the other day," "in olden days") or by way of a quotation (a "saying," a proverb) made in order to take advantage of an occasion and to modify an equilibrium by taking it by surprise. Its discourse is characterized more by a way of *exercising itself* than by the thing it indicates. And one must grasp a sense other than what is said. It produces effects, not objects. It is narration, not description. It is an *art* of saying. The audience makes no mistake on this account. It is quite capable of distinguishing art from a mere "trick" (what one has only *to know* in order to perform it)— and also from revelation/popularization (that which one *must know* indefinitely)—just as the ordinary people Kant refers to (as for him, where is *he*, then?) are capable of easily distinguishing the charlatan from the tightrope walker. Something in narration escapes the order of what it is sufficient or necessary to know, and, in its characteristics, concerns the *style* of tactics.

It is easy to recognize this art in Foucault's work: an art of suspense, of quotations, of ellipsis, of metonymy; an art of conjuncture (current events, the audience) and occasions (epistemological, political); in short, an art of making *"coups"* with the fictions of stories. Foucault does not owe his effectiveness primarily to his erudition (prodigious though it is), but rather to this art of speaking which is an art of thinking and of operating. With the most subtle procedures of rhetoric, by clever alternation of descriptive tableaux (exemplary "stories") and analytical tableaux (theoretical distinctions), he makes what he says appear evident to the public he has in view, he disturbs the fields into which he moves one after the other, creating a new disposition of the whole. But with its historiographical "description" this art tricks its other and modifies its law without replacing it by a different one. It does not have its own discourse. It does not say itself. It is the practice of nowhere (*non-lieu*): *fort*? *da*? There and not there. It pretends to be eclipsed by the erudition or the taxonomies that in fact it manipulates. A dancer disguised as an archivist. Nietzsche's laughter rings through the historian's text.

In order to grasp the relation between narration and tactics, we must locate a more explicit scientific model for it, in which the theory of practices takes precisely the form of a way of narrating them.

Telling "coups": Détienne

Marcel Détienne, who is a historian and an anthropologist, has deliberately chosen to tell stories. He does not examine Greek stories in order to treat them in the name of something other than themselves. He rejects the break that would make of them objects of knowledge and also objects to be known, dark caverns in which hidden "mysteries" are supposed to await the scientific investigation to receive a meaning. He does not assume that behind all these stories, secrets exist whose gradual unveiling would give him, in the background, his own place, that of interpretation. For him, these tales, stories, poems, and treatises are already practices. They say exactly what they do. They constitute an act which they intend to mean. There is no need to add a gloss that knows what they express without knowing it, nor to wonder *what* they are the metaphor of. They form a network of operations whose formal rules and clever "*coups*" are outlined by an enormous cast of characters.

In this space of textual practices, as in a chessgame in which the pieces, rules and players have been multiplied out to the scale of a whole literature, Détienne has an artist's sense for the innumerable moves that have already been executed (the memory of earlier moves is essential in every game of chess), but he plays the game himself; he makes other moves with this repertory: he *narrates* in his turn. He re-cites these tactical moves. To say what they say, there is no discourse outside of them. You ask what they "mean" ("*veulent*" *dire*)? I'll tell them to you again. When someone asked him about the meaning of a sonata, it is said, Beethoven merely played it over. It is the same with the recitation of the oral tradition as analyzed by J. Goody: it is a way of re-telling the consequences and combinations of formal operations, along with an art of "harmonizing" them with the circumstances and with the audience.[2]

The story does not express a practice. It does not limit itself to telling about a movement. It *makes* it. One understands it, then, if one enters into this movement oneself, as Détienne does. He expresses Greek practices by reciting Greek stories: "Once upon a time. . . ." *The Gardens of Adonis, La panthère parfumée, Dionysos Slain , La cuisine du sacrifice—* these are so many fables from a practicing raconteur.[3] He outlines Greek turns and tricks by playing out their stories in his own way on the contemporary scene. He protects them against museographical alteration by means of an art that historiography is losing after having long held it to be essential, and whose importance among other peoples is being rediscovered by anthropology, from Lévi-Strauss' *Mythologiques* to the essays in Bauman and Scherzer's *Ethnography of Speaking*:[4] the art of telling stories. He thus operates between what historiography itself practiced in the past and what anthropology is restoring today as a foreign object. In this interval we find the pleasure of storytelling taking on scientific importance. The storyteller falls in step with the lively pace of his fables. He follows them in all their turns and detours, thus exercising an art of thinking. Like the knight in chess, he crosses the immense chessboard of literature with the "curved" movement of these stories, like Ariadne's threads, formal games of practices. In that very action he "interprets" these fables as a pianist "interprets" a musical composition. He executes them, privileging two "figures" in which the Greek art of thinking is particularly active: the dance and combat, that is, the very figures that the writing of the story makes use of.

With Jean-Pierre Vernant, Détienne has written a book on the Greeks' *mētis*, called *Les ruses de l'intelligence.*[5] This book is a sequence of stories. It deals with a form of intelligence that is always "immersed in practice" and which combines "flair, sagacity, foresight, intellectual flexibility, deception, resourcefulness, vigilant watchfulness, a sense for opportunities, diverse sorts of cleverness, and a great deal of acquired experience."[6] Even though it is absent from the image that Greek thought constructed of itself, *mētis* is extraordinarily stable throughout Hellenism. It is close to everyday tactics through its "sleights of hand, its cleverness and its stratagems," and through the spectrum of behaviors that it includes, from know-how to trickiness.

Three elements in this analysis merit particular attention here, because they differentiate *mētis* more clearly from other sorts of behavior, but also because they are equally characteristic of the stories that tell about it. They are constituted by three relations of *mētis*, to the "situation," to disguise, and to a paradoxical invisibility. In the first place, *mētis* counts and plays on the right point in time (*kairos*): it is a temporal practice. Second, it takes on many different masks and metaphors: it is an undoing of the proper place (*le lieu propre*). Third, it disappears into its own action, as though lost in what it does, without any mirror that re-presents it: it has no image of itself. These characteristics of *mētis* can also be attributed to the story (*récit*). They thus suggest a "supplement" to Détienne and Vernant: the form of practical intelligence that they analyze and the manner in which they do it must also be connected by a theoretical link if storytelling narrativity is also something like *mētis*.

The art of memory and circumstances

In the relationship of forces in which it intervenes, *mētis* is the "ultimate weapon," the one that gives Zeus supremacy over the other gods. It is a principle of economy: obtain the maximum number of effects from the minimum force. It thus also defines an esthetics, as is well known. The multiplication of effects through the rarefaction of means is, for different reasons, the rule that organizes both an art of operating and the poetic art of speaking, painting or singing.

This economic relationship delimits *mētis* more than it indicates its dynamic. The "turn" or inversion that leads the operation from its point of departure (*less* force) to its destination (*more* effects) implies first of all the mediation of a body of *knowledge*, but a peculiar one whose characteristics are the duration of its acquisition and its composition as an unending summation of particular fragments. It is a matter of "age," say the texts: they oppose the "experience of the old man" to the "thoughtlessness of youth." This knowledge is composed of many moments and many heterogeneous elements. It has no general and abstract formulation, no proper place. It is a *memory*,[7] whose attainments are indissociable from the time of their acquisition and bear the marks of its particularities. Drawing its knowledge from a multitude of events among which it moves without possessing them (they are all *past*, each a loss of place but a fragment of time), it also computes and predicts "the multiple paths of the future" by combining antecedent or possible particularities.[8] A certain duration is thus introduced into the relationship of forces and changes it. *Mētis* in fact counts on an accumulated time, which is in its favor, to overcome a hostile composition of place. But its memory remains hidden (it has no determinable place) up to the instant in which it reveals itself, at the "right point in time" in a way that is still connected with time even though it contradicts its usual concealment in a temporal duration. The flashes of this memory illuminate the *occasion*.

The occasion is encyclopedic because of *mētis*'s ability to use through it its treasure of past experiences and to inventory multiple possibilities in it: it contains all this knowledge within the smallest volume. It concentrates the *most* knowledge in the *least* time. Reduced to its smallest format, in an act transforming the situation, this concrete encyclopedia is a virtual philosopher's stone! It recalls still more the mathematical theme of an identity correspondence between a circle and its center. But here extension means duration, and concentration means an instant. By means of this substitution of time for space, the correspondence of the unending series of experiences (the circle) with the punctual moment of their recapitulation (the center) could be regarded as the theoretical model of the occasion.

Limiting ourselves to these first elements, we can offer a schematic representation of the "turn," from its initial point (I)—less force—to its terminal point (IV)—more effects. We would then have something like this:

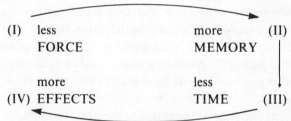

In (I), the force diminishes; in (II), memory–knowledge increases; in (III), time diminishes; in (IV), effects increase. These increases and diminutions are related inversely, yielding the following relationships: between (I) and (II), the less force there is, the more memory–knowledge is required; between (II) and (III), the more memory–knowledge there is, the less time is required: between (III) and (IV), the less time there is, the greater the effects.

The occasion is a nexus so important in all everyday practices, as well as in the related "popular" stories, that we must try here to clarify this preliminary outline. The occasion nevertheless constantly eludes attempts to define it, because it can be isolated neither from a conjuncture nor from an operation. It is a fact that cannot be detached from the "turn" or "trick" that produces it, because each time it is inserted in a sequence of elements, it distorts their relationships. Its presence causes *distortions* generated in the situation considered by the bringing together of *qualitatively heterogeneous dimensions* which are not merely contraries or contradictories. The index of this guileful process is the set of inversely proportional relationships noted above: they are comparable to the proportions and distortions that, through mirror effects (inversions, incurvations, reductions or enlargements) or perspectives (the farther it is, the smaller it is, etc.), permit the juxtaposition of *different* spaces in a single picture. But in the sequence into which the occasion is inserted, the juxtaposition of heteronomous dimensions concerns time and space, or state and action, etc. It is marked by inversely proportional ratios analogous to those which, in Pascal's work, articulate different "orders" and are of the type: *all the more* present because *less* visible; all the *fewer* because *more* favored by grace; etc.[9] Qualitatively, there are *passages into something else* through "twisted" relations, through successive reversals.

Among the qualitative differences linked by these inverse relationships, I shall point out at least two kinds whose insertion into a series requires two distinct sorts of reading:

1) A difference between *space and time* yields the paradigmatic sequence: in the composition of the initial place (I), the world of the memory (II) intervenes at the "right moment" (III) and produces modifications of the space (IV). According to this kind of difference, the series has a spatial organization as its beginning and its end; time is the intermediary, an oddity proceeding from the outside and producing the transition from one state of the places to the next. In short, between two "equilibria" comes a temporal irruption:

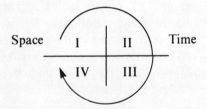

2) A second difference between *being* established (a state) and operating (a production and a transformation) is combined with the first. It plays moreover on an opposition between the visible and the invisible, without exactly corresponding to it. Along this axis, one finds the following paradigmatic sequence: given a visible establishment of forces (I)

and an invisible fund of memories (II), a punctual act of memory (III) produces visible effects in the established order (IV). The first part of the series is composed of two factual situations, in which invisible knowledge escapes visible power; then comes an operational part. By distinguishing between the being/operating cycle and the visible/invisible cycle one arrives at the following schema:

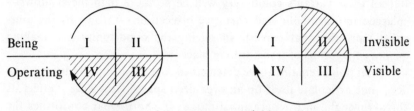

A summary tabulation of these elements yields:

	(I) Place	(II) Memory	(III) *Kairos*	(IV) Effects
Time		+	+	
Operation			+	+
Appearance	+		+	+

Memory mediates spatial transformations. In the mode of the "right point in time" (*kairos*), it produces a founding rupture or break. Its foreignness makes possible a transgression of the law of the place. Coming out of its bottomless and mobile secrets, a "*coup*" modifies the local order. The goal of the series is thus an operation that transforms the visible organization. But this change requires the invisible resources of a time which obeys other laws and which, taking it by surprise, steals something from the distribution owning the space.

This schema can be found in any number of stories. It is, as it were, their *minimal unit*. It can take a comic form in the memory that, at just the right moment, reverses a situation. In the exchange, "But . . . you must be my father!" "Good God, my daughter!," we see a pirouette due to the return of a time that the spatial distribution of the characters did not know about. There is a whodunit form in which the past, by coming back, overturns an established hierarchical order: "*He* must be the murderer, then!" The structure of the miracle has a similar form: out of another time, from a time that is alien, arises a "god" who has the characteristics of memory, that silent encyclopedia of singular acts, and who, in religious stories, represents with such fidelity the "popular" memory of those who have no place but who have time—"Patience!" With variations, each repeats the recourse to a different world from which can, *must*, come the blow that will change the established order. But all these variants could very well be no more than the shadows—enlarged into symbolic and narrative projections—thrown by the journalistic practice that consists in seizing the opportunity and making memory the means of transforming places.

A final point remains to be determined, the most important one: how does time articulate itself on an organized space? How does it effect its "breakthrough" in the occasional mode? In short, what constitutes the *implantation of memory in a place* that already forms an ensemble? That implantation is the moment which calls for a tightrope-walker's talent and a sense of tactics; it is the instant of art. Now it is clear that this implantation is neither localized nor determined by memory-knowledge. The occasion is taken advantage of, not created. It is furnished by the conjuncture, that is, by *external* circumstances in which a sharp eye can see the new and favorable ensemble they will constitute, given *one more detail*. A supplementary stroke, and it will be "right." In order for there to be a practical "harmony," there is lacking only a little something, a scrap which becomes precious in these particular circumstances and which the invisible treasury of the memory will provide. But the fragment to be drawn from this fund can be inserted only into a disposition imposed from the outside, in order to transform it into an unstable, makeshift harmony. In its practical form, memory has no ready-made organization that it could settle there. It is mobilized relative to what happens—something unexpected that it is clever enough to transform into an opportunity. It inserts itself into something encountered by chance, on the other's ground.

Like those birds that lay their eggs only in other species' nests, memory produces in a place that does not belong to it. It receives its form and its implantation from external circumstances, even if it furnishes the content (the missing detail). Its mobilization is inseparable from an *alteration*. More than that, memory derives its interventionary force from its very capacity to be altered—unmoored, mobile, lacking any fixed position. Its permanent mark is that it is formed (and forms its "capital") by *arising from the other* (a circumstance) and by *losing it* (it is no more than a memory). There is a double alteration, both of memory, which works when something affects it, and of its object, which is remembered only when it has disappeared. Memory is in decay when it is no longer capable of this alteration. It constructs itself from events that are independent of it, and it is linked to the expectation that something alien to the present will or must occur. Far from being the reliquary or trash can of the past, it sustains itself by *believing* in the existence of possibilities and by vigilantly awaiting them, constantly on the watch for their appearance.

Standing in the same relation to time that an "art" of war has to manipulations of space, an "art" of memory develops an aptitude for always being in the other's place without possessing it, and for profiting from this alteration without destroying itself through it. This ability is not a power (even if its narration may be). It has rather been given the name of *authority*: what has been "drawn" from the collective or individual memory and "authorizes" (makes possible) a reversal, a change in order or place, a transition into something different, a "metaphor" of practice or of discourse. Thus we find a subtle manipulation of "authorities" in every popular tradition. Memory comes from somewhere else, it is outside of itself, it moves things about. The tactics of its art are related to what it is, and to its disquieting familiarity. I would like to underline a few of its procedures, those which are particularly responsible for organizing the occasion in everyday modes of behavior: the play of alteration, the metonymic practice of singularity and (but this is ultimately only a general effect) a confusing and guileful (*retorse*) mobility.

1) Practical memory is regulated by the manifold activity of *alteration*, not merely because it is constituted only by being marked by external occurrences and by accumulating these successive blazons and tattoos inscribed by the other, but also because these invisible inscriptions are "recalled" to the light of day only through new circumstances. The manner in which they are recalled corresponds to that in which they were inscribed. Perhaps memory is no more than this "recall" or call on the part of the other, leaving its mark like a kind of overlay on a body that has always already been altered without knowing it. This originary and secret writing "emerges" little by little, in the very spots where memory is touched: memory is played by circumstances, just as a piano is played by a musician and music emerges from it when its keys are touched by the hands. Memory is a sense of the other. Hence it develops along with relationships—in "traditional" societies as in love—whereas it atrophies

when proper places become autonomous. It responds more than it records, up to the moment when, losing its mobile fragility and becoming incapable of new alterations, it can only repeat its initial responses.

This system of responsive alteration organizes, from moment to moment, the tact accompanying insertion into a circumstantial ensemble. The occasion, seized on the ground, is the very transformation of touch into response, a "reversion" of this surprise which is expected without being foreseen: what the event inscribes, no matter how fleeting and rapid it may be, is reversed, reverts back to it in the form of a word or an act: a flash repartee. The vivacity and appropriateness of this repartee are inseparable from their dependence on the instants which occur and from the vigilance that they mark all the more because there is less of a proper place to protect oneself and oneself's memory against their occurrence.

2) This response is *singular*. Within the ensemble in which it occurs, it is merely *one more detail*—an action, a word—so well-placed as to reverse the situation. But what else could memory provide? It is composed of individual bits and fragments. One detail, many details, are memories. Each of them, when it emerges in a shadowy setting, is relative to an ensemble which lacks it. Each memory shines like a metonymy in relation to this whole. From a picture, there remains only the delicious wound of this deep blue. From a body, the luminosity of its eyes, or the texture of a bit of white glimpsed through a gap in a hairdo. These particulars have the force of demonstratives: *that* fellow who was going by all bent over . . . , *that* odor, which came from some undetermined source. . . . Sharp details, intense particulars already function in the memory as they intervene in the occasion. The same tact is exercised in both cases, the same art of connecting a concrete detail and a conjuncture in a relation which, in the memory, is suggested as the trace of an event, and in the occasion, operates through the production of an accord or "harmony."

3) The oddest thing is no doubt the *mobility* of this memory in which details are never *what* they are: they are not objects, for they are elusive as such; not fragments, for they yield the ensemble they forget; not totalities, since they are not self-sufficient; not stable, since each recall alters them. This "space" of a moving nowhere has the subtlety of a cybernetic world. It probably constitutes (but this reference is more indicative than explanatory, referring to what we do not know) the model of the art of operating or of that *mētis* which, in seizing occasions,

constantly restores the unexpected pertinence of time in places where powers are distributed.

Stories

Everything seems the same in the structure into which the detail inserts itself, and yet both its functioning and its equilibrium are changed. Both contemporary scientific analyses that reduce memory to its "social frameworks"[10] and the clerical techniques that in the Middle Ages so cleverly transformed it into a composition of places and thus prepared the modern mutation of time into a quantifiable and regulatable space,[11] forget or reject its detours, even when the latter offer the major advantage of explaining by what procedures and for what legitimate strategic reasons the occasion—that indiscreet instant, that poison—has been controlled by the spatialization of scientific discourse. As the constitution of a proper place, scientific writing ceaselessly reduces time, that fugitive element, to the normality of an observable and readable system. In this way, surprises are averted. Proper maintenance of the place eliminates these criminal tricks.

But they return, not only surreptitiously and silently in this scientific activity itself[12] and not only in daily practices which, though they no longer have a discourse, are nonetheless extant, but also in rambling, wily, everyday stories. To recognize them in these stories all we have to do is not limit ourselves to examining their forms or repetitive structures (though this is also a necessary task). A certain know-how is at work here, in which all the characteristics of the art of memory can be discerned. I offer just one example. The significance of a story that is well known, and therefore classifiable, can be reversed by a single "circumstantial" detail. To "recite" it is to play on this *extra* element hidden in the felicitous stereotypes of the commonplace. The "insignificant detail" inserted into the framework that supports it makes the commonplace produce other effects. He that hath ears to hear, let him hear. The finely tuned ear can discern in the *saying* the difference introduced by the *act of saying* (*it*) here and now, and remains attentive to these guileful tricks on the part of the storyteller.

It would be interesting to examine more closely the turns that transform into occasions and opportunities the stories of the collective treasury of legends or everyday conversation and which concern in large measure, once again, rhetoric.[13] But one can already take as a preliminary hypothesis that in the art of telling about ways of operating, the latter is already at work. Thus it is exemplary that Détienne and Vernant should have made themselves the storytellers of this "labyrinthine intelligence" ("*intelligence en dédales*"), as Françoise Frontisi so well terms it.[14] This discursive practice of the story (*l'histoire*) is both its art and its discourse.

At bottom, this is all a very old story. When he grew old, Aristotle, who is not generally considered exactly a tightrope dancer, liked to lose himself in the most labyrinthine and subtle of discourses. He had then arrived at the age of *mētis*: "The more solitary and isolated I become, the more I come to like stories."[15] He had explained the reason admirably: as in the older Freud, it was a connoisseur's admiration for the tact that composed harmonies and for its art of doing it by surprise: "The lover of myth is in a sense a lover of Wisdom, for myth is composed of wonders."[16]

Part III
Spatial Practices

Chapter VII   Walking in the City

SEEING Manhattan from the 110th floor of the World Trade Center. Beneath the haze stirred up by the winds, the urban island, a sea in the middle of the sea, lifts up the skyscrapers over Wall Street, sinks down at Greenwich, then rises again to the crests of Midtown, quietly passes over Central Park and finally undulates off into the distance beyond Harlem. A wave of verticals. Its agitation is momentarily arrested by vision. The gigantic mass is immobilized before the eyes. It is transformed into a texturology in which extremes coincide—extremes of ambition and degradation, brutal oppositions of races and styles, contrasts between yesterday's buildings, already transformed into trash cans, and today's urban irruptions that block out its space. Unlike Rome, New York has never learned the art of growing old by playing on all its pasts. Its present invents itself, from hour to hour, in the act of throwing away its previous accomplishments and challenging the future. A city composed of paroxysmal places in monumental reliefs. The spectator can read in it a universe that is constantly exploding. In it are inscribed the architectural figures of the *coincidatio oppositorum* formerly drawn in miniatures and mystical textures. On this stage of concrete, steel and glass, cut out between two oceans (the Atlantic and the American) by a frigid body of water, the tallest letters in the world compose a gigantic rhetoric of excess in both expenditure and production.[1]

Voyeurs or walkers

To what erotics of knowledge does the ecstasy of reading such a cosmos belong? Having taken a voluptuous pleasure in it, I wonder what is the source of this pleasure of "seeing the whole," of looking down on, totalizing the most immoderate of human texts.

To be lifted to the summit of the World Trade Center is to be lifted out of the city's grasp. One's body is no longer clasped by the streets that turn and return it according to an anonymous law; nor is it possessed, whether as player or played, by the rumble of so many differences and by the nervousness of New York traffic. When one goes up there, he leaves behind the mass that carries off and mixes up in itself any identity of authors or spectators. An Icarus flying above these waters, he can ignore the devices of Daedalus in mobile and endless labyrinths far below. His elevation transfigures him into a voyeur. It puts him at a distance. It transforms the bewitching world by which one was "possessed" into a text that lies before one's eyes. It allows one to read it, to be a solar Eye, looking down like a god. The exaltation of a scopic and gnostic drive: the fiction of knowledge is related to this lust to be a viewpoint and nothing more.

Must one finally fall back into the dark space where crowds move back and forth, crowds that, though visible from on high, are themselves unable to see down below? An Icarian fall. On the 110th floor, a poster, sphinx-like, addresses an enigmatic message to the pedestrian who is for an instant transformed into a visionary: *It's hard to be down when you're up.*

The desire to see the city preceded the means of satisfying it. Medieval or Renaissance painters represented the city as seen in a perspective that no eye had yet enjoyed.[2] This fiction already made the medieval spectator into a celestial eye. It created gods. Have things changed since technical procedures have organized an "all-seeing power"?[3] The totalizing eye imagined by the painters of earlier times lives on in our achievements. The same scopic drive haunts users of architectural productions by materializing today the utopia that yesterday was only painted. The 1370 foot high tower that serves as a prow for Manhattan continues to construct the fiction that creates readers, makes the complexity of the city readable, and immobilizes its opaque mobility in a transparent text.

Is the immense texturology spread out before one's eyes anything more than a representation, an optical artifact? It is the analogue of the facsimile produced, through a projection that is a way of keeping aloof, by the space planner urbanist, city planner or cartographer. The panorama-city is a "theoretical" (that is, visual) simulacrum, in short a picture, whose condition of possibility is an oblivion and a misunderstanding of practices. The voyeur-god created by this fiction, who, like Schreber's God, knows only cadavers,[4] must disentangle himself from the murky intertwining daily behaviors and make himself alien to them.

The ordinary practitioners of the city live "down below," below the thresholds at which visibility begins. They walk—an elementary form of this experience of the city; they are walkers, *Wandersmänner*, whose bodies follow the thicks and thins of an urban "text" they write without being able to read it. These practitioners make use of spaces that cannot be seen; their knowledge of them is as blind as that of lovers in each other's arms. The paths that correspond in this intertwining, unrecognized poems in which each body is an element signed by many others, elude legibility. It is as though the practices organizing a bustling city were characterized by their blindness.[5] The networks of these moving, intersecting writings compose a manifold story that has neither author nor spectator, shaped out of fragments of trajectories and alterations of spaces: in relation to representations, it remains daily and indefinitely other.

Escaping the imaginary totalizations produced by the eye, the everyday has a certain strangeness that does not surface, or whose surface is only its upper limit, outlining itself against the visible. Within this ensemble, I shall try to locate the practices that are foreign to the "geometrical" or "geographical" space of visual, panoptic, or theoretical constructions. These practices of space refer to a specific form of *operations* ("ways of operating"), to "another spatiality"[6] (an "anthropological," poetic and mythic experience of space), and to an *opaque and blind* mobility characteristic of the bustling city. A *migrational*, or metaphorical, city thus slips into the clear text of the planned and readable city.

1. From the concept of the city to urban practices

The World Trade Center is only the most monumental figure of Western urban development. The atopia-utopia of optical knowledge has long had the ambition of surmounting and articulating the contradictions arising from urban agglomeration. It is a question of managing a growth of human agglomeration or accumulation. "The city is a huge monastery," said Erasmus. Perspective vision and prospective vision constitute the twofold projection of an opaque past and an uncertain future onto a

surface that can be dealt with. They inaugurate (in the sixteenth century?) the transformation of the urban *fact* into the *concept* of a city.
Long before the concept itself gives rise to a particular figure of history,
it assumes that this fact can be dealt with as a unity determined by an
urbanistic *ratio*. Linking the city to the concept never makes them
identical, but it plays on their progressive symbiosis: to plan a city is
both to *think the very plurality* of the real and to make that way of
thinking the plural *effective*; it is to know how to articulate it and be
able to do it.

An operational concept?

The "city" founded by utopian and urbanistic discourse[7] is defined by
the possibility of a threefold operation:

1. The production of its *own* space (*un espace propre*): rational
organization must thus repress all the physical, mental and political
pollutions that would compromise it;

2. the substitution of a nowhen, or of a synchronic system, for the
indeterminable and stubborn resistances offered by traditions; univocal
scientific strategies, made possible by the flattening out of all the data in
a plane projection, must replace the tactics of users who take advantage
of "opportunities" and who, through these trap-events, these lapses in
visibility, reproduce the opacities of history everywhere;

3. finally, the creation of a *universal* and anonymous *subject* which is
the city itself: it gradually becomes possible to attribute to it, as to its
political model, Hobbes' State, all the functions and predicates that were
previously scattered and assigned to many different real subjects—
groups, associations, or individuals. "The city," like a proper name, thus
provides a way of conceiving and constructing space on the basis of a
finite number of stable, isolatable, and interconnected properties.

Administration is combined with a process of elimination in this place
organized by "speculative" and classificatory operations.[8] On the one
hand, there is a differentiation and redistribution of the parts and functions of the city, as a result of inversions, displacements, accumulations,
etc.; on the other there is a rejection of everything that is not capable of
being dealt with in this way and so constitutes the "waste products" of a
functionalist administration (abnormality, deviance, illness, death, etc.).
To be sure, progress allows an increasing number of these waste products

to be reintroduced into administrative circuits and transforms even deficiencies (in health, security, etc.) into ways of making the networks of order denser. But in reality, it repeatedly produces effects contrary to those at which it aims: the profit system generates a loss which, in the multiple forms of wretchedness and poverty outside the system and of waste inside it, constantly turns production into "expenditure." Moreover, the rationalization of the city leads to its mythification in strategic discourses, which are calculations based on the hypothesis or the necessity of its destruction in order to arrive at a final decision.[9] Finally, the functionalist organization, by privileging progress (i.e., time), causes the condition of its own possibility—space itself—to be forgotten; space thus becomes the blind spot in a scientific and political technology. This is the way in which the Concept-city functions; a place of transformations and appropriations, the object of various kinds of interference but also a subject that is constantly enriched by new attributes, it is simultaneously the machinery and the hero of modernity.

Today, whatever the avatars of this concept may have been, we have to acknowledge that if in discourse the city serves as a totalizing and almost mythical landmark for socioeconomic and political strategies, urban life increasingly permits the re-emergence of the element that the urbanistic project excluded. The language of power is in itself "urbanizing," but the city is left prey to contradictory movements that counterbalance and combine themselves outside the reach of panoptic power. The city becomes the dominant theme in political legends, but it is no longer a field of programmed and regulated operations. Beneath the discourses that ideologize the city, the ruses and combinations of powers that have no readable identity proliferate; without points where one can take hold of them, without rational transparency, they are impossible to administer.

The return of practices

The Concept-city is decaying. Does that mean that the illness afflicting both the rationality that founded it and its professionals afflicts the urban populations as well? Perhaps cities are deteriorating along with the procedures that organized them. But we must be careful here. The ministers of knowledge have always assumed that the whole universe was threatened by the very changes that affected their ideologies and their positions. They transmute the misfortune of their theories into theories of misfortune. When they transform their bewilderment into "catastrophes," when they seek to enclose the people in the "panic" of their discourses, are they once more necessarily right?

Rather than remaining within the field of a discourse that upholds its privilege by inverting its content (speaking of catastrophe and no longer of progress), one can try another path: one can try another path: one can analyze the microbe-like, singular and plural practices which an urbanistic system was supposed to administer or suppress, but which have outlived its decay; one can follow the swarming activity of these procedures that, far from being regulated or eliminated by panoptic administration, have reinforced themselves in a proliferating illegitimacy, developed and insinuated themselves into the networks of surveillance, and combined in accord with unreadable but stable tactics to the point of constituting everyday regulations and surreptitious creativities that are merely concealed by the frantic mechanisms and discourses of the observational organization.

This pathway could be inscribed as a consequence, but also as the reciprocal, of Foucault's analysis of the structures of power. He moved it in the direction of mechanisms and technical procedures, "minor instrumentalities" capable, merely by their organization of "details," of transforming a human multiplicity into a "disciplinary" society and of managing, differentiating, classifying, and hierarchizing all deviances concerning apprenticeship, health, justice, the army, or work.[10] "These often miniscule ruses of discipline," these "minor but flawless" mechanisms, draw their efficacy from a relationship between procedures and the space that they redistribute in order to make an "operator" out of it. But what *spatial practices* correspond, in the area where discipline is manipulated, to these apparatuses that produce a disciplinary space? In the present conjuncture, which is marked by a contradiction between the collective mode of administration and an individual mode of reappropriation, this question is no less important, if one admits that spatial practices in fact secretly structure the determining conditions of social life. I would like to follow out a few of these multiform, resistance, tricky and stubborn procedures that elude discipline without being outside the field in which it is exercised, and which should lead us to a theory of everyday practices, of lived space, of the disquieting familiarity of the city.

2. The chorus of idle footsteps

> "The goddess can be recognized by her step"
> Virgil, *Aeneid*, I, 405

Their story begins on ground level, with footsteps. They are myriad, but do not compose a series. They cannot be counted because each unit has a qualitative character: a style of tactile apprehension and kinesthetic appropriation. Their swarming mass is an innumerable collection of singularities. Their intertwined paths give their shape to spaces. They weave places together. In that respect, pedestrian movements form one of these "real systems whose existence in fact makes up the city."[11] They are not localized; it is rather they that spatialize. They are no more inserted within a container than those Chinese characters speakers sketch out on their hands with their fingertips.

It is true that the operations of walking on can be traced on city maps in such a way as to transcribe their paths (here well-trodden, there very faint) and their trajectories (going this way and not that). But these thick or thin curves only refer, like words, to the absence of what has passed by. Surveys of routes miss what was: the act itself of passing by. The operation of walking, wandering, or "window shopping," that is, the activity of passers-by, is transformed into points that draw a totalizing and reversible line on the map. They allow us to grasp only a relic set in the nowhen of a surface of projection. Itself visible, it has the effect of making invisible the operation that made it possible. These fixations constitute procedures for forgetting. The trace left behind is substituted for the practice. It exhibits the (voracious) property that the geographical system has of being able to transform action into legibility, but in doing so it causes a way of being in the world to be forgotten.

Pedestrian speech acts

A comparison with the speech act will allow us to go further[12] and not limit ourselves to the critique of graphic representations alone, looking from the shores of legibility toward an inaccessible beyond. The act of walking is to the urban system what the speech act is to language or to the statements uttered.[13] At the most elementary level, it has a triple "enunciative" function: it is a process of *appropriation* of the topographical system on the part of the pedestrian (just as the speaker appropriates and takes on the language); it is a spatial acting-out of the place (just as the speech act is an acoustic acting-out of language); and it implies *relations* among differentiated positions, that is, among pragmatic "contracts" in the form of movements (just as verbal enunciation is an "allocution," "posits another opposite" the speaker and puts contracts between interlocutors into action).[14] It thus seems possible to give a preliminary definition of walking as a space of enunciation.

We could moreover extend this problematic to the relations between the act of writing and the written text, and even transpose it to the relationships between the "hand" (the touch and the tale of the paintbrush [*le et la geste du pinceau*]) and the finished painting (forms, colors, etc.). At first isolated in the area of verbal communication, the speech act turns out to find only one of its applications there, and its linguistic modality is merely the first determination of a much more general distinction between the *forms used* in a system and the *ways of using* this system (i.e., *rules*), that is, between two "different worlds," since "the same things" are considered from two opposite formal viewpoints.

Considered from this angle, the pedestrian speech act has three characteristics which distinguish it at the outset from the spatial system: the present, the discrete, the "phatic."

First, if it is true that a spatial order organizes an ensemble of possibilities (e.g., by a place in which one can move) and interdictions (e.g., by a wall that prevents one from going further), then the walker actualizes some of these possibilities. In that way, he makes them exist as well as emerge. But he also moves them about and he invents others, since the crossing, drifting away, or improvisation of walking privilege, transform or abandon spatial elements. Thus Charlie Chaplin multiplies the possibilities of his cane: he does other things with the same thing and he goes beyond the limits that the determinants of the object set on its utilization. In the same way, the walker transforms each spatial signifier into something else. And if on the one hand he actualizes only a few of the possibilities fixed by the constructed order (he goes only here and not there), on the other he increases the number of possibilities (for example, by creating shortcuts and detours) and prohibitions (for example, he forbids himself to take paths generally considered accessible or even obligatory). He thus makes a selection. "The user of a city picks out certain fragments of the statement in order to actualize them in secret."[15]

He thus creates a discreteness, whether by making choices among the signifiers of the spatial "language" or by displacing them through the use he makes of them. He condemns certain places to inertia or disappearance and composes with others spatial "turns of phrase" that are "rare," "accidental" or illegitimate. But that already leads into a rhetoric of walking.

In the framework of enunciation, the walker constitutes, in relation to his position, both a near and a far, a *here* and a *there*. To the fact that the adverbs *here* and *there* are the indicators of the locutionary seat in verbal communication[16]—a coincidence that reinforces the parallelism between linguistic and pedestrian enunciation—we must add that this location (*here—there*) (necessarily implied by walking and indicative of a present appropriation of space by an "I") also has the function of introducing an other in relation to this "I" and of thus establishing a conjunctive and disjunctive articulation of places. I would stress particularly the "phatic" aspect, by which I mean the function, isolated by Malinowski and Jakobson, of terms that initiate, maintain, or interrupt contact, such as "hello," "well, well," etc.[17] Walking, which alternately follows a path and has followers, creates a mobile organicity in the environment, a sequence of phatic *topoi*. And if it is true that the phatic function, which is an effort to ensure communication, is already characteristic of the language of talking birds, just as it constitutes the "first verbal function acquired by children," it is not surprising that it also gambols, goes on all fours, dances, and walks about, with a light or heavy step, like a series of "hellos" in an echoing labyrinth, anterior or parallel to informative speech.

The modalities of pedestrian enunciation which a plane representation on a map brings out could be analyzed. They include the kinds of relationship this enunciation entertains with particular paths (or "statements") by according them a truth value ("alethic" modalities of the necessary, the impossible, the possible, or the contingent), an epistemological value ("epistemic" modalities of the certain, the excluded, the plausible, or the questionable) or finally an ethical or legal value ("deontic" modalities of the obligatory, the forbidden, the permitted, or the optional).[18] Walking affirms, suspects, tries out, transgresses, respects, etc., the trajectories it "speaks." All the modalities sing a part in this chorus, changing from step to step, stepping in through proportions, sequences, and intensities which vary according to the time, the path taken and the walker. These enunciatory operations are of an unlimited diversity. They therefore cannot be reduced to their graphic trail.

Walking rhetorics

The walking of passers-by offers a series of turns (*tours*) and detours that can be compared to "turns of phrase" or "stylistic figures." There is a rhetoric of walking. The art of "turning" phrases finds an equivalent in an art of composing a path (*tourner un parcours*). Like ordinary language,[19] this art implies and combines styles and uses. *Style* specifies "a linguistic structure that manifests on the symbolic level . . . an individual's fundamental way of being in the world";[20] it connotes a singular. Use defines the social phenomenon through which a system of communication manifests itself in actual fact; it refers to a norm. Style and use both have to do with a "way of operating" (of speaking, walking, etc.), but style involves a peculiar processing of the symbolic, while use refers to elements of a code. They intersect to form a style of use, a way of being and a way of operating.[21]

In introducing the notion of a "residing rhetoric" ("*rhétorique habitante*"), the fertile pathway opened up by A. Médam[22] and systematized by S. Ostrowetsky[23] and J.-F. Augoyard,[24] we assume that the "tropes" catalogued by rhetoric furnish models and hypotheses for the analysis of ways of appropriating places. Two postulates seem to me to underlie the validity of this application: 1) it is assumed that practices of space also correspond to manipulations of the basic elements of a constructed order; 2) it is assumed that they are, like the tropes in rhetoric, deviations relative to a sort of "literal meaning" defined by the urbanistic system. There would thus be a homology between verbal figures and the figures of walking (a stylized selection among the latter is already found in the figures of dancing) insofar as both consist in "treatments" or operations bearing on isolatable units,[25] and in "ambiguous dispositions" that divert and displace meaning in the direction of equivocalness[26] in the way a tremulous image confuses and multiplies the photographed object. In these two modes, the analogy can be accepted. I would add that the geometrical space of urbanists and architects seems to have the status of the "proper meaning" constructed by grammarians and linguists in order to have a normal and normative level to which they can compare the drifting of "figurative" language. In reality, this faceless "proper" meaning (*ce "propre" sans figure*) cannot be found in current use, whether verbal or pedestrian; it is merely the fiction produced by a use that is also particular, the metalinguistic use of science that distinguishes itself by that very distinction.[27]

The long poem of walking manipulates spatial organizations, no matter how panoptic they may be: it is neither foreign to them (it can take place only within them) nor in conformity with them (it does not receive its identity from them). It creates shadows and ambiguities within them. It inserts its multitudinous references and citations into them (social models, cultural mores, personal factors). Within them it is itself the effect of successive encounters and occasions that constantly alter it and make it the other's blazon: in other words, it is like a peddler, carrying something surprising, transverse or attractive compared with the usual choice. These diverse aspects provide the basis of a rhetoric. They can even be said to define it.

By analyzing this "modern art of everyday expression" as it appears in accounts of spatial practices,[28] J.-F. Augoyard discerns in it two especially fundamental stylistic figures: synecdoche and asyndeton. The predominance of these two figures seems to me to indicate, in relation to two complementary poles, a formal structure of these practices. *Synecdoche* consists in "using a word in a sense which is part of another meaning of the same word."[29] In essence, it names a part instead of the whole which includes it. Thus "sail" is taken for "ship" in the expression "a fleet of fifty sails"; in the same way, a brick shelter or a hill is taken for the park in the narration of a trajectory. *Asyndeton* is the suppression of linking words such as conjunctions and adverbs, either within a sentence or between sentences. In the same way, in walking it selects and fragments the space traversed; it skips over links and whole parts that it omits. From this point of view, every walk constantly leaps, or skips like a child, hopping on one foot. It practices the ellipsis of conjunctive *loci*.

In reality, these two pedestrian figures are related. Synecdoche expands a spatial element in order to make it play the role of a "more" (a totality) and take its place (the bicycle or the piece of furniture in a store window stands for a whole street or neighborhood). Asyndeton, by elision, creates a "less," opens gaps in the spatial continuum, and retains only selected parts of it that amount almost to relics. Synecdoche replaces totalities by fragments (a *less* in the place of a *more*); asyndeton disconnects them by eliminating the conjunctive or the consecutive (nothing in place of something). Synecdoche makes more dense: it amplifies the detail and miniaturizes the whole. Asyndeton cuts out: it undoes continuity and undercuts its plausibility. A space treated in this way and shaped by practices is transformed into enlarged singularities and separate islands.[30] Through these swellings, shrinkings, and fragmentations, that is, through these rhetorical operations a spatial phrasing of an analogical (composed of juxtaposed citations) and elliptical (made of gaps, lapses, and allusions) type is created. For the technological system of a coherent and totalizing space that is "linked" and simultaneous, the figures of pedestrian rhetoric substitute trajectories that have a mythical structure, at least if one understands by "myth" a discourse relative to the place/nowhere (or origin) of concrete existence, a story jerry-built out of elements taken from common sayings, an allusive and fragmentary story whose gaps mesh with the social practices it symbolizes.

Figures are the acts of this stylistic metamorphosis of space. Or rather, as Rilke puts it, they are moving "trees of gestures." They move even the rigid and contrived territories of the medico-pedagogical institute in which retarded children find a place to play and dance their "spatial stories."[31] These "trees of gestures" are in movement everywhere. Their forests walk through the streets. They transform the scene, but they cannot be fixed in a certain place by images. If in spite of that an illustration were required, we could mention the fleeting images, yellowish-green and metallic blue calligraphies that howl without raising their voices and emblazon themselves on the subterranean passages of the city, "embroideries" composed of letters and numbers, perfect gestures of violence painted with a pistol, Shivas made of written characters, dancing graphics whose fleeting apparitions are accompanied by the rumble of subway trains: New York graffiti.

If it is true that *forests of gestures* are manifest in the streets, their movement cannot be captured in a picture, nor can the meaning of their movements be circumscribed in a text. Their rhetorical transplantation carries away and displaces the analytical, coherent proper meanings of urbanism; it constitutes a "wandering of the semantic"[32] produced by masses that make some parts of the city disappear and exaggerate others, distorting it, fragmenting it, and diverting it from its immobile order.

3. Myths: what "makes things go"

The figures of these movements (synecdoches, ellipses, etc.) characterize both a "symbolic order of the unconscious" and "certain typical processes of subjectivity manifested in discourse."[33] The similarity between "discourse"[34] and dreams[35] has to do with their use of the same "stylistic procedures"; it therefore includes pedestrian practices as well. The "ancient catalog of tropes" that from Freud to Benveniste has furnished an appropriate inventory for the rhetoric of the first two registers of expression is equally valid for the third. If there is a parallelism, it is not only because enunciation is dominant in these three areas, but also because its discursive (verbalized, dreamed, or walked) development is organized as a relation between the *place* from which it proceeds (an origin) and the nowhere it produces (a way of "going by").

From this point of view, after having compared pedestrian processes to linguistic formations, we can bring them back down in the direction of oneiric figuration, or at least discover on that other side what, in a spatial practice, is inseparable from the dreamed place. To walk is to lack a place. It is the indefinite process of being absent and in search of a proper. The moving about that the city multiplies and concentrates makes the city itself an immense social experience of lacking a place—an experience that is, to be sure, broken up into countless tiny deportations (displacements and walks), compensated for by the relationships and intersections of these exoduses that intertwine and create an urban fabric, and placed under the sign of what ought to be, ultimately, the place but is only a name, the City. The identity furnished by this place is all the more symbolic (named) because, in spite of the inequality of its citizens' positions and profits, there is only a pullulation of passer-by, a network of residences temporarily appropriated by pedestrian traffic, a shuffling among pretenses of the proper, a universe of rented spaces haunted by a nowhere or by dreamed-of places.

Names and symbols

An indication of the relationship that spatial practices entertain with that absence is furnished precisely by their manipulations of and with "proper" names. The relationships between the direction of a walk (*le sens de la marche*) and the meaning of words (*le sens des mots*) situate two sorts of apparently contrary movements, one extrovert (to walk is to go outside), the other introvert (a mobility under the stability of the signifier). Walking is in fact determined by semantic tropisms; it is attracted and repelled by nominations whose meaning is not clear, whereas the city, for its part, is transformed for many people into a "desert" in which the meaningless, indeed the terrifying, no longer takes the form of shadows but becomes, as in Genet's plays, an implacable light that produces this urban text without obscurities, which is created by a technocratic power everywhere and which puts the city-dweller under control (under the control of what? No one knows): "The city keeps us under its gaze, which one cannot bear without feeling dizzy," says a resident of Rouen.[36] In the spaces brutally lit by an alien reason, proper names carve out pockets of hidden and familiar meanings. They "make sense"; in other words, they are the impetus of movements, like vocations and calls that turn or divert an itinerary by giving it a meaning (or a direction) (*sens*) that was previously unforeseen. These names create a nowhere in places; they change them into passages.

A friend who lives in the city of Sèvres drifts, when he is in Paris, toward the rue des Saints-*Pères* and the rue de *Sèvres*, even though he is going to see his mother in another part of town: these names articulate a sentence that his steps compose without his knowing it. Numbered streets and street numbers (112th St., or 9 rue Saint-Charles) orient the magnetic field of trajectories just as they can haunt dreams. Another friend unconsciously represses the streets which have names and, by this fact, transmit her—orders or identities in the same way as summonses and classifications; she goes instead along paths that have no name or signature. But her walking is thus still controlled negatively by proper names.

What is it then that they spell out? Disposed in constellations that hierarchize and semantically order the surface of the city, operating chronological arrangements and historical justifications, these words (*Borrégo, Botzaris, Bougainville . . .*) slowly lose, like worn coins, the value engraved on them, but their ability to signify outlives its first definition. *Saints-Pères, Corentin Celton, Red Square . . .* these names make themselves available to the diverse meanings given them by passers-by; they detach themselves from the places they were supposed to define and serve as imaginary meeting-points on itineraries which, as metaphors, they determine for reasons that are foreign to their original value but may be recognized or not by passers-by. A strange toponymy that is detached from actual places and flies high over the city like a foggy geography of "meanings" held in suspension, directing the physical deambulations below: *Place de l'Étoile, Concorde, Poissonnière . . .* These constellations of names provide traffic patterns: they are stars directing itineraries. "The Place de la Concorde does not exist," Malaparte said, "it is an idea."[37] It is much more than an "idea." A whole series of comparisons would be necessary to account for the magical powers proper names enjoy. They seem to be carried as emblems by the travellers they direct and simultaneously decorate.

Linking acts and footsteps, opening meanings and directions, these words operate in the name of an emptying-out and wearing-away of their primary role. They become liberated spaces that can be occupied. A rich indetermination gives them, by means of a semantic rarefaction, the function of articulating a second, poetic geography on top of the geography of the literal, forbidden or permitted meaning. They insinuate other routes into the functionalist and historical order of movement. Walking follows them: "I fill this great empty space with a beautiful name."[38] People are put in motion by the remaining relics of meaning, and sometimes by their waste products, the inverted remainders of great ambitions.[39] Things that amount to nothing, or almost nothing, sym-bolize and orient walkers' steps: names that have ceased precisely to be "proper."

In these symbolizing kernels three distinct (but connected) functions of the relations between spatial and signifying practices are indicated (and perhaps founded): the *believable*, the *memorable*, and the *primitive*. They designate what "authorizes" (or makes possible or credible) spatial appropriations, what is repeated in them (or is recalled in them) from a silent and withdrawn memory, and what is structured in them and continues to be signed by an in-fantile (*in-fans*) origin. These three symbolic mechanisms organize the topoi of a discourse on/of the city (legend, memory, and dream) in a way that also eludes urbanistic systematicity. They can already be recognized in the functions of proper names: they make habitable or believable the place that they clothe with a word (by emptying themselves of their classifying power, they acquire that of "permitting" something else); they recall or suggest phantoms (the dead who are supposed to have disappeared) that still move about, concealed in gestures and in bodies in motion; and, by naming, that is, by imposing an injunction proceeding from the other (a story) and by altering functionalist identity by detaching themselves from it, they create in the place itself that erosion or nowhere that the law of the other carves out within it.

Credible things and memorable things: habitability

By a paradox that is only apparent, the discourse that makes people believe is the one that takes away what it urges them to believe in, or never delivers what it promises. Far from expressing a void or describing a lack, it creates such. It makes room for a void. In that way, it opens up clearings; it "allows" a certain play within a system of defined places. It "authorizes" the production of an area of free play (*Spielraum*) on a checkerboard that analyzes and classifies identities. It makes places habitable. On these grounds, I call such discourse a "local authority." It is a crack in the system that saturates places with signification and indeed so reduces them to this signification that it is "impossible to breathe in them." It is a symptomatic tendency of functionalist totalitarianism (including its programming of games and celebrations) that it seeks precisely to eliminate these local authorities, because they compromise the univocity of the system. Totalitarianism attacks what it quite correctly calls *superstitions*: supererogatory semantic overlays that insert themselves "over and above" and "in excess,"[40] and annex to a past or poetic realm a part of the land the promoters of technical rationalities and financial profitabilities had reserved for themselves.

Ultimately, since proper names are already "local authorities" or "superstitions," they are replaced by numbers: on the telephone, one no longer dials *Opera*, but 073. The same is true of the stories and legends that haunt urban space like superfluous or additional inhabitants. They are the object of a witch-hunt, by the very logic of the techno-structure. But their extermination (like the extermination of trees, forests, and hidden places in which such legends live)[41] makes the city a "suspended symbolic order."[42] The habitable city is thereby annulled. Thus, as a woman from Rouen put it, no, here "there isn't any place special, except for my own home, that's all. . . . There isn't anything." Nothing "special": nothing that is marked, opened up by a memory or a story, signed by something or someone else. Only the cave of the home remains believable, still open for a certain time to legends, still full of shadows. Except for that, according to another city-dweller, there are only "places in which one can no longer believe in anything."[43]

It is through the opportunity they offer to store up rich silences and wordless stories, or rather through their capacity to create cellars and garrets everywhere, that local legends (*legenda*: what is *to be read*, but also what *can be read*) permit exits, ways of going out and coming back in, and thus habitable spaces. Certainly walking about and traveling substitute for exits, for going away and coming back, which were formerly made available by a body of legends that places nowadays lack. Physical moving about has the itinerant function of yesterday's or today's "superstitions." Travel (like walking) is a substitute for the legends that used to open up space to something different. What does travel ultimately produce if it is not, by a sort of reversal, "an exploration of the deserted places of my memory," the return to nearby exoticism by way of a detour through distant places, and the "discovery" of relics and legends: "fleeting visions of the French countryside," "fragments of music and poetry,"[44] in short, something like an "uprooting in one's origins (Heidegger)? What this walking exile produces is precisely the body of legends that is currently lacking in one's own vicinity; it is a fiction, which moreover has the double characteristic, like dreams or pedestrian rhetoric, of being the effect of displacements and condensations.[45] As a corollary, one can measure the importance of these signifying practices (to tell oneself legends) as practices that invent spaces.

From this point of view, their contents remain revelatory, and still more so is the principle that organizes them. Stories about places are makeshift things. They are composed with the world's debris. Even if the literary form and the actantial schema of "superstitions" correspond to stable models whose structures and combinations have often been analyzed over the past thirty years, the materials (all the rhetorical details of their "manifestation") are furnished by the leftovers from nominations, taxonomies, heroic or comic predicates, etc., that is, by fragments of scattered semantic places. These heterogeneous and even contrary elements fill the homogeneous form of the story. Things *extra* and *other* (details and excesses coming from elsewhere) insert themselves into the accepted framework, the imposed order. One thus has the very relationship between spatial practices and the constructed order. The surface of this order is everywhere punched and torn open by ellipses, drifts, and leaks of meaning: it is a sieve-order.

The verbal relics of which the story is composed, being tied to lost stories and opaque acts, are juxtaposed in a collage where their relations are not thought, and for this reason they form a symbolic whole.[46] They are articulated by lacunae. Within the structured space of the text, they thus produce anti-texts, effects of dissimulation and escape, possibilities of moving into other landscapes, like cellars and bushes: "*ô massifs, ô pluriels*."[47] Because of the process of dissemination that they open up, stories differ from *rumors* in that the latter are always injunctions, initiators and results of a levelling of space, creators of common movements that reinforce an order by adding an activity of making people believe things to that of making people do things. Stories diversify, rumors totalize. If there is still a certain oscillation between them, it seems that today there is rather a stratification: stories are becoming private and sink into the secluded places in neighborhoods, families, or individuals, while the rumors propagated by the media cover everything and, gathered under the figure of the City, the masterword of an anonymous law, the substitute for all proper names, they wipe out or combat any superstitions guilty of still resisting the figure.

The dispersion of stories points to the dispersion of the memorable as well. And in fact memory is a sort of anti-museum: it is not localizable. Fragments of it come out in legends. Objects and words also have hollow places in which a past sleeps, as in the everyday acts of walking, eating, going to bed, in which ancient revolutions slumber. A memory is only a Prince Charming who stays just long enough to awaken the Sleeping Beauties of our wordless stories. "*Here*, there used to be a bakery." "*That's* where old lady Dupuis used to live." It is striking here that the places people live in are like the presences of diverse absences. What can be seen designates what is no longer there: "you *see*, here there used to be . . . ," but it can no longer be seen. Demonstratives indicate the invisible identities of the visible: it is the very definition of a place, in fact, that it is composed by these series of displacements and effects among the fragmented strata that form it and that it plays on these moving layers.

"Memories tie us to that place. . . . It's personal, not interesting to anyone else, but after all that's what gives a neighborhood its character."[48] There is no place that is not haunted by many different spirits hidden there in silence, spirits one can "invoke" or not. Haunted places are the only ones people can live in—and this inverts the schema of the *Panopticon*. But like the gothic sculptures of kings and queens that once adorned Notre-Dame and have been buried for two centuries in the basement of a building in the rue de la Chaussée-d'Antin,[49] these "spirits," themselves broken into pieces in like manner, do not *speak* any more than they *see*. This is a sort of knowledge that remains silent. Only hints of what is known but unrevealed are passed on "just between you and me."

Places are fragmentary and inward-turning histories, pasts that others are not allowed to read, accumulated times that can be unfolded but like stories held in reserve, remaining in an enigmatic state, symbolizations encysted in the pain or pleasure of the body. "I feel good here":[50] the well-being under-expressed in the language it appears in like a fleeting glimmer is a spatial practice.

Childhood and metaphors of places

> Metaphor consists in giving the thing
> a name that belongs to something
> else.
>
> Aristotle, *Poetics* 1457b

The memorable is that which can be dreamed about a place. In this place that is a palimpsest, subjectivity is already linked to the absence that structures it as existence and makes it "be there," *Dasein*. But as we have seen, this being-there acts only in spatial practices, that is, in *ways of moving into something different* (*manières de passer à l'autre*). It must ultimately be seen as the repetition, in diverse metaphors, of a decisive and originary experience, that of the child's differentiation from the mother's body. It is through that experience that the possibility of space and of a localization (a "not everything") of the subject is inaugurated. We need not return to the famous analysis Freud made of this matrix-experience by following the game played by his eighteen-month-old grandson, who threw a reel away from himself, crying *oh-oh-oh* in pleasure, *fort*! (i.e., "over there," "gone," or "no more") and then pulled it back with the piece of string attached to it with a delighted *da*! (i.e., "here," "back again");[51] it suffices here to remember this (perilous and satisfied) process of detachment from indifferentiation in the mother's body, whose substitute is the spool: this departure of the mother (sometimes she disappears by herself, sometimes the child makes her disappear) constitutes localization and exteriority against the background of an absence. There is a joyful manipulation that can make the maternal object "go away" and make *oneself* disappear (insofar as one considers oneself identical with that object), making it possible to be *there* (because) *without* the other but in a necessary relation to what has disappeared; this manipulation is an "original spatial structure."

No doubt one could trace this differentiation further back, as far as the naming that separates the foetus identified as masculine from his mother—but how about the female foetus, who is from this very moment introduced into another relationship to space? In the initiatory game, just as in the "joyful activity" of the child who, standing before a mirror, sees itself as *one* (it is *she* or *he*, seen as a whole) but *another* (*that*, an image with which the child identifies itself),[52] what counts is the process of this "spatial captation" that inscribes the passage toward the other as the law of being and the law of place. To practice space is thus to repeat the joyful and silent experience of childhood; it is, in a place, *to be other and to move toward the other.*

Thus begins the walk that Freud compares to the trampling underfoot of the mother-land.[53] This relationship of oneself to oneself governs the internal alterations of the place (the relations among its strata) or the pedestrian unfolding of the stories accumulated in a place (moving about the city and travelling). The childhood experience that determines spatial practices later develops its effects, proliferates, floods private and public spaces, undoes their readable surfaces, and creates within the planned city a "metaphorical" or mobile city, like the one Kandinsky dreamed of: "a great city built according to all the rules of architecture and then suddenly shaken by a force that defies all calculation."[54]

Chapter VIII   Railway Navigation and Incarceration

A TRAVELLING INCARCERATION. Immobile inside the train, seeing immobile things slip by. What is happening? Nothing is moving inside or outside the train.

The unchanging traveller is pigeonholed, numbered, and regulated in the grid of the railway car, which is a perfect actualization of the rational utopia. Control and food move from pigeonhole to pigeonhole: "Tickets, please . . . " "Sandwiches? Beer? Coffee? . . . " Only the restrooms offer an escape from the closed system. They are a lovers' phantasm, a way out for the ill, an escapade for children ("Wee-wee!")—a little space of irrationality, like love affairs and sewers in the *Utopias* of earlier times. Except for this lapse given over to excesses, everything has its place in a gridwork. Only a rationalized cell travels. A bubble of panoptic and classifying power, a module of imprisonment that makes possible the production of an order, a closed and autonomous insularity—that is what can traverse space and make itself independent of local roots.

Inside, there is the immobility of an order. Here rest and dreams reign supreme. There is nothing to do, one is in the *state* of reason. Everything is in its place, as in Hegel's *Philosophy of Right*. Every being is placed there like a piece of printer's type on a page arranged in military order. This order, an organizational system, the quietude of a certain reason, is the condition of both a railway car's and a text's movement from one place to another.

Outside, there is another immobility, that of things, towering mountains, stretches of green field and forest, arrested villages, colonnades of buildings, black urban silhouettes against the pink evening sky, the twinkling of nocturnal lights on a sea that precedes or succeeds our histories. The train generalizes Dürer's *Melancholia*, a speculative experience of the world: being outside of these things that stay there, detached and absolute, that leave us without having anything to do with

111

this departure themselves; being deprived of them, surprised by their ephemeral and quiet strangeness. Astonishment in abandonment. However, these things do not move. They have only the movement that is brought about from moment to moment by changes in perspective among their bulky figures. They have only *trompe-l'oeil* movements. They do not change their place any more than I do; vision alone continually undoes and remakes the relationships between these fixed elements.

Between the immobility of the inside and that of the outside a certain *quid pro quo* is introduced, a slender blade that inverts their stability. The chiasm is produced by the windowpane and the rail. These are two themes found in Jules Verne, the Victor Hugo of travel literature: the porthole of the *Nautilus*, a transparent caesura between the fluctuating feelings of the observer and the moving about of an oceanic reality; the iron rail whose straight line cuts through space and transforms the serene identities of the soil into the speed with which they slip away into the distance. The windowpane is what allows us to *see*, and the rail, what allows us to *move through*. These are two complementary modes of separation. The first creates the spectator's distance: You shall not touch; the more you see, the less you hold—a dispossession of the hand in favor of a greater trajectory for the eye. The second inscribes, indefinitely, the injunction to pass on; it is its order written in a single but endless line: go, leave, this is not your country, and neither is that—an imperative of separation which obliges one to pay for an abstract ocular domination of space by leaving behind any proper place, by losing one's footing.

The windowglass and the iron (rail) line divide, on the one hand, the traveller's (the putative narrator's) interiority and, on the other, the power of being, constituted as an object without discourse, the strength of an exterior silence. But paradoxically it is the silence of these things put at a distance, behind the windowpane, which, from a great distance, makes our memories speak or draws out of the shadows the dreams of our secrets. The isolation of the voting booth produces thoughts as well as separations. Glass and iron produce speculative thinkers or gnostics. This cutting-off is necessary for the birth, outside of these things but not without them, of unknown landscapes and the strange fables of our private stories.

Only the partition makes noise. As it moves forward and creates two inverted silences, it taps out a rhythm, it whistles or moans. There is a beating of the rails, a vibrato of the windowpanes—a sort of rubbing together of spaces at the vanishing points of their frontier. These junctions have no place. They indicate themselves by passing cries and momentary noises. These frontiers are illegible; they can only be heard as a single stream of sounds, so continuous is the tearing off that annihilates the points through which it passes.

These sounds also indicate, however, as do their results, the Principle responsible for all the action taken away from both travellers and nature: the machine. As invisible as all theatrical machinery, the locomotive organizes from afar all the echoes of its work. Even if it is discreet and indirect, its orchestra indicates what makes history, and, like a rumor, guarantees that there is still some history. There is also an accidental element in it. Jolts, brakings, surprises arise from this motor of the system. This residue of events depend on an invisible and single actor, recognizable only by the regularity of the rumbling or by the sudden miracles that disturb the order. The machine is the *primum mobile*, the solitary god from which all the action proceeds. It not only divides spectators and beings, but also connects them; it is a mobile sym-bol between them, a tireless shifter, producing changes in the relationships between immobile elements.

There is something at once incarcerational and navigational about railroad travel; like Jules Verne's ships and submarines, it combines dreams with technology. The "speculative" returns, located in the very heart of the mechanical order. Contraries coincide for the duration of a journey. A strange moment in which a society fabricates spectators and transgressors of spaces, with saints and blessed souls placed in the halos-holes (*auréoles-alvéoles*) of its railway cars. In these places of laziness and thoughtfulness, paradisiacal ships sailing between two social meeting-points (business deals and families, drab, almost imperceptible violences), atopical liturgies are pronounced, parentheses of prayers to no one (to whom are all these travelling dreams addressed?). Assemblies no longer obey hierarchies of dogmatic orders; they are organized by the gridwork of technocratic discipline, a mute rationalization of laissez-faire individualism.

To get in, as always, there was a price to be paid. The historical threshold of beatitude: history exists where there is a price to be paid. Repose can be obtained only through payment of this tax. In any case the blessed in trains are humble, compared to those in airplanes, to whom it is granted, for a few dollars more, a position that is more abstract (a cleaning-up of the countryside and filmed simulacra of the world) and more perfect (statues sitting in an aerial museum), but enjoying an excess that is penalized by a diminution of the ("melancholy") pleasure of seeing what one is separated from.

And, also as always, one has to get out: there are only lost paradises. Is the terminal the end of an illusion? There is another threshold, composed of momentary bewilderments in the airlock constituted by the train station. History begins again, feverishly, enveloping the motionless framework of the wagon: the blows of his hammer make the inspector aware of cracks in the wheels, the porter lifts the bags, the conductors move back and forth. Visored caps and uniforms restore the network of an order of work within the mass of people, while the wave of travellers/ dreamers flows into the net composed of marvellously expectant or preventively justiciary faces. Angry cries. Calls. Joys. In the mobile world of the train station, the immobile machine suddenly seems monumental and almost incongruous in its mute, idol-like inertia, a sort of god undone.

Everyone goes back to work at the place he has been given, in the office or the workshop. The incarceration-vacation is over. For the beautiful abstraction of the prison are substituted the compromises, opacities and dependencies of a workplace. Hand-to-hand combat begins again with a reality that dislodges the spectator without rails or window-panes. There comes to an end the Robinson Crusoe adventure of the travelling noble soul that could believe itself *intact* because it was surrounded by glass and iron.

Chapter IX Spatial Stories

"Narration created humanity."
Pierre Janet, *L'Evolution de la mémoire et la notion de temps*, 1928, p. 261.

I N MODERN ATHENS, the vehicles of mass transportation are called *metaphorai*. To go to work or come home, one takes a "metaphor"— a bus or a train. Stories could also take this noble name: every day, they traverse and organize places; they select and link them together; they make sentences and itineraries out of them. They are spatial trajectories.

In this respect, narrative structures have the status of spatial syntaxes. By means of a whole panoply of codes, ordered ways of proceeding and constraints, they regulate changes in space (or moves from one place to another) made by stories in the form of places put in linear or interlaced series: from here (Paris), one goes there (Montargis); this place (a room) includes another (a dream or a memory); etc. More than that, when they are represented in descriptions or acted out by actors (a foreigner, a city-dweller, a ghost), these places are linked together more or less tightly or easily by "modalities" that specify the kind of passage leading from the one to the other: the transition can be given an "epistemological" modality concerning knowledge (for example: "it's not certain that this is the Place de la République"), an "alethic" one concerning existence (for example, "the land of milk and honey is an improbable end-point"), or a deontic one concerning obligation (for example: "from this point, you have to go over to that one"). . . . These are only a few notations among many others, and serve only to indicate with what subtle complexity stories, whether everyday or literary, serve us as means of mass transportation, as *metaphorai*.

Every story is a travel story—a spatial practice. For this reason, spatial practices concern everyday tactics, are part of them, from the alphabet of spatial indication ("It's to the right," "Take a left"), the beginning of a story the rest of which is written by footsteps, to the daily "news" ("Guess who I met at the bakery?"), television news reports ("Teheran: Khomeini is becoming increasingly isolated . . . "), legends (Cinderellas living in hovels), and stories that are told (memories and fiction of foreign lands or more or less distant times in the past). These narrated adventures, simultaneously producing geographies of actions and drifting into the commonplaces of an order, do not merely constitute a "supplement" to pedestrian enunciations and rhetorics. They are not satisfied with displacing the latter and transposing them into the field of language. In reality, they organize walks. They make the journey, before or during the time the feet perform it.

These proliferating metaphors—sayings and stories that organize places through the displacements they "describe" (as a mobile point "describes" a curve)—what kind of analysis can be applied to *them*? To mention only the studies concerning spatializing *operations* (and not spatial systems), there are numerous works that provide methods and categories for such an analysis. Among the most recent, particular attention can be drawn to those referring to a semantics of space (John Lyons on "Locative Subjects" and "Spatial Expressions"),[1] a psycholinguistics of perception (Miller and Johnson-Laird on "the hypothesis of localization"),[2] a sociolinguistics of descriptions of places (for example, William Labov's),[3] a phenomenology of the behavior that organizes "territories" (for example, the work of Albert E. Scheflen and Norman Ashcraft),[4] an "ethnomethodology" of the indices of localization in conversation (for example, by Emanuel A. Schegloff),[5] or a semiotics viewing culture as a spatial metalanguage (for example, the work of the Tartu School, especially Y. M. Lotman, B. A. Ouspenski),[6] etc. Just as signifying practices, which concern the ways of putting language into effect, were taken into consideration after linguistic systems had been investigated, today spatializing practices are attracting attention now that the codes and taxonomies of the spatial order have been examined. Our investigation belongs to this "second" moment of the analysis, which moves from structures to actions. But in this vast ensemble, I shall consider only *narrative actions*; this will allow us to specify a few elementary forms of practices organizing space: the bipolar distinction between "map" and "itinerary," the procedures of delimitation or "marking boundaries" ("*bornage*") and "enunciative focalizations" (that is, the indication of the body within discourse).

"Spaces" and "places"

At the outset, I shall make a distinction between space (*espace*) and place (*lieu*) that delimits a field. A place (*lieu*) is the order (of whatever kind) in accord with which elements are distributed in relationships of coexistence. It thus excludes the possibility of two things being in the same location (*place*). The law of the "proper" rules in the place: the elements taken into consideration are *beside* one another, each situated in its own "proper" and distinct location, a location it defines. A place is thus an instantaneous configuration of positions. It implies an indication of stability.

A *space* exists when one takes into consideration vectors of direction, velocities, and time variables. Thus space is composed of intersections of mobile elements. It is in a sense actuated by the ensemble of movements deployed within it. Space occurs as the effect produced by the operations that orient it, situate it, temporalize it, and make it function in a polyvalent unity of conflictual programs or contractual proximities. On this view, in relation to place, space is like the word when it is spoken, that is, when it is caught in the ambiguity of an actualization, transformed into a term dependent upon many different conventions, situated as the act of a present (or of a time), and modified by the transformations caused by successive contexts. In contradistinction to the place, it has thus none of the univocity or stability of a "proper."

In short, *space is a practiced place*. Thus the street geometrically defined by urban planning is transformed into a space by walkers. In the same way, an act of reading is the space produced by the practice of a particular place: a written text, i.e., a place constituted by a system of signs.

Merleau-Ponty distinguished a "geometrical" space ("a homogeneous and isotropic spatiality," analogous to our "place") from another "spatiality" which he called an "anthropological space." This distinction depended on a distinct problematic, which sought to distinguish from "geometrical" univocity the experience of an "outside" given in the form of space, and for which "space is existential" and "existence is spatial." This experience is a relation to the world; in dreams and in perception, and because it probably precedes their differentiation, it expresses "the same essential structure of our being as a being situated in relationship to a milieu"—being situated by a desire, indissociable from a "direction of existence" and implanted in the space of a landscape. From this point of view "there are as many spaces as there are distinct spatial experiences."[7] The perspective is determined by a "phenomenology" of existing in the world.

In our examination of the daily practices that articulate that experience, the opposition between "place" and "space" will rather refer to two sorts of determinations in stories: the first, a determination through objects that are ultimately reducible to the *being-there* of something dead, the law of a "place" (from the pebble to the cadaver, an inert body always seems, in the West, to found a place and give it the appearance of a tomb); the second, a determination through *operations* which, when they are attributed to a stone, tree, or human being, specify "spaces" by the actions of historical *subjects* (a movement always seems to condition the production of a space and to associate it with a history). Between these two determinations, there are passages back and forth, such as the putting to death (or putting into a landscape) of heroes who transgress frontiers and who, guilty of an offense against the law of the place, best provide its restoration with their tombs; or again, on the contrary, the awakening of inert objects (a table, a forest, a person that plays a certain role in the environment) which, emerging from their stability, transform the place where they lay motionless into the foreignness of their own space.

Stories thus carry out a labor that constantly transforms places into spaces or spaces into places. They also organize the play of changing relationships between places and spaces. The forms of this play are numberless, fanning out in a spectrum reaching from the putting in place of an immobile and stone-like order (in it, nothing moves except discourse itself, which, like a camera panning over a scene, moves over the whole panorama), to the accelerated succession of actions that multiply spaces (as in the detective novel or certain folktales, though this spatializing frenzy nevertheless remains circumscribed by the textual place). It would be possible to construct a typology of all these stories in terms of identification of places and actualization of spaces. But in order to discern in them the modes in which these distinct operations are combined, we need criteria and analytical categories—a necessity that leads us back to travel stories of the most elementary kind.

Tours and maps

Oral descriptions of places, narrations concerning the home, stories about the streets, represent a first and enormous corpus. In a very

precise analysis of descriptions New York residents gave of their apartments, C. Linde and W. Labov recognize two distinct types, which they
call the "map" and the "tour." The first is of the type: "The girls' room is
next to the kitchen." The second: "You turn right and come into the
living room." Now, in the New York corpus, only three percent of the
descriptions are of the "map" type. All the rest, that is, virtually the
whole corpus, are of the "tour" type: "You come in through a low door,"
etc. These descriptions are made for the most part in terms of *operations*
and show "how to enter each room." Concerning this second type, the
authors point out that a circuit or "tour" is a speech-act (an act of
enunciation) that "furnishes a minimal series of paths by which to go
into each room"; and that the "path" is a series of units that have the
form of vectors that are either "static" ("to the right," "in front of you,"
etc.) or "mobile" ("if you turn to the left," etc.).[8]

In other words, description oscillates between the terms of an alternative: either *seeing* (the knowledge of an order of places) or *going* (spatializing actions). Either it presents a *tableau* ("there are . . . "), or it
organizes *movements* ("you enter, you go across, you turn . . . "). Of
these two hypotheses, the choices made by the New York narrators
overwhelmingly favored the second.

Leaving Linde and Labov's study aside (it is primarily concerned with
the rules of the social interactions and conventions that govern "natural
language," a problem we will come back to later), I would like to make
use of these New York stories—and other similar stories[9]—to try to
specify the relationships between the indicators of "tours" and those of
"maps," where they coexist in a single description. How are *acting* and
seeing coordinated in this realm of ordinary language in which the former is so obviously dominant? The question ultimately concerns the
basis of the everyday narrations, the relation between the itinerary (a
discursive series of operations) and the map (a plane projection totalizing observations), that is, between two symbolic and anthropological
languages of space. Two poles of experience. It seems that in passing
from "ordinary" culture to scientific discourse, one passes from one pole
to the other.

In narrations concerning apartments or streets, manipulations of space
or "tours" are dominant. This form of description usually determines the
whole style of the narration. When the other form intervenes, it has the
characteristic of being *conditioned* or *presupposed* by the first. Examples
of tours conditioning a map: "If you turn to the right, there is . . . ", or
the closely related form, "If you go straight ahead, you'll see . . . " In

both cases, an action permits one to see something. But there are also cases in which a tour assumes a place indication: "There, there's a door, you take the next one"—an element of mapping is the presupposition of a certain itinerary. The narrative fabric in which describers (*descripteurs*) of itineraries predominate is thus punctuated by describers of the map type which have the function of indicating either an *effect* obtained by the tour ("you see . . . ") or a *given* that it postulates as its limit ("there is a wall"), its possibility ("there's a door"), or an obligation ("there's a one-way street"), etc. The chain of spatializing operations seems to be marked by references to what it produces (a representation of places) or to what it implies (a local order). We thus have the structure of the travel story: stories of journeys and actions are marked out by the "citation" of the places that result from them or authorize them.

From this angle, we can compare the combination of "tours" and "maps" in everyday stories with the manner in which, over the past five centuries, they have been interlaced and then slowly dissociated in literary and scientific representations of space. In particular, if one takes the "map" in its current geographical form, we can see that in the course of the period marked by the birth of modern scientific discourse (i.e., from the fifteenth to the seventeenth century) the map has slowly disengaged itself from the itineraries that were the condition of its possibility. The first medieval maps included only the rectilinear marking out of itineraries (performative indications chiefly concerning pilgrimages), along with the stops one was to make (cities which one was to pass through, spend the night in, pray at, etc.) and distances calculated in hours or in days, that is, in terms of the time it would take to cover them on foot.[10] Each of these maps is a memorandum prescribing actions. The tour to be made is predominant in them. It includes the map elements, just as today the description of a route to be taken accompanies a hasty sketch already on paper, in the form of citations of places, a sort of dance through the city: "20 paces straight ahead, then turn to the left, then another 40 paces. . . ." The drawing articulates spatializing practices, like the maps of urban routes, arts of actions and stories of paces, that serve the Japanese as "address books,"[11] or the wonderful fifteenth-century Aztec map describing the exodus of the Totomihuacas. This drawing outlines not the "route" (there wasn't one) but the "log" of their journey on foot—an outline marked out by footprints with regular gaps between them and by pictures of the successive events that took place in the course of the journey (meals, battles, crossings of rivers or mountains, etc.): not a "geographical map" but "history book."[12]

Between the fifteenth and the seventeenth centuries, the map became more autonomous. No doubt the proliferation of the "narrative" figures that have long been its stock-in-trade (ships, animals, and characters of all kinds) still had the function of indicating the operations—travelling, military, architectural, political or commercial—that make possible the fabrication of a geographical plan.[13] Far from being "illustrations," iconic glosses on the text, these figurations, like fragments of stories, mark on the map the historical operations from which it resulted. Thus the sailing ship painted on the sea indicates the maritime expedition that made it possible to represent the coastlines. It is equivalent to a describer of the "tour" type. But the map gradually wins out over these figures; it colonizes space; it eliminates little by little the pictural figurations of the practices that produce it. Transformed first by Euclidean geometry and then by descriptive geometry, constituted as a formal ensemble of abstract places, it is a "theater" (as one used to call atlases) in which the same system of projection nevertheless juxtaposes two very different elements: the data furnished by a tradition (Ptolemy's *Geography*, for instance) and those that came from navigators (portulans, for example). The map thus collates on the same plane heterogeneous places, some *received* from a tradition and others *produced* by observation. But the important thing here is the erasure of the itineraries which, presupposing the first category of places and conditioning the second, makes it possible to move from one to the other. The map, a totalizing stage on which elements of diverse origin are brought together to form the tableau of a "state" of geographical knowledge, pushes away into its prehistory or into its posterity, as if into the wings, the operations of which it is the result or the necessary condition. It remains alone on the stage. The tour describers have disappeared.

The organization that can be discerned in stories about space in everyday culture is inverted by the process that has isolated a system of geographical places. The difference between the two modes of description obviously does not consist in the presence or absence of practices (they are at work everywhere), but in the fact that maps, constituted as proper places in which to *exhibit the products* of knowledge, form tables of *legible* results. Stories about space exhibit on the contrary the operations that allow it, within a constraining and non-"proper" place, to mingle its elements anyway, as one apartment-dweller put it concerning the rooms in his flat: "One can mix them up" ("*On peut les triturer*").[14] From the folktale to descriptions of residences, an exacerbation of "practice" ("*faire*") (and thus of enunciation), actuates the stories narrating tours in places that, from the ancient cosmos to contemporary public housing developments, are all forms of an imposed order.

In a pre-established geography, which extends (if we limit ourselves to the home) from bedrooms so small that "one can't do anything in them" to the legendary, long-lost attic that "could be used for everything,"[15] everyday stories tell us what one can do in it and make out of it. They are treatments of space.

Marking out boundaries

As operations on places, stories also play the everyday role of a mobile and magisterial tribunal in cases concerning their delimitation. As always, this role appears more clearly at the second degree, when it is made explicit and duplicated by juridical discourse. In the traditional language of court proceedings, magistrates formerly "visited the scene of the case at issue" ("*se transportaient sur les lieux*") (transports and juridical metaphors), in order to "hear" the contradictory *statements* (*dits*) made by the parties to a dispute concerning debatable boundaries. Their "interlocutory judgment," as it was called, was an "operation of marking out boundaries" (*bornage*). Written in a beautiful hand by the court clerk on parchments where the writing sometimes flowed into (or was inaugurated by?) drawings outlining the boundaries, these interlocutory judgments were in sum nothing other than meta-stories. They combined together (the work of a scribe collating variants) the opposing stories of the parties involved: "Mr. Mulatier declares that his grandfather planted this apple tree on the edge of his field. . . . Jeanpierre reminds us that Mr. Bouvet maintains a dungheap on a piece of land of which he is supposed to be the joint owner with his brother André. . . ." Genealogies of places, legends about territories. Like a critical edition, the judge's narration reconciles these versions. The narration is "established" on the basis of "primary" stories (those of Mr. Mulatier, Jeanpierre, and so many others), stories that already have the function of *spatial legislation* since they determine rights and divide up lands by "acts" or discourses about actions (planting a tree, maintaining a dungheap, etc.).

These "operations of marking out boundaries," consisting in narrative contracts and compilations of stories, are composed of fragments drawn from earlier stories and fitted together in makeshift fashion (*bricolés*). In this sense, they shed light on the formation of myths, since they also have the function of founding and articulating spaces. Preserved in the court records, they constitute an immense travel literature, that is, a literature concerned with actions organizing more or less extensive social cultural areas. But this literature itself represents only a tiny part (the part that is written about disputed points) of the oral narration that interminably labors to compose spaces, to verify, collate, and displace their frontiers.

The ways of "conducting" a story offer, as Pierre Janet pointed out,[16] a very rich field for the analysis of spatiality. Among the questions that depend on it, we should distinguish those that concern dimensions (extensionality), orientation (vectorality), affinity (homographies), etc. I shall stress only a few of its aspects that have to do with delimitation itself, the primary and literally "fundamental" question: it is the partition of space that structures it. Everything refers in fact to this differentiation which makes possible the isolation and interplay of distinct spaces. From the distinction that separates a subject from its exteriority to the distinctions that localize objects, from the home (constituted on the basis of the wall) to the journey (constituted on the basis of a geographical "elsewhere" or a cosmological "beyond"), from the functioning of the urban network to that of the rural landscape, there is no spatiality that is not organized by the determination of frontiers.

In this organization, the story plays a decisive role. It "describes," to be sure. But "every description is more than a fixation," it is "a culturally creative act."[17] It even has distributive power and performative force (it does what it says) when an ensemble of circumstances is brought together. Then it founds spaces. Reciprocally, where stories are disappearing (or else are being reduced to museographical objects), there is a loss of space: deprived of narrations (as one sees it happen in both the city and the countryside), the group or the individual regresses toward the disquieting, fatalistic experience of a formless, indistinct, and nocturnal totality. By considering the role of stories in delimitation, one can see that the primary function is to *authorize* the establishment, displacement or transcendence of limits, and as a consequence, to set in opposition, within the closed field of discourse, two movements that intersect (setting and transgressing limits) in such a way as to make the story a sort of "crossword" decoding stencil (a dynamic partitioning of space) whose essential narrative figures seem to be the *frontier* and the *bridge*.

1. *Creating a theater of actions.* The story's first function is to authorize, or more exactly, to *found.* Strictly speaking, this function is

ize, or more exactly, to *found*. Strictly speaking, this function is not juridical, that is, related to laws or judgments. It depends rather on what Georges Dumézil analyzes in connection with the Indo-European root *dhē*, "to set in place," and its derivatives in Sanskrit (*dhātu*) and Latin (*fās*). The Latin noun "*fās*," he writes, "is properly speaking the mystical foundation, which is in the invisible world, and without which all forms of conduct that are enjoined or authorized by *ius* (human law) and, more generally speaking, all human conduct, are doubtful, perilous, and even fatal. *Fās* cannot be subjected to analysis or casuistry, as *ius* can: *fās* can no more be broken up into parts than its name can be declined." A *foundation* either exists or it doesn't: *fās est* or *fās non est*. "A time or a place are said to be *fasti* or *nefasti* [auspacious or inauspacious] depending on whether they provide or fail to provide human action with this necessary foundation."[18]

In the Western parts of the Indo-European world, this function has been divided in a particular way among different institutions—in contrast to what happened in ancient India, where different roles were played in turn by the same characters. Occidental culture created its own ritual concerning *fās*, which was carried out in Rome by specialized priests called *fētiāles*. It was practiced "before Rome undertook any action with regard to a foreign nation," such as a declaration of war, a military expedition, or an alliance. The ritual was a procession with three centrifugal stages, the first within Roman territory but near the frontier, the second on the frontier, the third in foreign territory. The ritual action was carried out before every civil or military action because it is designed to *create the field* necessary for political or military activities. It is thus also a *repetitio rerum*: both a renewal and a repetition of the originary founding acts, a *recitation* and a citation of the genealogies that could legitimate the new enterprise, and a *prediction* and a promise of success at the beginning of battles, contracts, or conquests. As a general repetition before the actual representation, the rite, a narration in acts, precedes the historical realization. The tour or procession of the *fētiāles* opens a space and provides a foundation for the operations of the military men, diplomats, or merchants who dare to cross the frontiers. Similarly in the *Vedas*, Viṣṇu, "by his footsteps, opens the zone of space in which Indra's military action must take place." The *fās* ritual is a foundation. It "provides space" for the actions that will be undertaken; it "creates a field" which serves as their "base" and their "theater."[19]

This founding is precisely the primary role of the story. It opens a legitimate *theater* for practical *actions*. It creates a field that authorizes dangerous and contingent social actions. But it differs in three ways from the function the Roman ritual so carefully isolated: the story founds *fās* in a form that is fragmented (not unique and whole), miniaturized (not on a national scale), and polyvalent (not specialized). It is *fragmented*, not only because of the diversification of social milieus, but especially because of the increasing heterogeneity (or because of a heterogeneity that is increasingly obvious) of the authorizing "references": the excommunication of territorial "divinities," the deconsecration of places haunted by the story-spirit, and the extension of neutral areas deprived of legitimacy have marked the disappearance and fragmentation of the narrations that organized frontiers and appropriations. (Official historiography—history books, television news reports, etc.—nevertheless tries to make everyone believe in the existence of a national space.) It is *miniaturized*, because socioeconomic technocratization confines the significance of *fās* and *nefas* to the level of the family unit or the individual, and leads to the multiplication of "family stories," "life stories," and psychoanalytical narrations. (Gradually cut loose from these particular stories, public justifications nevertheless continue to exist in the form of blind rumors, or resurface savagely in class or race conflicts). It is finally *polyvalent*, because the mixing together of so many micro-stories gives them functions that change according to the groups in which they circulate. This polyvalence does not affect the relational origins of narrativity, however: the ancient ritual that creates fields of action is recognizable in the "fragments" of narration planted around the obscure thresholds of our existence; these buried fragments articulate without its knowing it the "biographical" story whose space they found.

A narrative activity, even if it is multiform and no longer unitary, thus continues to develop where frontiers and relations with space abroad are concerned. Fragmented and disseminated, it is continually concerned with marking out boundaries. What it puts in action is once more the *fās* that "authorizes" enterprises and precedes them. Like the Roman *fētiāles*, stories "go in a procession" ahead of social practices in order to open a field for them. Decisions and juridical combinations themselves come only afterwards, like the statements and acts of Roman law (*iūs*), arbitrating the areas of action granted to each party,[20] participating themselves in the activities for which *fās* provided a "foundation."

According to the rules that are proper to them, the magistrates' "interlocutory judgments" operate within the aggregate of heterogeneous
spaces that have already been created and established by the innumerable
forms of an oral narrativity composed of family or local stories, cus-
tomary or professional "poems" and "recitations" of paths taken or
countrysides traversed. The magistrates' judgments do not create these
theaters of action, they articulate and manipulate them. They presuppose
the narrative authorities that the magistrates "hear" compare, and put
into hierarchies. Preceding the judgment that regulates and settles, there
is a founding narration.

2. *Frontiers and bridges.* Stories are actuated by a contradiction that
is represented in them by the relationship between the frontier and the
bridge, that is, between a (legitimate) space and its (alien) exteriority. In
order to account for contradiction, it is helpful to go back to the elementary units. Leaving aside morphology (which is not our concern
here) and situating ourselves in the perspective of a pragmatics and,
more precisely, a syntax aimed at determining "programs" or series of
practices through which space is appropriated, we can take as our point
of departure the "region," which Miller and Johnson-Laird define as a
basic unit: the place where programs and actions interact. A "region" is
thus the space created by an interaction.[21] It follows that in the same
place there are as many "regions" as there are interactions or intersections of programs. And also that the determination of space is dual and
operational, and, in a problematics of enunciation, related to an "interlocutory" process.

In this way a dynamic contradiction between each delimitation and its
mobility is introduced. On the one hand, the story tirelessly marks out
frontiers. It multiplies them, but in terms of interactions among the
characters—things, animals, human beings: the acting subjects (*actants*)
divide up among themselves places as well as predicates (simple, crafty,
ambitious, silly, etc.) and movements (advancing, withdrawing, going
into exile, returning, etc.). Limits are drawn by the points at which the
progressive appropriations (the acquisition of predicates in the course of
the story) and the successive displacements (internal or external movements) of the acting subjects meet. Both appropriations and displacements depend on a dynamic distribution of possible goods and functions
in order to constitute an increasingly complex network of differentia-
tions, a combinative system of spaces. They result from the operation of

distinctions resulting from encounters. Thus, in the obscurity of their unlimitedness, bodies can be distinguished only where the "contacts" ("*touches*") of amorous or hostile struggles are inscribed on them. This is a paradox of the frontier: created by contacts, the points of differentiation between two bodies are also their common points. Conjunction and disjunction are inseparable in them. Of two bodies in contact, which one possesses the frontier that distinguishes them? Neither. Does that amount to saying: no one?

The theoretical and practical problem of the frontier: to whom does it belong? The river, wall or tree *makes* a frontier. It does not have the character of a nowhere that cartographical representation ultimately presupposes. It has a mediating role. So does the story that gives it voice: "Stop," says the forest the wolf comes out of. "Stop!" says the river, revealing its crocodile. But this actor, by virtue of the very fact that he is the mouthpiece of the limit, creates communication as well as separation; more than that, he establishes a border only by saying what crosses it, having come from the other side. He articulates it. He is *also* a passing through or over. In the story, the frontier functions as a third element. It is an "in-between"—a "space between," *Zwischenraum*, as Morgenstern puts it in a marvelous and ironic poem on "closure" (*Zaun*), which rhymes with "space" (*Raum*) and "to see through" (*hindurchzu-schaun*).[22] It is the story of a picket fence (*Lattenzaun*):

Es war einmal ein Lattenzaun mit Zwischenraum, hindurchzu- schaun.	One time there was a picket fence with space to gaze from hence to thence.

A middle place, composed of interactions and inter-views, the frontier is a sort of void, a narrative sym-bol of exchanges and encounters. Passing by, an architect suddenly appropriates this "in-between space" and builds a great edifice on it:

Ein Architekt, der dieses sah, stand eines Abends plötzlich da—	An architect who saw this sight approached it suddenly one night,

und nahm den Zwischenraum
  heraus
und baute draus ein grosses Haus.
	removed the spaces from the
	  fence
	and built of them a residence.

Transformation of the void into a plenitude, of the in-between into an established place. The rest goes without saying. The Senate "takes on"

the monument—the Law establishes itself in it—and the architect escapes
to Afri-or-America:

| Drum zog ihn der Senat auch ein. | the senate had to intervene. |

| Der Architekt jedoch entfloh | The architect, however, flew |
| nach Afri-od-Ameriko | to Afri- or Americoo. |

(Max Knight, trans.)

The Architect's drive to cement up the picket fence, to fill in and build
up "the space in-between," is also his illusion, for without knowing it he
is working toward the political freezing of the place and there is nothing
left for him to do, when he sees his work finished, but to flee far away
from the blocs of the law.

In contrast, the story privileges a "logic of ambiguity" through its
accounts of interaction. It "turns" the frontier into a crossing, and the
river into a bridge. It recounts inversions and displacements: the door
that closes is precisely what may be opened; the river is what makes
passage possible; the tree is what marks the stages of advance; the picket
fence is an ensemble of interstices through which one's glances pass.

The *bridge* is ambiguous everywhere: it alternately welds together and
opposes insularities. It distinguishes them and threatens them. It liberates
from enclosure and destroys autonomy. Thus, for example, it occurs as
a central and ambivalent character in the stories of the Noirmoutrins,
before, during, and after the construction of a bridge between La Fosse
and Fromentine in Vendée in 1972.[23] It carries on a double life in innumerable memories of places and everyday legends, often summed up
in proper names, hidden paradoxes, ellipses in stories, riddles to be
solved: Bridgehead, Bridgenorth, Bridgetown, Bridgewater, Bridgman,
Cambridge, Trowbridge, etc.

Justifiably, the bridge is the index of the diabolic in the paintings
where Bosch invents his modifications of spaces.[24] As a transgression of
the limit, a disobedience of the law of the place, it represents a departure,
an attack on a state, the ambition of a conquering power, or the flight of
an exile; in any case, the "betrayal" of an order. But at the same time as
it offers the possibility of a bewildering exteriority, it allows or causes
the re-emergence beyond the frontiers of the alien element that was
controlled in the interior, and gives ob-jectivity (that is, expression and
re-presentation) to the alterity which was hidden inside the limits, so
that in recrossing the bridge and coming back within the enclosure the
traveler henceforth finds there the exteriority that he had first sought by

going outside and then fled by returning. Within the frontiers, the alien is already there, an exoticism or sabbath of the memory, a disquieting familiarity. It is as though delimitation itself were the bridge that opens the inside to its other.

Delinquencies?

What the map cuts up, the story cuts across. In Greek, narration is called "diegesis": it establishes an itinerary (it "guides") and it passes through (it "transgresses"). The space of operations it travels in is made of movements: it is *topological*, concerning the deformations of figures, rather than *topical*, defining places. It is only ambivalently that the limit circumscribes in this space. It plays a double game. It does the opposite of what it says. It hands the place over to the foreigner that it gives the impression of throwing out. Or rather, when it marks a stopping place, the latter is not stable but follows the variations of encounters between programs. Boundaries are transportable limits and transportations of limits; they are also *metaphorai*.

In the narrations that organize spaces, boundaries seem to play the role of the Greek *xoana*, statuettes whose invention is attributed to the clever Daedalus: they are crafty like Daedalus and mark out limits only by moving themselves (and the limits). These straight-line indicators put emphasis on the curves and movements of space. Their distributive work is thus completely different from that of the divisions established by poles, pickets or stable columns which, planted in the earth, cut up and compose an order of places.[25] They are also transportable limits.

Today, narrative operations of boundary-setting take the place of these enigmatic describers of earlier times when they bring movement in through the very act of fixing, in the name of delimitation. Michelet already said it: when the aristocracy of the great Olympian gods collapsed at the end of Antiquity, it did not take down with it "the mass of indigenous gods, the populace of gods that still possessed the immensity of fields, forests, woods, mountains, springs, intimately associated with the life of the country. These gods lived in the hearts of oaks, in the swift, deep waters, and could not be driven out of them. . . . Where are they? In the desert, on the heath, in the forest? Yes, but also and especially in the home. They live on in the most intimate of domestic habits."[26] But they also live on in our streets and in our apartments. They were perhaps after all only the agile representatives of narrativity, and of narrativity in its most *delinquent* form. The fact that they have changed their names (every power is toponymical and initiates its order of places by naming them) takes nothing away from the multiple, insidious, moving force. It survives the avatars of the great history that debaptises and rebaptises them.

If the delinquent exists only by displacing itself, if its specific mark is to live not on the margins but in the interstices of the codes that it undoes and displaces, if it is characterized by the privilege of the *tour* over the *state*, then the story is delinquent. Social delinquency consists in taking the story literally, in making it the principle of physical existence where a society no longer offers to subjects or groups symbolic outlets and expectations of spaces, where there is no longer any alternative to disciplinary falling-into-line or illegal drifting away, that is, one form or another of prison and wandering outside the pale. Inversely, the story is a sort of delinquency in reserve, maintained, but itself displaced and consistent, in traditional societies (ancient, medieval, etc.), with an order that is firmly established but flexible enough to allow the proliferation of this challenging mobility that does not respect places, is alternately playful and threatening, and extends from the microbe-like forms of everyday narration to the carnivalesque celebrations of earlier days.[27]

It remains to be discovered, of course, what actual changes produce this delinquent narrativity in a society. In any event, one can already say that in matters concerning space, this delinquency begins with the inscription of the body in the order's text. The opacity of the body in movement, gesticulating, walking, taking its pleasure, is what indefinitely organizes a *here* in relation to an *abroad*, a "familiarity" in relation to a "foreignness." A spatial story is in its minimal degree a *spoken* language, that is, a linguistic system that distributes places insofar as it is *articulated* by an "enunciatory focalization," by an act of practicing it. It is the object of "proxemics."[28] Before we return to its manifestations in the organization of memory, it will suffice here to recall that, in this focalizing enunciation, space appears once more as a *practiced* place.

Part IV
Uses of Language

Chapter X   The Scriptural Economy

> "Only words that stride onward,
> passing from mouth to mouth, leg-
> ends and songs, keep a people alive"
> N. F. S. Grundtvig[1]

T HE DEDICATION TO Grundtvig, the Danish poet and prophet whose
pathways all lead toward "the living word" (*det levende ord*), the
Grail of orality, authorizes today, as the Muses did in earlier
ages, a quest for lost and ghostly voices in our "scriptural" societies. I
am trying to hear these fragile ways in which the body makes itself heard
in the language, the multiple voices set aside by the triumphal *conquista*
of the economy that has, since the beginning of the "modern age" (i.e.,
since the seventeenth or eighteenth century), given itself the name of
writing. My subject is orality, but an orality that has been changed by
three or four centuries of Western fashioning. We no longer believe, as
Grundtvig (or Michelet) did, that, behind the doors of our cities, in the
nearby distance of the countryside, there are vast poetic and "pagan"
pastures where one can still hear songs, myths, and the spreading murmur of the *folkelighed*[2] (a Danish word that cannot be translated: it
means "what belongs to the people"). These voices can no longer be
heard except within the interior of the scriptural systems where they
recur. They move about, like dancers, passing lightly through the field of
the other.

The installation of the scriptural apparatus of modern "discipline," a
process that is inseparable from the "reproduction" made possible by the

131

development of printing, was accompanied by a double isolation from the "people" (in opposition to the "bourgeoisie") and from the "voice" (in opposition to the written). Hence the conviction that far, too far away from economic and administrative powers, "the People speaks." This speech is alternately seductive and dangerous, unique, lost (despite violent and brief outbreaks), constituted as the "Voice of the people" by its very repression, the object of nostalgic longing, observation and regulation, and above all of the immense campaign that has rearticulated it on writing by means of education. Today it is "recorded" in every imaginable way, normalized, audible everywhere, but only when it has been "cut" (as one "cuts a record"), and thus mediated by radio, television, or the phonograph record, and "cleaned up" by the techniques of diffusion. Where it does manage to infiltrate itself, the sound of the body often becomes an imitation of this part of itself that is produced and reproduced by the media—i.e., the copy of its own artifact.

It is thus useless to set off in quest of this voice that has been simultaneously colonized and mythified by recent Western history. There is, moreover, no such "pure" voice, because it is always determined by a system (whether social, familial, or other) and codified by a way of receiving it. Even if the voices of each group composed a sonic landscape—a site of sounds—that was easily recognizable, a dialect—an accent—can be discerned by the mark it leaves on a language, like a delicate perfume; even if a particular voice can be distinguished among countless others by the way it caresses or irritates the body that hears it, like a musical instrument played by an invisible hand, there is no unique unity among the sounds of presence that the enunciatory act gives a language in speaking it. Thus we must give up the fiction that collects all these sounds under the sign of a "Voice," of a "Culture" of its own—or of the great Other's. Rather, orality insinuates itself, like one of the threads of which it is composed, into the network—an endless tapestry—of a scriptural economy.

It is through an analysis of this economy, of its historical implantation, of its rules and the instruments of its success—a vast program for which I shall substitute a mere sketch—that one can best begin to locate the points at which voices slip into the great book of our law. I shall try simply to outline the historical configuration that has been created in our society by the disjunction between writing and orality, in order to indicate some of its effects and to point out a few current displacements that take the form of tasks to be accomplished.

I want to make clear at the outset that in referring to writing and orality I am not postulating two opposed terms whose contradiction could be transcended by a third, or whose hierarchization could be inverted. I am not interested in returning to one of the "metaphysical oppositions" (writing vs. orality, language vs. speech-acts, etc.) concerning which Jacques Derrida has very correctly said that "they have as their ultimate reference . . . the presence of a value or of a *meaning* (*sens*) that is supposed to be anterior to difference."[3] In the thought that asserts them, these antinomies postulate the principle of a unique origin (a founding archeology) or a final reconciliation (a teleological concept), and thus a discourse that is maintained by this referential unity. On the contrary, although this is not the place to explain my reasons in detail, I shall assume that plurality is originary; that difference is constitutive of its terms; and that language must continually conceal the structuring work of division beneath a sym-bolic order.

In the perspective of cultural anthropology, we must moreover not forget that:

1) These "unities" (e.g., writing and orality) are the result of reciprocal distinctions within successive and interconnected historical configurations. For this reason, they cannot be isolated from these historical determinations or raised to the status of general categories.

2) Since these distinctions present themselves as the relation between the delimitation of a field (e.g., language) or a system (e.g., writing) and what it constitutes as its outside or its remainder (speech or orality), the two terms are not equivalent or comparable, either with respect to their coherence (the definition of one presupposes that the other remains undefined) or with respect to their operativity (the one that is productive, predominant, and articulated puts the other in a position of inertia, subjection, and opaque resistance). It is thus impossible to assume that they would function in homologous ways if only the signs were reversed. They are incommensurable; the difference between them is qualitative.

Writing: a "modern" mythical practice

Scriptural practice has acquired a mythical value over the past four centuries by gradually reorganizing all the domains into which the Occidental ambition to compose its history, and thus to compose history itself, has been extended. I mean by "myth" a fragmented discourse which is articulated on the heterogeneous practices of a society and which also articulates them symbolically. In modern Western culture, it is no longer a discourse that plays this role, but rather a transport, in other words a practice: writing. The origin is no longer what is narrated, but rather the multiform and murmuring activity of producing a text and producing society as a text. "Progress" is scriptural in type. In very diverse ways, orality is defined by (or as) that from which a "legitimate" practice—whether in science, politics, or the classroom, etc.—must differentiate itself. The "oral" is that which does not contribute to progress; reciprocally, the "scriptural" is that which separates itself from the magical world of voices and tradition. A frontier (and a front) of Western culture is established by that separation. Thus one can read above the portals of modernity such inscriptions as "Here, to work is to write," or "Here only what is written is understood." Such is the internal law of that which has constituted itself as "Western."

What is writing, then? I designate as "writing" the concrete activity that consists in constructing, on its own, blank space (*un espace propre*)—the page—a text that has power over the exteriority from which it has first been isolated. At this elementary level, three elements are decisive.

First, the *blank page*: a space of its own delimits a place of production for the subject. It is a place where the ambiguities of the world have been exorcised. It assumes the withdrawal and the distance of a subject in relation to an area of activities. It is made available for a partial but regulatable operation. A separation divides the traditional cosmos, in which the subject remained possessed by the voices of the world. An autonomous surface is put before the eye of the subject who thus accords himself the field for an operation of his own. This is the Cartesian move of making a distinction that initiates, along with a *place* of writing, the mastery (and isolation) of a subject confronted by an *object*. In front of his blank page, every child is already put in the position of the industrialist, the urban planner, or the Cartesian philosopher—the position of having to manage a space that is his own and distinct from all others and in which he can exercise his own will.

Then *a text* is constructed in this place. Linguistic fragments or materials are treated (factory-processed, one might say) in this space according to methods that can be made explicit and in such a way as to produce an order. A series of articulated operations (gestural or mental)— that is what writing *literally* is—traces on the page the trajectories that sketch out words, sentences, and finally a system. In other terms, on the blank page, an itinerant, progressive, and regulated practice—a "walk"—

composes the artefact of another "world" that is not received but rather made. The model of a productive reason is written on the nowhere of the paper. In many different forms, this text constructed on a proper space is the fundamental and generalized utopia of the modern West.

Thirdly, this construction is not merely a game. To be sure, in every society, play is a stage on which the formality of practices is represented, but the condition of its possibility is that it be detached from actual social practices. On the contrary, the "meaning" ("*sens*") of scriptural play, the production of a system, a space of formalization, refers to the reality from which it has been distinguished *in order to change it*. Its goal is social efficacity. It manipulates its exteriority. The writing laboratory has a "strategic" function: either an item of information received from tradition or from the outside is collected, classified, inserted into a system and thereby transformed, or the rules and models developed in this place (which is not governed by them) allow one to act on the environment and to transform it. The island of the page is a transitional place in which an industrial inversion is made: what comes in is something "received," what comes out is a "product." The things that go in are the indexes of a certain "passivity" of the subject with respect to a tradition; those that come out, the marks of his power of fabricating objects. The scriptural enterprise transforms or retains within itself what it receives from its outside and creates internally the instruments for an appropriation of the external space. It stocks up what it sifts out and gives itself the means to expand. Combining the power of *accumulating* the past and that of making the alterity of the universe *conform* to its models, it is capitalist and conquering. The scientific laboratory and industry (the latter correctly defined by Marx as the "book" of "science")[4] are governed by the same schema. And so is the modern city: it is a circumscribed space in which the will to collect and store up an external population and the will to make the countryside conform to urban models are realized.

Revolution itself, that "modern" idea, represents the scriptural project at the level of an entire society seeking to *constitute itself* as a blank page with respect to the past, to write itself by itself (that is, to produce itself as its own system) and to produce *a new history* (*refaire l'histoire*) on the model of what it fabricates (and this will be "progress"). It is necessary only for this ambition to multiply scriptural operations in economic, administrative, or political areas in order for the project to be realized. Today, by an inversion that indicates that a threshold in this development has been crossed, the scriptural system moves forward on its own; it is becoming self-moving and technocratic; it transforms the subjects that controlled it into operators of the writing machine that orders and uses them. A cybernetic society.

It is thus not without reason that for the past three centuries learning to write has been the very definition of entering into a capitalist and conquering society. Such is its fundamental initiatory *practice.* It was only when the disturbing effects of this prodigious growth of writing were noticed that we came to have doubts about modern children's education by means of a scriptural practice.

I shall give only one example of this structuring practice, but one that has the status of a myth. It is one of the rare myths that modern Occidental society has been able to create (it has generally replaced the myths of traditional societies by practices): Defoe's *Robinson Crusoe.* This novel combines the three elements I distinguished above: the island that isolates a place of one's own, the production of a system of objects by a dominant subject, and the transformation of a "natural" world. It is the romance of writing. Moreover, in Defoe's work, the awakening of Robinson to the capitalist and conquering task of writing his island is inaugurated by the decision to write his diary, to give himself in that way a space in which he can master time and things, and to thus constitute for himself, along with the blank page, an initial island in which he can produce what he wants. It is not surprising that since Rousseau, who wanted his Émile to read only this book, Robinson Crusoe has been both the model recommended to the "modern" educators of future technicians without voices, and the dream of children that want to create a universe without a father.

In analyzing *writing*, this modern mythical practice, I do not in any way deny that we all owe it a great deal, especially those of us who are more or less intellectuals, and therefore the children, professionals, and beneficiaries of writing in a society which draws its strength from it. I would even point out two further aspects of writing that will make the dynamic of this strength clearer. They are connected with my subject because they concern the relation between writing and the loss of an identifying Spoken Word, on the one hand, and on the other, a new treatment of language by the speaking subject.

One could hardly overestimate the importance of the fundamental relationship between Western culture and what was for centuries considered writing par excellence, the Bible. If we simplify history (I am constructing an artifact, knowing that a model is judged not by the proofs advanced in support of it, but by the results it produces in interpretation), one can say that before the "modern" period, that is, until the sixteenth or seventeenth century, this writing (Holy Scripture) speaks. The sacred text is a voice, it teaches (the original sense of *documentum*), it is the advent of a "meaning" (*un "vouloir-dire"*) on the part of a God who expects the reader (in reality, the listener) to have a "desire to hear and understand" (*un "vouloir-entendre"*) on which access to truth depends. For reasons analyzed elsewhere, the modern age is formed by discovering little by little that this Spoken Word is no longer heard, that it has been altered by textual corruptions and the avatars of history. One can no longer hear it. "Truth" no longer depends on the attention of a receiver who assimilates himself to the great identifying message. It is the result of work—historical, critical, economic work. It depends on a "will to do" (*un vouloir-faire*). The voice that today we consider altered or extinguished is above all that great cosmological Spoken Word that we notice no longer reaches us: it does not cross the centuries separating us from it. There is a disappearance of the places established by a spoken word, a loss of the identities that people believed they received from a spoken word. A work of mourning. Henceforth, identity depends on the production, on the endless moving on (or detachment and cutting loose) that this loss makes necessary. Being is measured by doing.

Writing is progressively being overturned by this development. Another writing is imposed little by little in scientific, erudite or political forms: it is no longer something that speaks, but something made. Still linked to what is disappearing, indebted to what is moving away into the distance like a past but remains an origin, this new writing must be a practice, the endless production of an identity that is supported only by an activity (*un faire*), a moving on (*une marche*) that always depends on something else to provide an available space for its advance, to the degree that the voice proper to Christian culture becomes its other and that the presence given in the signifier (the very definition of voice) is transformed into a past. The capitalist scriptural conquest is articulated on that loss and on the gigantic effort of "modern" societies to redefine themselves without that voice. The revolutionary task is only a major result of this effort. It is inseparable from the message that up to that point had always signified their end for other civilizations (none of them survived the death of its gods): "Our gods no longer speak to us—God is dead."

Along with writing, the relationship to language was also transformed. The two are always interdependent, but the relationship to language must also be stressed in order to be able to grasp the form in which the spoken word comes back with a new importance today. Another historical outline may be used to suggest it. The turning point that inaugurates the modern age is marked first, in the seventeenth century, by a devaluation of the statement (*l'énoncé*) and a concentration on the act enunciating it (*l'énonciation*). When the speaker's identity was certain ("God speaks in the world"), attention was directed toward the deciphering of his statements, the "mysteries" of the world. But when this certitude is disturbed along with the political and religious institutions that guaranteed it, the questioning is directed toward the possibility of finding substitutes for the unique speaker: who is going to speak? and to whom? The disappearance of the First Speaker creates the problem of communication, that is, of a language that has to be *made* and not just *heard and understood.* In the vast sea of a progressively disseminated language, a world without closure or anchorage (it becomes doubtful, eventually improbable, that a Unique subject will appropriate it and make it speak), every particular discourse attests to the absence of the position which the organization of a cosmos formerly assigned to the individual, and thus to the necessity of carving out a position by one's own way of treating a particular area of language. In other words, it is because he loses his position that the individual comes into being as a *subject.* The place a cosmological language formerly assigned to him and which was understood as a "vocation" and a placement in the order of the world, becomes a "nothing," a sort of void, which drives the subject to make himself the master of a space and to set himself up as a producer of writing.

Because of this isolation of the subject, language ob-jectifies itself, becoming a field to be plowed rather than to be deciphered, a disorderly nature that has to be cultivated. The dominant ideology is transformed into a technique that has for its essential program to *make* language and no longer to *read* it. Language itself has to be fabricated, "written." For Condillac, constructing a science and constructing a language amount to the same task, just as for the revolutionaries of 1790 establishing the revolution required the creation and imposition of a national French language.[5] This implies a distancing of the living body (both traditional and individual) and thus also of everything which remains, among the people, linked to the earth, to the place, to orality or to non-verbal tasks. The mastery of language guarantees and isolates a new power, a "bourgeois" power, that of making history and fabricating languages. This power, which is essentially scriptural, challenges not only the privilege of "birth," that is, of the aristocracy, but also defines the code governing socioeconomic promotion and dominates, regulates, or selects according to its norms all those who do not possess this mastery of language. Writing becomes a principle of the social hierarchization that formerly privileged the middle class and now privileges the technocrat. It functions as the law of an educational system organized by the dominant class, which can make language (whether rhetorical or mathematical) its instrument of production. Here again Robinson Crusoe sheds light on the situation: the subject of writing is the master, and his man Friday is the worker, who has a tool other than language.

Inscriptions of the law on the body

This historical mutation does not transform the whole organization that structures a society through writing. It initiates another use, a new way of using that organization, a different functioning. It is therefore necessary to connect its establishment with the virtually immemorial effort to place the (social and/or individual) body under the law of writing. This effort preceded the historical form that writing has taken in modern times. It will outlive this particular form. It is interwoven into this form and determines it like a continuing archeology whose name and status we are unable to determine. What is at stake is the relation between the law and the body—a body is itself defined, delimited, and articulated by what writes it.

There is no law that is not inscribed on bodies. Every law has a hold on the body. The very idea of an individual that can be isolated from the group was established along with the necessity, in penal justice, of having a body that could be marked by punishment, and in matrimonial law, of having a body that could be marked with a price in transactions among collectivities. From birth to mourning after death, law "takes hold of" bodies in order to make them its text. Through all sorts of initiations (in rituals, at school, etc.), it transforms them into tables of the law, into living tableaux of rules and customs, into actors in the drama organized by a social order. And for Kant and Hegel, there is even no law unless there is capital punishment, that is, unless in extreme cases the body signifies by its destruction the absolute power of the letter and of the norm—a questionable assertion. However that may be, it remains that the law constantly writes itself on bodies. It engraves itself on parchments made from the skin of its subjects. It articulates them in a juridical corpus. It makes its book out of them. These writings carry out two complementary operations: through them, living beings are "packed into a text" (in the sense that products are canned or packed), transformed into signifiers of rules (a sort of "intextuation") and, on the other hand, the reason or *Logos* of a society "becomes flesh" (an incarnation).

A whole tradition tells the story: the skin of the servant is the parchment on which the master's hand writes. Thus Dromio the slave says to his master Antipholus of Ephesus in *The Comedy of Errors*: "If the skin were parchment and the blows you gave were ink. . . ."[6] Shakespeare indicated in this way the first place of writing and the relationship of mastery that the law entertains with its subject through the gesture of "working him over" (*lui faire la peau*). Every power, including the power of law, is written first of all on the backs of its subjects. Knowledge does the same. Thus Western ethnological science is written on the space that the body of the other provides for it. One might thus assume that parchments and papers are put in place of our skins and that when, in good times, they have been substituted for it, they form a sort of protective coating around it. Books are only metaphors of the body. But in times of crisis, paper is no longer enough for the law, and it writes itself again on the bodies themselves. The printed text refers to what is printed on our body, brands it with a red-hot iron with the mark of the Name and of the Law, and ultimately affects it with pain and/or pleasure so as to turn it into a symbol of the Other, something *said, called, named.* The printed setting represents the social and amorous experience of being the writing of something one cannot identify: "My body will be no more than the graph that you write on it, a signifier that no one but you can decipher. But who are you, Law who transforms the body into your sign?" The act of suffering oneself to be written by the group's law is oddly accompanied by a pleasure, that of being recognized (but one does not know by whom), of becoming an identifiable and legible word in a social language, of being changed into a fragment within an anonymous text, of being inscribed in a symbolic order that has neither owner nor author. Every printed text repeats this ambivalent experience of the body written by the law of the other. In some cases it is only a distant and worn metaphor of this experience that no longer works on incarnate writing: in others, it is a living memory of this experience aroused when reading touches the body at the points where the scars of the unknown text have long been imprinted.[7]

In order for the law to be written on bodies, an apparatus is required that can mediate the relation between the former and the latter. From the instruments of scarification, tatooing, and primitive initiation to those of penal justice, tools work on the body. Formerly the tool was a flint knife or a needle. Today the instruments range from the policeman's billyclub to handcuffs and the box reserved for the accused in the courtroom. These tools compose a series of objects whose purpose is to inscribe the force of the law on its subject, to tattoo him in order to make him demonstrate the rule, to produce a "copy" that makes the norm legible. This series forms an in-between; it borders on the law (it is the law that provides it with weapons) and it aims at the body (in order to mark it). An offensive frontier, it organizes social space: it separates the text and the body, but it also links them, by permitting the acts that will make the textual "fiction" of the model reproduced and realized by the body.

This panoply of instruments for writing can be isolated. It is put in reserve in storage places or in museums. It can be collected, before or after use. It remains there, ready for use or left over after use. This hardware can be used on bodies that are still far away, unknown, and can be re-employed in the service of laws other than those whose "application" they have made possible. These objects made for squeezing, holding up, cutting, opening, or confining bodies are displayed in fantastic showcases: shining iron and steel, dense wood, solid and abstract figures arranged like lines of print, instruments, curved or straight, constraining or bruising, that outline the movements of a suspended justice and already mold the parts of the body that are to be branded but are still absent. Between the laws that change and the living beings that pass by, the exhibits of these stable tools punctuate space, form networks and branching patterns, referring on one side to the symbolic corpus and on the other to carnal beings. No matter how disseminated it may be (like the tiny bones of a skeleton), this panoply outlines in dotted line the relations between rules and bodies that are equally mobile. In detached pieces, it is the writing machine (*la machine à écrire*) of the Law—the mechanical system of a social articulation.

From one body to another

This machinery transforms individual bodies into a body politic. It makes these bodies produce the text of a law. Another machinery runs parallel to the first, but it is medical or surgical in type, and not juridical. It is in the service of an individual and not a collective "therapeutics." The body it treats is distinguished from the group. After having long been only a "member"—arm, leg, or head—of the social unit or a place in which cosmic forces or "spirits" intersected, it has slowly emerged as a whole, with its *own* illnesses, equilibriums, deviations and abnormalities. A long historical development stretching from the fifteenth to the eighteenth century was required before the individual body could be "isolated" in the way one "isolates" an element in chemistry or microphysics; before it could become the basic unit of a society, after a time of transition in which it appeared as a miniaturization of the political or celestial order—a "microcosm."[8] A change in sociocultural axioms occurs when the unit referred to gradually ceases to be the body politic in order to become the individual body, and when the reign of a *juridical* politics begins to be replaced by the reign of a *medical* politics, that of the representation, administration, and well-being of individuals.

Individualistic and medical classification delimits a "bodily" space of its own in which a combinative system of elements and the laws governing their exchanges can be analyzed. From the seventeenth to the eighteenth century, the idea of a physics of bodies in movement within this very body haunts medicine,[9] until this scientific model is replaced in the nineteenth century by one based on thermodynamics and chemistry. The dream of a mechanics of distinct elements correlated by propulsive forces, pressures, changes in equilibrium and maneuvers of every kind. The opera of the body: a complex machinery of pumps, pipes, filters, and levers, through which liquids circulate and organs respond to each other.[10] The identification of the pieces and their operations makes it possible to substitute artificial parts for those that wear out or have some defect, and even to construct automatons. The body can be repaired. It can be educated. It can even be fabricated. The panoply of orthopedic instruments and means of treatment expands in proportion to what one can henceforth take apart and repair, cut off, replace, take out, add, correct, or straighten. The network of these tools becomes more complex and extensive. It still remains in place today, in spite of the transition to a chemical medicine and to cybernetic models. Count-less delicate steel instruments are adjusted to the innumerable possibilities that the mechanization of the body offers them.

But has their proliferation modified their functioning? In changing jobs, moving from the "application" of the law to that of surgical and orthopedic medicine, the apparatus of tools retains the function of marking or shaping bodies in the name of a law. If the *textual corpus* (scientific, ideological, and mythological) has been transformed, if bodies have become more autonomous with respect to the cosmos and take on the appearance of mechanical constructions, the task of relating the textual corpus to these bodies remains, no doubt emphasized by the multiplication of the possible means of treatment, but still defined by the writing of a text on bodies, by the incarnation of knowledge. The stability of the instrumentation. A strange functional inertia of these tools that are nevertheless active in cutting, gripping, shaping the flesh constantly offered up to a creation that makes it into bodies in a society.

A necessity (a destiny?) seems to be indicated by these steel and nickel objects: the necessity that introduces the law into the flesh by means of iron and that, in a culture, neither authorizes nor recognizes as bodies flesh that has not been written out by the tool. Even when, at the beginning of the 19th century, medical ideology is slowly inverted, as a therapeutics of extraction (the disorder is caused by an excess, some-thing extra or superfluous—which has to be taken out of the body through bleeding, purging, etc.) is for the most part replaced by a thera-peutics of addition (the disorder is a lack, a deficit, which has to be compensated for or replaced by drugs, supports, etc.), the apparatus of *instrumentality* continues to play its role of writing social knowledge's new text on the body in place of the old one, just as the harrow in Kafka's story "In the Penal Colony" remains the same even if one can change the normative text that it engraves on the backs of the tortured one.

No doubt Kafka's mythical machine takes on, through the ages, less violent forms—and perhaps also forms less capable of eliciting the final sparkle of pleasure that the story's narrator glimpses in the eyes of the dying men wounded by the writing of the Other. At least the analysis of the system allows us to determine the variants and the different speeds and rates of the machine that makes bodies the inscription of a text, and to ask ourselves for what eye this writing, which cannot be read by its supports, is intended.

Mechanisms of incarnation

From the seventeenth-century movement that attracted Puritan reformers as well as jurists to the medical theorists of the doctors who were known precisely as *Physicians*, a great ambition arose: to produce a new history on the basis of a text.[11] The myth of the Reformation is that the Scriptures provide, in the midst of a corrupt society and a decadent Church, a model one can use to re-form both society and the Church. A return to the origins, not only those of the Christian West, but also that of the universe itself, to find a genesis giving a body to the *Logos* and incarnating it so that it can once again but in a different way "become flesh." The variants of this myth are found everywhere, in this time of Renascences, along with the utopian, philosophical, scientific, political or religious conviction that Reason must be able to establish or restore a world, and that it is no longer a matter of deciphering the secrets of an order or a hidden Author, but of *producing* an order so that it can be *written* on the body of an uncivilized or depraved society. Writing acquires the right to reclaim, subdue or educate history.[12] It becomes a power in the hands of a "bourgeoisie" that substitutes the instrumentality of the letter for the privilege of birth, a privilege linked to the hypothesis that the world as it is, is right. Writing becomes science and politics, with the assurance, soon transformed into an axiom of Enlightenment or revolution, that theory must transform nature by inscribing itself on it. It becomes violence, cutting its way through the irrationality of superstitious peoples or regions still under the spell of sorcery.

Printing represents this articulation of the text on the body through writing. The order thought (the text conceived) produces itself as a body (books) which repeats it, forming paving stones and paths, networks of rationality through the incoherence of the universe. The process later becomes more widespread and diverse. At this point it is only the metaphor of the more successfully rationalized techniques that later transform living beings themselves into the printed texts of an order. But the fundamental idea is already present in this logos that becomes books and in these books which the Age of Enlightenment thought would produce a new history. It could also have as its symbol the "constitutions" that proliferate in the eighteenth and nineteenth centuries: they give the text the status of being "applicable" to public or private bodies, of defining them and thus finding its effectiveness.

This grand mythical and reforming passion functions on the basis of three terms that characterize it: first, a model or "fiction," i.e., a *text*; second, the instruments of its application or writing, i.e., *tools*; third, the material which is both the support and the incarnation of the model, i.e., a nature, essentially a *flesh*, which writing changes into a *body*. Using tools to make a body conform to its definition in a social discourse: that is the movement. It sets out from a normative idea whose vehicles are a code of economic exchanges or the variants of this code presented by stories from the common legendary lore and by the new products of scientific knowledge. At the beginning, there is a fiction determined by a "symbolic" system that acts as a law, and thus a representation (a theater) or a fable (a "saying") of the body. That is to say, a body is postulated as the signifier (the term) in a *contract*. This discursive image is supposed to inform an *unknown* "reality" formerly designated as "flesh." The transition from the fiction to the unknown that will give it a body is made by means of instruments that multiply and diversify the unpredictable resistances of the body to be (con)formed. An indefinite fragmentation of the apparatus is necessary in order to adjust and apply each of these sayings and/or types of knowlege about the body, which work as unifying models, to the opaque carnal reality that gradually reveals its complex organization as it resists successive efforts to modify and control it. Between the tool and the flesh, there is thus an interaction that shows itself on the one hand by a change in the fiction (a correction of knowledge) and, on the other, by the cry, which shrieks an inarticulable pain and constitutes the unthought part of bodily difference.

As the products of a craft, and later of an industry, these tools multiply around the images which they serve and which are the empty centers, the pure signifiers of social communication, "non-entities"; the tools represent in concrete form the tortuous knowledge, sharp sinuosities, perforating ruses, and incisive detours that penetration into the labyrinthine body requires and produces. In that way, they become the metallic vocabulary of the knowledge that they bring back from these expeditions. They are the figures of an experimental knowledge won through the pain of the bodies that change themselves into engravings and maps of these conquests. The flesh that has been cut out or added to, putrefied or put back together tells the story of the high deeds of all these tools, these incorruptible heroes. Over the span of a life or a fashion, they illustrate the actions of a tool. They are its human, ambulatory, and transitory stories.

But apparatuses have instrumental value if, and only if, a "nature" exterior to the model is assumed, if a "subject matter" is distinguished from informatory and reformatory operations. An outside is required for that sort of writing. When there is no separation between the text to be inscribed and the body that historicizes it, the system no longer functions. It is precisely the tools that establish that difference. They mark the gap without which everything becomes a disseminated writing, an indefinite combinative system of fictions and simulacra, or else, on the contrary, a continuum of natural forces, of libidinal drives and instinctual outpourings. Tools are the operators of writing and also its defenders. They protect the privilege that circumscribes it and distinguishes it from the bodies to be educated. Their networks maintain, vis-à-vis the textual instance they execute, an ontological referentiality—or a "reality"—they inform. But this barrier is gradually breaking down. The instruments are giving way little by little; they are almost anachronistic in the contemporary order, in which writing and machinery, no longer distinct, are themselves becoming the chance modalizations of programmatic matrices determined by a genetic code[13] and in which, of the "carnal" reality formerly subjected to writing, there perhaps remains no more than the cry—of pain or pleasure—an incongruous voice in the indefinite combinative system of simulations.

Losing its (mythical) ability to organize what can be thought, the three-part system composed of text, tool and body remains in the background. It survives, even though it is regarded as illicit by a cybernetically-oriented type of scientific knowledge. Partial and framented, it piles up on top of many other systems. Epistemological configurations are never replaced by the appearance of new orders; they compose strata that form the bedrock of a present. Relics and pockets of the instrumental system continue to exist everywhere, like those discharged officers who, after having symbolized a régime and an imperial *conquista*, still constituted networks and centers of the Napoleonic order throughout Restoration France. Tools take on a folkloric appearance. They nevertheless make up a discharged corps left behind by the defunct empire of mechanics. These populations of instruments oscillate between the status of memorable ruins and an intense everyday activity. They form an intermediary class of objects, some already put into retirement (in museums) and others still at work (operating in a multitude of secondary functions).[14] This beehive activity takes place on many different terrains, from bathrooms to the most advanced laboratories, from shops to operating rooms. Children of another age, they nevertheless pullulate in the midst of our own, in the gadgets or lancets that give us information on bodies.

The machinery of representation

Two main operations characterize their activities. The first seeks primarily to *remove* something excessive, diseased, or unesthetic from the body, or else to *add* to the body what it lacks. Instruments are thus distinguished by the action they perform: cutting, tearing out, extracting, removing, etc., or else inserting, installing, attaching, covering up, assembling, sewing together, articulating, etc.—without mentioning those substituted for missing or deteriorated organs, such as heart valves and regulators, prosthetic joints, pins implanted in the femur, artificial irises, substitute ear bones, etc.

From the inside or the outside, they correct an excess or a lack, but in relationship to what? As in the case of removing the hair from one's legs or putting mascara on one's eyelashes, having one's hair cut or having hair reimplanted, this activity of extracting or adding on is carried out by reference to *a code*. It keeps bodies within the limits set by a norm. In this respect, clothes themselves can be regarded as instruments through which a social law maintains its hold on bodies and its members, regulates them and exercises them through changes in fashion as well as through military maneuvers. The automobile, like a corset, also shapes them and makes them conform to a model of correct posture; it is an orthopedic and orthopractic instrument. The foods that are selected by traditions and sold in the markets of a society also shape bodies at the same time that they nourish them; they impose on bodies a form and a muscle tone that function like an identity card. Glasses, cigarettes, shoes, etc., reshape the physical "portrait" in their own ways. Is there a limit to the machinery by which a society represents itself in living beings and makes them its representations? Where does the disciplinary apparatus[15] end that displaces and corrects, adds or removes things from these bodies, malleable under the instrumentation of so many laws? To tell the truth, they become bodies only by conforming to these codes. Where and when is there ever anything bodily that is not written, remade, cultured, identified by the different tools which are part of a social symbolic code? Perhaps at the extreme limit of these tireless inscriptions, or perforating them with lapses, there remains only the cry: it escapes, it escapes them. From the first to the last cry, something else breaks out with them, the body's difference, alternately *in-fans* and ill-bred, intolerable in the child, the possessed, the madman or the sick—a lack of "good manners," like the howling of the baby in *Jeanne Dielman* or that of the vice-consul in *India Song.**

This first operation of removing or adding is thus only the corollary of another, more general operation, which consists in *making the body tell the code.* As we have seen, this work "realizes" a social language, gives it its effectiveness. This is an immense task of "machining" bodies to make them spell out an order.[16] Economic individualism is no less effective than totalitarianism in carrying out this articulation of the law by means of bodies. It just proceeds by different methods. Instead of crushing groups in order to mark them with the unique brand of a power, it atomizes them first and multiplies the constraining networks of exchange that shape individual units in conformity with the rules (or "fashions") of socioeconomic and cultural contracts. In both cases, one may wonder why it works. What desire or what need leads us to make our bodies the emblems of an identifying law? The hypotheses that answer this question show in another way the power of the links that tools forge between our in-fantile "natures" and the forms of social discourse.

The *credibility* of a discourse is what first makes believers act in accord with it. It produces practitioners. To make people believe is to make them act. But by a curious circularity, the ability to make people act—to write and to machine bodies—is precisely what makes people believe. Because the law is already applied with and on bodies, "incarnated" in physical practices, it can accredit itself and make people believe that it speaks in the name of the "real." It makes itself believable by saying: "This text has been dictated for you by Reality itself." People believe what they assume to be real, but this "reality" is assigned to a discourse by a belief that gives it a body inscribed by the law. The law requires an accumulation of corporeal capital in advance in order to make itself believed and practiced. It is thus inscribed because of what has already been inscribed: the witnesses, martyrs, or examples that make it credible to others. It imposes itself in this way on the subject of

---

* *Jeanne Dielman* is a film by Chantal Akerman, *India Song* a film by Marguerite Duras.

the law: "The ancients practiced it," or "Others have believed it and done it," or "You yourself already bear my signature on your body."

In other words, *normative* discourse "operates" only if it has already become a *story*, a text articulated on something real and speaking in its name, i.e., a law made into a story and historicized (*une loi historiée et historicisée*), recounted by bodies. Its being made into a story is the presupposition of its producing further stories and thereby making itself believed. And the tool ensures precisely the passage from discourse to the story through the interventions that incarnate the law by making bodies conform to it and thus make it appear to be recited by reality itself. From initiation ceremonies to tortures, every social orthodoxy makes use of instruments to give itself the form of a story and to produce the credibility attached to a discourse articulated by bodies.

Another dynamics completes the first and interlaces with it, the dynamics that leads living beings to become signs, to find in a discourse the means of transforming themselves into a unit of meaning, into an identity. To finally pass from this opaque and dispersed flesh, from this exorbitant and troubled life, to the limpidness of a *word*, to become a fragment of language, a single name, that can be read and quoted by others: this passion moves the ascetic armed with instruments for mortifying his flesh, or the philosopher who does the same to language, "recklessly," as Hegel put it. But it does not matter who the person is that is moved by this passion, eager to finally have or be a name, to be called, to be transformed into a *saying* (*dit*), even at the price of his life. The intextuation of the body corresponds to the incarnation of the law; it supports it, it even seems to establish it, and in any case it serves it. For the law plays on it: "Give me your body and I will give you meaning, I will make you a name and a word in my discourse." The two problematics maintain each other, and perhaps the law would have no power if it were not able to support itself on the obscure desire to exchange one's flesh for a glorious body, to be written, even if it means dying, and to be transformed into a recognized word. Here again, the only force opposing this passion to be a sign is the cry, a deviation or an ecstasy, a revolt or flight of that which, within the body, escapes the law of the named.

Perhaps all experience that is not a cry of pleasure or pain is recuperated by the institution. All experience that is not displaced or undone by this ecstasy is captured by "the love of the censor,"[17] collected and utilized by the discourse of the law. It is channeled and instrumented. It is written by the social system. Thus we must seek in the area of these cries what is not "remade" by the order of scriptural instrumentality.

"Celibate machines"

To the establishment of a new scriptural practice, marked on the sky of the eighteenth century by the laborious insularity of Robinson Crusoe, we can now compare its generalization as represented by the fantastic machines whose images emerge around 1910–1914 in the works of Alfred Jarry (*Le Surmâle*, 1902; *Le Docteur Faustroll*, 1911), Raymond Roussel (*Impressions d'Afrique*, 1910; *Locus Solus*, 1914), Marcel Duchamp (*Le Grand Verre: La mariée mise à nu par ses célibataires, même*, 1911–1925), Franz Kafka (*Die Strafkolonie*, 1914), etc.[18] These are the myths of an incarceration within the operations of a writing that constantly makes a machine of itself and never encounters anything but itself. There are no ways out except through fictions, painted windows, mirror-panes. No rips or rents other than written ones. These are comedies about people stripped naked and tortured, "automatic" stories about defoliations of meaning, theatrical ravagings of disintegrating faces. These productions are fantastic not in the indefiniteness of the reality that they make appear at the frontiers of language, *but in the relationship between the mechanisms that produce simulacra and the absence of anything else.* These novelistic or iconic fictions tell us that there is no entry or exit for writing, but only the endless play of its fabrications. If every event is an entry or an exit, then the myth tells the nowhere (*non-lieu*) of the event or of an event that does not take place (*qui n'a pas lieu*). The machine producing language is wiped clean of history, isolated from the obscenities of reality, ab-solute and without relation to the "celibate" other.

This is a "theoretical fiction," to borrow an expression from Freud, who sketched out in 1900 a sort of celibate machine that manufactured dreams—going forward during the day, and backward at night.[19] Such a fiction is written in a language without homeland and without body, with the whole repertory of a fatal exile or an impossible exodus. The solitary machine makes the Eros of the dead function, but this ritual of mourning (there is no other) is a comedy played within the tomb of the departed (*l'absent(e)*). There are no dead in the field of graphic and linguistic operations. The "torture" of the separation or putting to death of the body remains literary. Wounding, torturing, killing, it develops within the confines of the page. Celibacy is scriptural. Characters transformed into cylinders, drums, ruins, and springs put together and painted on the "glass" where their perspective representation mixes with the objects located behind (the glass is a window) and in front (the glass is a mirror) represent not only, in the painting-glass-mirror constituted by Duchamp's *La Mariée mise à nu* hanging in the library of Miss Dreier's country house,[20] the dissemination of the subject of painting, but the lure of communication that the transparency of the pane of glass promises. A laughable tragedy of language: being mixed together by an optical effect, these elements are neither coherent nor conjoined. Spectators that happen to look at them associate but do not articulate them. Stripped naked (*mise à nu*) by a mechanically organized deterioration, the bride (*la mariée*) is never married to a reality of a meaning.

To be sure, only an erotic drive, a desire for the absent other, is capable of putting the productive apparatus in motion, but it aims at something that will never be *there* and that makes the voyeur's gaze obsessive when he is gripped by his double reflected on the mirror, moving in the middle of the things offered/refused in the windowpane-mirror. In the reflected image, the spectator sees himself dispersed among what cannot be grasped (the painted images of things). The graph painted on Marcel Duchamp's glass figures the trompe-l'oeil image of a stripping-naked by and for voyeur-spectators who will always remain celibate. The vision indicates and frustrates the absent communication. Other celibate machines function in the same way, identifying sex with its mechanical image and sexuality with an optical illusion. Thus, in Alfred Jarry's *Les Jours et les nuits*, an inscription hangs over the glass wall that encircles the island of the nereid, a woman surrounded by glass in the midst of a military décor; the inscription speaks of "the man who passionately embraces his Double through the glass": "The glass takes on life at one point and becomes a sexual organ, and being and image make love through the wall."[21] On this "island of lubricious glass," machines produce a giant windowpane which shapes itself into whatever sexual organ is required at whatever point it happens to be touched. In the same way, in *Les Dix mille milles*, a pane of glass separates the woman shut up in a railway car from the males on bicycles who race against the train.

These tragi-comedies, fragments of myths, recognize the impossibility of communication, of which language is both the promise and the phantasm. A poetics, once again, has preceded theory. Since then, reflection has moved in that direction. In Lacan's work, the category of "*lalangue*" connects speaking with the impossibility of conjoining ("there is no sexual relationship"); it connects the very possibility of language to the impossibility of the communication it is supposed to produce. A linguist adds: "Just as the philosopher's language is the place of the impossibility of mutual knowledge, *lalangue* is the place of the impossibility of the sexual relationship."[22] Among desiring subjects, there remains only the possibility of loving the language that substitutes itself for their communication. And that is indeed a model of language furnished by the machine, which is made of differentiated and combined parts (like every enunciation) and develops, through the interplay of its mechanisms, the logic of a celibate narcissism.

"It is a matter of *exhausting* the meaning of words, of playing with them until one has done violence to their most secret attributes, and pronounced at last the total divorce between the term and the expressive content that we usually give it."[23] Henceforth, the important thing is neither *what is said* (a content), nor the *saying* itself (an act), but rather the *transformation*, and the invention of still unsuspected mechanisms that will allow us to multiply the transformations.[24]

The time is thus over in which the "real" appeared to come into the text to be manufactured and exported. The time is over when writing seemed to make love with the violence of things and place them in a rational order. Verism was merely apparent, the theater of verisimilitude. After Zola, came Jarry, Roussel, Duchamp, *et al.*, that is, the "theoretical fictions" of the impossible other and of a writing given over to its own mechanisms or to its solitary erections. The text mimes its own death and makes it ridiculous. No one any longer respects this writing, this exquisite cadaver. It is no more than the illusory sacrament of the real, a space of laughter at the expense of yesterday's axioms. In it is deployed the ironic and meticulous work of mourning.

The key parts of the writing triumphant in Defoe's work are compromised: the blank page is only a pane of glass to which representation is attracted by what it excluded; the written text, closed on itself, loses the referent that authorized it; expansionist utility is inverted into the "sterile gratuitousness" of a celibate Don Juan or of a "widower" having no generation other than a symbolizing one, a man without woman and without nature, without an other. Writing has become an "inscription island," a *locus solus*, a "penal colony"—a laborious dream, occupied by this "impossible" to which or about which it thinks it "speaks."

It is through this stripping naked of the modern myth of writing that the celibate machine becomes, in a derisive mode, blasphemy. It attacks the Occidental ambition to articulate the reality of things on a text and to reform it. It takes away the *appearance* of being (i.e., of content, of meaning) that was the sacred secret of the Bible, transformed by four centuries of bourgeois writing into the power of the letter and the numeral. Perhaps this anti-myth is still ahead of our history, even if it is repeatedly confirmed by the erosion of scientific certainties, the massive "boredom" of people at school, or the progressive metaphorizaıion of administrative discourses. Or perhaps it has simply been placed "alongside" a galloping technocratization, like a suggestive para-dox, a little white pebble.

Chapter XI   Quotations of Voices

Vox . . .
Nympha fugax
(Voice . . . fleeting nymph)
G. Cossart, *Orationes et Carmina,*
1675[1]

ROBINSON CRUSOE already indicated himself how a crack appeared in his scriptural empire. For a time, his enterprise was in fact interrupted, and haunted, by an absent other that returned to the shores of the island, by "the print of a man's naked foot on the shore." The instability of the limits set: the frontier yields to something foreign. On the margins of the page, the mark of an "apparition" disturbs the order that a capitalizing and methodical labor had constructed. It elicits "fluttering thoughts," "whimsies," and "terror" in Robinson Crusoe.[2] The conquering bourgeois is transformed into a man "beside himself," made wild himself by this (wild) clue that reveals nothing. He is almost driven out of his mind. He dreams, and has nightmares. He loses his confidence in a world governed by the Great Clockmaker. His arguments abandon him. Driven out of the productive asceticism that took the place of meaning for him, he lives through diabolical day after day, obsessed by the cannibalistic desire to devour the unknown intruder or by the fear of being devoured himself.

On the written page, there thus appears a smudge—like the scribbling of a child on the book which is the local authority. A lapse insinuates itself into language. The territory of appropriation is altered by the mark of something which is not there and does not happen (like myth).[3] Robinson will see someone (Friday) and will recover the power of mastery when he has the opportunity to see, that is, when the absent other shows himself. Then he will be once again within his order. Disorder is due to the mark of something past and passing, to the "practically nothing" of a passing-by. The violence that oscillates between the drive to devour and the fear of being eaten arises from what we could call a "presence of absence," following Hadewijch of Antwerp. The other, here, does not constitute a system hidden beneath the one Robinson writes. The island is not a palimpsest in which it is possible to reveal, decode, and decipher a system covered up by an order that is super-imposed on it but of the same type. What marks itself and passes on has no text of its own (*texte propre*). The latter is spoken only by the owner's discourse (*le discours du propriétaire*) and resides only in his place. The only language available to difference is interpretive delirium—the dreams and "whimsies" of Robinson himself.

Defoe's 1719 novel already indicates the nowhere (a trace or mark, which eats into borders) and the fantastic modality (an interpretive madness) of what will intervene as voice in the field of writing, even though Defoe considers only a silent marking of the text by small part of the body (a bare foot), and not the voice itself, which is a marking of language by the body. He also gives this form and these modalities a name: they have to do, Robinson says, with something *wild*. Naming is not here the "painting" of a reality any more than it is elsewhere; it is a performative act organizing what it enunciates. It does what it says, and constitutes the savagery it declares. Just as one excommunicates by naming, the name "wild" both creates and defines what the scriptural economy situates outside of itself. It is moreover immediately given its essential predicate: the wild is transitory; it marks itself (by smudges, lapses, etc.) but it does not write itself. It alters a place (it disturbs), but it does not establish a place.

The "theoretical fiction" invented by Defoe thus outlines a *form* of alterity in relation to writing, a form that will also impose its identity on the voice, since when Friday appears, he is confronted by an alternative destined to have a long history: he must either cry out (a "wild" out-break that calls for interpretation and correction through pedagogical—or psychiatric—treatment) or else make his body the vehicle of the dominant language (by becoming "his master's voice," a docile body that executes the order, incarnates reason and receives the status of being a substitute for enunciation, and is thus no longer the act but the acting out of the other's "saying"). In turn, the voice will also insinuate itself into the text as a mark or trace, an effect or metonymy of the body, a transitory citation like Cossart's "nymph"—*Nympha fugax*, a transitory fugitive, an indiscreet ghost, a "pagan" or "wild" reminiscence in the scriptural economy, a disturbing sound from a different tradition, and a pre-text for interminable interpretive productions.

We must still determine a few of the historical forms imposed on orality by the end of its confinement. Because of its exclusion on the grounds of economic neatness and efficiency, the voice appears essentially in the form of *quotation*, which is homologous, in the field of the written, with the mark of the bare foot left on Robinson's island. In scriptural culture, quotation links interpretive effects (it makes the production of texts possible) and effects of alteration (it dis-quiets the text). It operates between these two poles defining its extreme forms: on the one hand, the *quotation–pre-text*, which serves to fabricate texts (assumed to be commentaries or analyses) on the basis of relics selected from an oral tradition functioning as an authority; on the other, the *quotation-reminiscence*, marking in language the fragmented and unexpected return (like the intrusion of voices from outside) of oral relationships that are structuring but repressed by the written. These seem to be limiting cases, beyond which we are no longer concerned with the voice. In the first case, quotations become the means by which discourse proliferates; in the second, it lets them out and they interrupt it.

Focusing only on these two variants, I shall call the first "the science of fables" (from the name it was so frequently given in the eighteenth century), and the second "returns and turns of voices" ("*retours et tours de voix*") (since their returns, like those of swallows in the spring, are accompanied by subtle modalities and procedures, in the manner of the turns or tropes of rhetoric, and take the form of itineraries that squat on unoccupied lands, of "films for voices," as Marguerite Duras puts it, of ephemeral rounds—"*un petit tour et puis s'en va*"). The outline of these two forms can serve as a preliminary to the examination of oral practices, by making clear a few aspects of the framework that still leaves voices ways of speaking.

Displaced enunciation

A general problematic traverses and determines these forms and must be recalled in introducing them. I shall approach it from its linguistic side. From this point of view, Robinson Crusoe participates in and refers to an historical displacement of the problem of enunciation, that is to say, of the "act of speaking" or *speech-act*. The problem of the speaker and of his identity became acute with the breakdown of the world that was assumed to be spoken and speaking: who speaks when there is no longer a divine Speaker who founds every particular enunciation? The question was apparently settled by the system that furnished the subject with a place guaranteed and measured by his scriptural production.[4] In a laissez-faire economy where isolated and competitive activities are supposed to contribute to a general rationality, the work of writing gives birth to both the product and its author. Henceforth, in theory, there is no longer any need for voices in these industrious workshops. Thus the classical age had as its primary task the creation of scientific and technical "languages" separated from nature and intended to transform it (an act symbolized by Robinson's act of beginning his project by writing his journal, or "record book" ("*livre de raison*")); each of these systems of "writing" (*écritures*) places its "bourgeois" producers beyond doubt and confirms the conquests that this autonomous instrument allows them to make on the body of the world.

A new king comes into being: the individual subject, an imperceptible master. The privilege of being himself the god that was formerly "separated" from his creation and defined by a *genesis* is transferred to the man shaped by enlightened culture. Of course, the bourgeois heirs of the Judeo-Christian God make a selection among his attributes: the new god writes, but he does not speak; he is an author, but he is not grasped corporeally in an interlocution. The disturbance of enunciation is thus liquidated a priori, before coming back to us today as the problem of communication. The growing fabrication of objective schedulings, put under the banner of "progress," can also be regarded as the autobiographical story of its promoters: their achievements tell their story. The history that is made is their history, by a double break which on the one hand isolates operations, subjects of power and knowledge, and on the other, reduces nature to the status of an inexhaustible fund against the background of which its products appear and from which they are wrested. The immunity from which these new creators benefit in their solitude, and the inertia of the nature which is provided for their expeditions: these two historical postulates have broken off oral communications between the masters (who do not speak) and the universe (which no longer speaks), and made possible, over the past three centuries, the over-emphasized labor which mediates their relations and which, fabricating men-gods, transforming the universe, becomes the central and silent strategy of a new history.

However, the question that was theoretically eliminated by this labor returns to haunt us: who is speaking? to whom? But it reappears outside of this writing that has been transformed into a means and an effect of production. It arises *alongside*, coming from beyond the frontiers reached by the expansion of the scriptural enterprise. "Something" *different* speaks again and presents itself to the masters in the various forms of non-labor—the savage, the madman, the child, even woman; then, often recapitulating the preceding, in the form of a voice or the cries of the People excluded from the written; and still later, under the sign of the unconscious, the language that is supposed to continue to "speak" in the bourgeois and the "intellectuals" without their knowing it. Here we see a kind of speech emerging or maintaining itself, but as what "escapes" from the domination of a sociocultural economy, from the organization of reason, from the grasp of education, from the power of an elite and, finally, from the control of the enlightened consciousness.

To each form of this alien enunciation corresponds a scientific and social mobilization: civilizing colonization, psychiatry, pedagogy, the education of the people, psychoanalysis, etc.—ways of re-establishing writing in these emancipated areas. But the important thing here is rather the phenomenon that serves as a point of departure (and a vanishing point) for all these reconquests: the displacement of *saying* (speech) and *doing* (writing) from their central position. *The place from which one speaks is outside the scriptural enterprise.* The uttering occurs outside the places in which systems of statements are composed. One no longer knows where speaking comes from, and one understands less and less how writing, which articulates power, could speak.

The first victim of this dichotomy was no doubt rhetoric: it claimed to make out of speech a way of manipulating the other's will, establishing adhesions and contracts, coordinating or modifying social practices, and thus shaping history. It has gradually been excluded from the area of the sciences. And it is not accidental that it reappears where legends prosper; or that Freud re-establishes it in the exiled and unproductive area of dreams in which an unconscious sort of "speech" makes its return. This division, already so clear in the eighteenth century in growing opposition between techniques (or sciences) and *opera*,[5] or, more specifically, in the linguistic distinction between the consonant (which is written reason) and the vowel (which is breath, a special effect of the body),[6] seems finally to have received its scientific status and legitimacy in the distinction Saussure established between "*langue*" and "*parole*." Thus, the "primordial thesis" (Hjelmslev) of the *Course in General Linguistics* separates the "social" from the "individual," and the "essential" from "what is accessory and more or less accidental."[7] It presupposes as well that *"language (langue)* exists only in order to govern *speech acts (parole)."*[8] The corollaries which specify this thesis (itself dependent on the Saussurian "first principle," i.e., the arbitrariness of the sign), and which oppose the synchronic to discrete occurrences, indicate the tradition Saussure generalizes by elevating it to the status of a science, a tradition which, through two centuries of history, has constituted as the postulate of scriptural enterprise the break between the statement (an object that can be written) and enunciation (the act of speaking). This does not, of course, take into consideration another ideological tradition also present in Saussure's work, the tradition which opposes the "creativity" of the speech-act to the "system of language."[9]

Even displaced, set aside or considered as a remainder, enunciation cannot be dissociated from the system of statements. To point out only two socio-historical forms of this re-articulation, we can distinguish between writing's effort to master the "voice" that it cannot be but without which it nevertheless cannot exist, on the one hand, and the illegible returns of voices cutting across statements and moving like strangers through the house of language, like imagination.

The science of fables

Taking up first the *science of fables*, we find that it touches on all the learned or elitist hermeneutics of speech—of savage, religious, insane, childlike, or popular speech—as they have been elaborated over the past two centuries by ethnology, "the science of religions," psychiatry, pedagogy and political or historiographical procedures seeking to introduce the "voice of the people" into the authorized language. An immense field, reaching from the "explanations" of ancient or exotic fables in the eighteenth century to the pioneering work of Oscar Lewis in "giving a voice" to the *Children of Sanchez* and a point of departure for so many "life stories."[10] These different "heterologies" (sciences of the different) have the common characteristic of attempting to *write the voice*. The voice reaching us from a great distance must find a place in the text. Thus primitive orality has to be written in the ethnological discourse: the "genius" of "mythologies" and religious "fables" (as the *Encyclopédie* puts it) has to be written in a scholarly discipline, or the "voice of the people" has to be written in Michelet's historiography. What is audible, but far away, will thus be transformed into texts in conformity with the Western desire to read its products.

The heterological operations seems to depend on the fulfillment of two conditions: an object, defined as a "fable," and an instrument, translation. To define the position of the other (primitive, religious, mad, childlike, or popular) as a "fable" is not merely to identify it with "what speaks" (*fari*), but with a speech that "does not know" what it says. When it is serious, enlightened or scientific analysis does indeed assume that something essential is expressed in the myths produced by the primitive, the dogmas of the believer, the child's babbling, the language of dreams or the gnomic conversations of common people, but it also assumes that these forms of speech do not understand what they say that is important. The "fable" is thus a word full of meaning, but what it says "implicitly" becomes "explicit" only through scholarly exegesis. By this trick, research accords itself in advance, through its very object, a certain necessity and a location. It is sure of being always able to place interpretation in the lack of knowledge that undercuts the fable's speech. Surreptitiously, the distance from which the foreign voice comes is transformed into the gap that separates the concealed (unconscious) truth of the voice from the lure of its manifestation. The domination of scriptural labor is thus founded *de jure* by the very "fable" structure that is in reality its historical product.

There exists an instrument allowing this domination to pass from a *de jure* to a *de facto* status: *translation*. This is a mechanism, perfected over the generations, that makes it possible to move from one language to another, to eliminate exteriority by transferring it to interiority, and to transform the unpredictable or non-sensical "noises" uttered by voices into (scriptural, produced, and "comprehended") "messages." As one can still see in Hjelmslev's work, this notion of translation assumes the "translatability" of all languages (whether iconic, gestural, or voiced) into "natural everyday language." On the basis of this axiom, analysis can reduce all expressions to the form that has been developed in a particular field but which is assumed to be "non-specific" and endowed with a "universal character."[11] From that point on, all the successive operations become legitimate: transcription, which changes the oral into the written; the construction of a model which treats the fable as a linguistic system; the production of a meaning, which results from the working of this model on what has been changed into a text; etc. It is impossible to consider each of the stages of the factory-like labor that thus transforms the material given it in the form of a "fable" into written and readable cultural products. I would stress only the importance of transcription, a common practice considered as obviously justified, for, by first substituting the written for the oral (for example, in the transcription of a folk tale), it makes it possible to believe that the written product of the analysis made on this written document has something to do with oral literature.

These tricks guaranteeing in advance the success of scriptural operations have, however, a strange fact as the condition of their possibility. In contrast to the so-called exact sciences, whose development is determined by the autonomy of a field of research, "heterological" sciences engender their products by means of a passage through or by way of the other. They advance according to a "sexual" process that posits the arrival of the other, the different, as a detour necessary for their progress. In the perspectives we have adopted here, that means that orality remains indefinitely something exterior without which writing does not function. *The voice makes people write.* Such is the relationship Michelet's historiography has to "the voice of the people," which nevertheless, he says, he has never "succeeded in making speak"; such also is the relationship Freud's psychoanalytic writing has to his patient Dora's pleasure, which "eluded" him all through the oral exchange in her treatment.

From ethnology to pedagogy, we see that the guaranteed success of writing hinges on an initial defeat and lack, as if discourse were constructed as the result and occultation of a loss that is the condition of its possibility, as if the meaning of all scriptural conquests were that they multiply products that substitute for an absent voice, without ever succeeding in capturing it, in bringing it inside the frontiers of the text, in suppressing it as an alien element. In other words, modern writing cannot be in the place of presence. We have already seen that scriptural practice arises precisely from a gap between presence and the system. It is formed on the basis of a fracture in the antique unity of the Scripture that spoke. Its condition is its non-identity with itself.

All "heterological" literature can thus be considered as the result of this fracture. It tells both what it does with orality (it alters it) and it remains altered with and by the voice. Texts thus express an altered voice in the writing the voice makes necessary by its insurmountable difference. In this literature, we have thus a first image of the voice simultaneously "cited" (as before a court of law) and "altered"—a lost voice, erased even within the object itself (the "fable") whose scriptural construction it makes possible. But this "sexual" functioning of heterological writing, a functioning that never succeeds entirely, transforms it into an erotics: it is the inaccessibility of its "object" that makes it produce.

The sounds of the body

From this formation, I shall distinguish another modern figure: the "voices of the body." An example of this other scene is furnished by the opera, which gradually established itself at around the same time the scriptural model organized techniques and social practices in the eighteenth century. A space for voices, the opera allows an enunciation to speak that in its most elevated moments detaches itself from statements, disturbs and interferes with syntax, and wounds or pleasures, in the audience, those places in the body that have no language either. Thus in Verdi's *Macbeth*, in Lady Macbeth's mad aria, the voice that is at first supported by the orchestra soon continues alone after the orchestra has fallen silent, follows the curve of the melody a moment longer, vacillates, slowly slips away from its path, gets lost and finally disappears into silence. One voice among others breaching the discourse in which it constitutes a parenthesis and a deviation.

On the modern stage the oral trajectories are as individual as the bodies and as opaque to meaning, which is always general. Thus one cannot "evoke" them (like the "spirits" and voices of earlier ages) except in the way Marguerite Duras has presented "the film of voices": "Voices of women . . . they come from a nocturnal, elevated space, from a balcony overhanging the void, the totality. They are linked by desire. Desire each other. . . . Do not know we exist. Do not know that people hear them." *Destroy, she said*: "Writing has ended."[12]

Even philosophy, from Deleuze's *Anti-Oedipus* to Lyotard's *Libidinal Economy*, has labored to hear these voices again and thus to create auditory space. This is a reversal that is leading psychoanalysis to pass from a "science of dreams" to the experience of what speaking voices change in the dark grotto of the bodies that hear them. The literary text is modified by becoming the ambiguous depth in which sounds that cannot be reduced to a meaning move about. A plural body in which ephemeral oral rumors circulate: that is what this dismembered writing becomes, a "stage for voices." It makes the reduction of the drive to a sign impossible. It tends to create, as composer Maurice Ohana did in his composition *Cries for Twelve Mixed Voices*. One no longer *knows* what it is, if not altered and altering voices.

In scholarly writing, it is nothing other than the return of the voices through which the social body "speaks" in quotations, sentence fragments, the tonalities of "words," the sounds things make. "Those were my parents' words," says Helias, "those were my father's words":[13] a voiced spell attached to bits of language. This glossolalia disseminated in vocal fragments includes words that become sounds again: for example, Marie-Jeanne "probably likes to use certain words for the sound that they make in her mouth and ears."[14] Or noises that become words, such as "the noise" that the pinecone-toy (*cochon de pin*) makes when it twitches around on the floor.[15] Or rhymes, counting jingles, *jibidis* and *jabadaos*, sound-envelopes of lost meanings and present memories:[16]

> Hickory, dickory, dock,
> The mouse ran up the clock.
> The clock struck one,
> The mouse ran down,
> Hickory, dickory, dock.

Through the legends and phantoms whose audible citations continue to haunt everyday life, one can maintain a tradition of the body, which is heard but not seen.

These are the reminiscences of bodies lodged in ordinary language and marking its path, like white pebbles dropped through the forest of signs. An amorous experience, ultimately. Incised into the prose of the passage from day to day, without any possible commentary or translation, the poetic sounds of quoted fragments remain. "There are" everywhere such resonances produced by the body when it is touched, like "moans" and sounds of love, cries breaking open the text that they make proliferate around them, enunciative gaps in a syntagmatic organization of statements. They are the linguistic analogues of an erection, or of a nameless pain, or of tears: voices without language, enunciations flowing from the remembering and opaque body when it no longer has the space that the voice of the other offers for amorous or indebted speech. Cries and tears: an aphasic enunciation of what appears without one's knowing where it came from (from what obscure debt or writing of the body), without one's knowing how it could be said except through the other's voice.

These contextless voice-gaps, these "obscene" citations of bodies, these sounds waiting for a language, seem to certify, by a "disorder" secretly referred to an unknown order, that there is something else, something other. But at the same time, they narrate interminably (it goes on murmuring endlessly) the expectation of an impossible presence that transforms into its own body the traces it has left behind. These quotations of voices mark themselves on an everyday prose that can only produce some of their effects—in the form of statements and practices.

Chapter XII   Reading as Poaching

"To arrest the meanings of words
once and for all, that is what Terror
wants."
Jean-Francois Lyotard, *Rudiments
païens*

S OME TIME AGO, Alvin Toffler announced the birth of a "new
species" of humanity, engendered by mass artistic consumption.
This species–in–formation, migrating and devouring its way
through the pastures of the media, is supposed to be defined by its "self
mobility."[1] It returns to the nomadic ways of ancient times, but now
hunts in artificial steppes and forests.

This prophetic analysis bears, however, only on the masses that con-
sume "art." An inquiry made in 1974 by a French government agency
concerned with cultural activities[2] shows to what extent this production
only benefits an elite. Between 1967 (the date of a previous inquiry made
by another agency, the INSEE) and 1974, public monies invested in the
creation and development of cultural centers reinforced the already
existing cultural inequalities among French people. They multiplied the
places of expression and symbolization, but, in fact, the same categories
profit from this expansion: culture, like money, "goes only to the rich."
The masses rarely enter these gardens of art. But they are caught and
collected in the nets of the media, by television (capturing 9 out of 10
people in France), by newspapers (8 out of 10), by books (7 out of 10, of
whom 2 read a great deal and, according to another survey made in
autumn 1978, 5 read more than they used to),[3] etc. Instead of an increasing nomadism, we thus find a "reduction" and a confinement: consumption, organized by this expansionist grid takes on the appearance of
something done by sheep progressively immobilized and "handled" as a
result of the growing mobility of the media as they conquer space. The
consumers settle down, the media keep on the move. The only freedom

supposed to be left to the masses is that of grazing on the ration of simulacra the system distributes to each individual.

That is precisely the idea I oppose: such an image of consumers is unacceptable.

The ideology of "informing" through books

This image of the "public" is not usually made explicit. It is nonetheless implicit in the "producers'" claim to *inform* the population, that is, to "give form" to social practices. Even protests against the vulgarization/ vulgarity of the media often depend on an analogous pedagogical claim; inclined to believe that its own cultural models are necessary for the people in order to educate their minds and elevate their hearts, the elite upset about the "low level" of journalism or television always assumes that the public is moulded by the products imposed on it. To assume that is to misunderstand the act of "consumption." This misunderstanding assumes that "assimilating" necessarily means "becoming similar to" what one absorbs, and not "making something similar" to what one is, making it one's own, appropriating or reappropriating it. Between these two possible meanings, a choice must be made, and first of all on the basis of a story whose horizon has to be outlined. "Once upon a time. . . ."

In the eighteenth century, the ideology of the Enlightenment claimed that the book was capable of reforming society, that educational popularization could transform manners and customs, that an elite's products could, if they were sufficiently widespread, remodel a whole nation. This myth of Education[4] inscribed a theory of consumption in the structures of cultural politics. To be sure, by the logic of technical and economic development that it mobilized, this politics was led to the present system that inverts the ideology that formerly sought to spread "Enlightenment." The means of diffusion are now dominating the ideas they diffuse. The medium is replacing the message. The "pedagogical" procedures for which the educational system was the support have developed to the point of abandoning as useless or destroying the professional "body" that perfected them over the span of two centuries: today, they make up the apparatus which, by realizing the ancient dream of enclosing *all* citizens and *each one* in particular, gradually destroys the goal, the convictions, and the educational institutions of the Enlightenment. In short, it is as though the *form* of Education's establishment had been too fully realized, by eliminating the very *content* that made it possible and which from that point on loses its social utility. But all through this evolution, the idea of producing a society by a "scriptural" system has continued to have as its corollary the conviction that although the public is more or less resistant, it is moulded by (verbal or iconic) writing, that it becomes similar to what it receives, and that it is *imprinted* by and like the text which is imposed on it.

This text was formerly found at school. Today, the text is society itself. It takes urbanistic, industrial, commercial, or televised forms. But the mutation that caused the transition from educational archeology to the technocracy of the media did not touch the assumption that consumption is essentially passive—an assumption that is precisely what should be examined. On the contrary, this mutation actually reinforced this assumption: the massive installation of standardized teaching has made the intersubjective relationships of traditional apprenticeship impossible; the "informing" technicians have thus been changed, through the systematization of enterprises, into bureaucrats cooped up in their specialities and increasingly ignorant of users; productivist logic itself, by isolating producers, has led them to suppose that there is no creativity among consumers; a reciprocal blindness, generated by this system, has ended up making both technicians and producers believe that initiative takes place only in technical laboratories. Even the analysis of the repression exercised by the mechanisms of this system of disciplinary enclosure continues to assume that the public is passive, "informed," processed, marked, and has no historical role.

The efficiency of production implies the inertia of consumption. It produces the ideology of consumption–as–a–receptacle. The result of class ideology and technical blindness, this legend is necessary for the system that distinguishes and privileges authors, educators, revolutionaries, in a word, "producers," in contrast with those who do not produce. By challenging "consumption" as it is conceived and (of course) confirmed by these "authorial" enterprises, we may be able to discover creative activity where it has been denied that any exists, and to relativize the exorbitant claim that *a certain kind* of production (real enough, but not the only kind) can set out to produce history by "informing" the whole of a country.

A misunderstood activity: reading

Reading is only one aspect of consumption, but a fundamental one. In a society that is increasingly written, organized by the power of modifying

things and of reforming structures on the basis of scriptural models
(whether scientific, economic, or political), transformed little by little
into combined "texts" (be they administrative, urban, industrial, etc.),
the binominal set production–consumption can often be replaced by its
general equivalent and indicator, the binominal set writing–reading.
The power established by the will to rewrite history (a will that is by
turns reformist, scientific, revolutionary, or pedagogical) on the basis of
scriptural operations that are at first carried out in a circumscribed field,
has as its corollary a major division between reading and writing.

"Modernization, modernity itself, is writing," says François Furet.
The generalization of writing has in fact brought about the replacement
of custom by abstract law, the substitution of the State for traditional
authorities, and the disintegration of the group to the advantage of the
individual. This transformation took place under the sign of a "cross-
breeding" of two distinct elements, the written and the oral. Furet and
Ozouf's recent study has indeed demonstrated the existence, in the less
educated parts of France, of a "vast semi-literacy, centered on reading,
instigated by the Church and by families, and aimed chiefly at girls."[5]
Only the schools have joined, with a link that has often remained extremely fragile, the ability to read and the ability to write. These abilities
were long separated, up until late in the nineteenth century, and even
today, the adult life of many of those who have been to school very
quickly dissociates "just reading" and writing; and we must thus ask
ourselves how reading proceeds where it is married with writing.

Research on the psycho-linguistics of comprehension[6] distinguishes
between "the lexical act" and the "scriptural act" in reading. It shows
that the schoolchild learns to read by a process that *parallels* his learning
to decipher; learning to read is not a *result* of learning to decipher:
reading meaning and *deciphering* letters correspond to two different
activities, even if they intersect. In other words, cultural memory (acquired through listening, through oral tradition) alone makes possible
and gradually enriches the strategies of semantic questioning whose
expectations the deciphering of a written text refines, clarifies, or corrects. From the child to the scientist, reading is preceded and made
possible by oral communication, which constitutes the multifarious
"authority" that texts almost never cite. It is as though the construction
of meanings, which takes the form of an expectation (waiting for something) or an anticipation (making hypotheses) linked to an oral transmission, was the initial block of stone that the decoding of graphic

materials progressively sculpted, invalidated, verified, detailed, in order to make way for acts of reading. The graph only shapes and carves the anticipation.

In spite of the work that has uncovered an autonomy of the practice of reading underneath scriptural imperialism, a *de facto* situation has been created by more than three centuries of history. The social and technical functioning of contemporary culture hierarchizes these two activities. To write is to produce the text; to read is to receive it from someone else without putting one's own mark on it, without remaking it. In that regard, the reading of the catechism or of the Scriptures that the clergy used to recommend to girls and mothers, by forbidding these Vestals of an untouchable sacred text to write continues today in the "reading" of the television programs offered to "consumers" who cannot trace their own writing on the screen where the production of the Other—of "culture"—appears. "The link existing between reading and the Church"[7] is reproduced in the relation between reading and the church of the media. In this mode, the construction of the social text by professional intellectuals (*clercs*) still seems to correspond to its "reception" by the faithful who are supposed to be satisfied to reproduce the models elaborated by the manipulators of language.

What has to be put in question is unfortunately not this division of labor (it is only too real), but the assimilation of reading to passivity. In fact, to read is to wander through an imposed system (that of the text, analogous to the constructed order of a city or of a supermarket). Recent analyses show that "every reading modifies its object,"[8] that (as Borges already pointed out) "one literature differs from another less by its text than by the way in which it is read,"[9] and that a system of verbal or iconic signs is a reservoir of forms to which the reader must give a meaning. If then "the book is a result (a construction) produced by the reader,"[10] one must consider the operation of the latter as a sort of *lectio*, the production proper to the "reader" ("*lecteur*").[11] The reader takes neither the position of the author nor an author's position. He invents in texts something different from what they "intended." He detaches them from their (lost or accessory) origin. He combines their fragments and creates something un-known in the space organized by their capacity for allowing an indefinite plurality of meanings. Is this "reading" activity reserved for the literary critic (always privileged in studies of reading), that is, once again, for a category of professional intellectuals (*clercs*), or can it be extended to all cultural consumers?

Such is the question to which history, sociology, or the educational theory ought to give us the rudiments of an answer.

Unfortunately, the many works on reading provide only partial clarifications on this point or depend on the experience of literary people. Research has been primarily concerned with the teaching of reading.[12] It has not ventured very far into the fields of history and ethnology, because of the lack of traces left behind by a practice that slips through all sorts of "writings" that have yet to be clearly determined (for example, one "reads" a landscape the way one reads a text).[13] Investigations of ordinary reading are more common in sociology, but generally statistical in type: they are more concerned with calculating the correlations between objects read, social groups, and places frequented more than with analyzing the very operation of reading, its modalities and its typology.[14]

There remains the literary domain, which is particularly rich today (from Barthes to Riffaterre or Jauss), once again privileged by writing but highly specialized: "writers" shift the "joy of reading" in a direction where it is articulated on an art of writing and on a pleasure of re-reading. In that domain, however, whether before or after Barthes, deviations and creativities are narrated that play with the expectations, tricks, and normativities of the "work read"; there theoretical models that can account for it are already elaborated.[15] In spite of all this, the story of man's travels through his own texts remains in large measure unknown.

"Literal" meaning, a product of a social elite

From analyses that follow the activity of reading in its detours, drifts across the page, metamorphoses and anamorphoses of the text produced by the travelling eye, imaginary or meditative flights taking off from a few words, overlappings of spaces on the militarily organized surfaces of the text, and ephemeral dances, it is at least clear, as a first result, that one cannot maintain the division separating the readable text (a book, image, etc.) from the act of reading. Whether it is a question of newspapers or Proust, the text has a meaning only through its readers; it changes along with them; it is ordered in accord with codes of perception that it does not control. It becomes a text only in its relation to the exteriority of the reader, by an interplay of implications and ruses between two sorts of "expectation" in combination: the expectation that organizes a *readable* space (a literality), and one that organizes a procedure necessary for the *actualization* of the work (a reading).[16]

It is a strange fact that the principle of this reading activity was formulated by Descartes more than three hundred years ago, in discussing contemporary research on combinative systems and on the example of ciphers (*chiffres*) or coded texts: "And if someone, in order to decode a cipher written with ordinary letters, thinks of reading a B everywhere he finds an A, and reading a C where he finds a B, and thus to substitute for each letter the one that follows it in alphabetic order and if, reading in this way, he finds words that have a meaning, he will not doubt that he has discovered the true meaning of this cipher in this way, even though it could very well be that the person who wrote it meant something quite different, giving a different meaning to each letter. . . ."[17] The operation of encoding, which is articulated on signifiers, produces the meaning, which is thus not defined by something deposited in the text, by an "intention," or by an activity on the part of the author.

What is then the origin of the Great Wall of China that circumscribes a "proper" in the text, isolates its semantic autonomy from everything else, and makes it the secret order of a "work?" Who builds this barrier constituting the text as a sort of island that no reader can ever reach? This fiction condemns consumers to subjection because they are always going to be guilty of infidelity or ignorance when confronted by the mute "riches" of the treasury thus set aside. The fiction of the "treasury" hidden in the work, a sort of strong-box full of meaning, is obviously not based on the productivity of the reader, but on the *social institution* that overdetermines his relation with the text.[18] Reading is as it were overprinted by a relationship of forces (between teachers and pupils, or between producers and consumers) whose instrument it becomes. The use made of the book by privileged readers constitutes it as a secret of which they are the "true" interpreters. It interposes a frontier between the text and its readers that can be crossed only if one has a passport delivered by these official interpreters, who transform their own reading (which is *also* a legitimate one) into an orthodox "literality" that makes other (equally legitimate) readings either heretical (not "in conformity" with the meaning of the text) or insignificant (to be forgotten). From this point of view, "literal" meaning is the index and the result of a social power, that of an elite. By its very nature available to a plural reading, the text becomes a cultural weapon, a private hunting reserve, the pretext for a law that legitimizes as "literal" the interpretation given by *socially* authorized professionals and intellectuals (*clercs*).

Moreover, if the reader's expression of his freedom through the text is tolerated among intellectuals (*clercs*) (only someone like Barthes can take this liberty), it is on the other hand denied students (who are scornfully driven or cleverly coaxed back to the meaning "accepted" by their teachers) or the public (who are carefully told "what is to be thought" and whose inventions are considered negligible and quickly silenced).

It is thus social hierarchization that conceals the reality of the practice of reading or makes it unrecognizable. Formerly, the Church, which instituted a social division between its intellectual clerks and the "faithful," ensured the Scriptures the status of a "Letter" that was supposed to be independent of its readers and, in fact, possessed by its exegetes: the autonomy of the text was the reproduction of sociocultural relationships within the institution whose officials determined what parts of it should be read. When the institution began to weaken, the reciprocity between the text and its readers (which the institution hid) appeared, as if by withdrawing the Church had opened to view the indefinite plurality of the "writings" produced by readings. The creativity of the reader grows as the institution that controlled it declines. This process, visible from the Reformation onward, already disturbed the pastors of the seventeenth century. Today, it is the socio-political mechanisms of the schools, the press, or television that isolate the text controlled by the teacher or the producer from its readers. But behind the theatrical décor of this new orthodoxy is hidden (as in earlier ages)[19] the silent, transgressive, ironic or poetic activity of readers (or television viewers) who maintain their reserve in private and without the knowledge of the "masters."

Reading is thus situated at the point where *social* stratification (class relationships) and *poetic* operations (the practitioner's constructions of a text) intersect: a social hierarchization seeks to make the reader conform to the "information" distributed by an elite (or semi-elite); reading operations manipulate the reader by insinuating their inventiveness into the cracks in a cultural orthodoxy. One of these two stories conceals what is not in conformity with the "masters" and makes it invisible to them; the other disseminates it in the networks of private life. They thus both collaborate in making reading into an unknown out of which emerge, on the one hand, only the experience of the *literate* readers (theatricalized and dominating), and on the other, rare and partial, like bubbles rising from the depths of the water, the indices of a *common* poetics.

An "exercise in ubiquity," that "impertinent absence"

The autonomy of the reader depends on a transformation of the social relationships that overdetermine his relation to texts. This transformation is a necessary task. This revolution would be no more than another totalitarianism on the part of an elite claiming for itself the right to conceal different modes of conduct and substituting a new normative education for the previous one, were it not that we can count on the *fact* that there *already* exists, though it is surreptitious or even repressed, an experience other than that of passivity. A politics of reading must thus be articulated on an analysis that, describing practices that have long been in effect, makes them politicizable. Even pointing out a few aspects of the operation of reading will already indicate how it eludes the law of information.

"I read and I daydream. . . . My reading is thus a sort of impertinent absence. Is reading an exercise in ubiquity?"[20] An initial, indeed initiatory, experience: to read is to be elsewhere, where *they* are not, in another world;[21] it is to constitute a secret scene, a place one can enter and leave when one wishes; to create dark corners into which no one can see within an existence subjected to technocratic transparency and that implacable light that, in Genet's work, materializes the hell of social alienation. Marguerite Duras has noted: "Perhaps one always reads in the dark. . . . Reading depends on the obscurity of the night. Even if one reads in broad daylight, outside, darkness gathers around the book."[22]

The reader produces gardens that miniaturize and collate a world, like a Robinson Crusoe discovering an island; but he, too, is "possessed" by his own fooling and jesting that introduces plurality and difference into the written system of a society and a text. He is thus a novelist. He deterritorializes himself, oscillating in a nowhere between what he invents and what changes him. Sometimes, in fact, like a hunter in the forest, he spots the written quarry, follows a trail, laughs, plays tricks, or else like a gambler, lets himself be taken in by it. Sometimes he loses the fictive securities of reality when he reads: his escapades exile him from the assurances that give the self its location on the social checkerboard. *Who* reads, in fact? Is it I, or some part of me? "It isn't *I* as a truth, but I as uncertainty about myself, reading these texts that lead to perdition. The more I read them, the less I understand them, and everything is going from bad to worse."[23]

This is a common experience, if one believes testimony that cannot be quantified or quoted, and not only that of "learned" readers. This experience is shared by the readers of *True Romances*, *Farm Journal* and *The Butcher and Grocery Clerk's Journal*, no matter how popularized or technical the spaces traversed by the Amazon or Ulysses of everyday life.

Far from being writers—founders of their own place, heirs of the peasants of earlier ages now working on the soil of language, diggers of wells and builders of houses—readers are travellers; they move across lands belonging to someone else, like nomads poaching their way across fields they did not write, despoiling the wealth of Egypt to enjoy it themselves. Writing accumulates, stocks up, resists time by the establishment of a place and multiplies its production through the expansionism of reproduction. Reading takes no measures against the erosion of time (one forgets oneself *and* also forgets), it does not keep what it acquires, or it does so poorly, and each of the places through which it passes is a repetition of the lost paradise.

Indeed, reading has no place: Barthes reads Proust in Stendhal's text;[24] the television viewer reads the passing away of his childhood in the news reports. One viewer says about the program she saw the previous evening: "It was stupid and yet I sat there all the same." What place captivated her, which was and yet was not that of the image seen? It is the same with the reader: his place is not *here* or *there*, one or the other, but neither the one nor the other, simultaneously inside and outside, dissolving both by mixing them together, associating texts like funerary statues that he awakens and hosts, but never owns. In that way, he also escapes from the law of each text in particular, and from that of the social milieu.

Spaces for games and tricks

In order to characterize this activity of reading, one can resort to several models. It can be considered as a form of the *bricolage* Lévi-Strauss analyzes as a feature of "the savage mind," that is, an arrangement made with "the materials at hand," a production "that has no relationship to a project," and which readjusts "the residues of previous construction and destruction."[25] But unlike Lévi-Strauss's "mythological universes," if this production also arranges events, it does not compose a unified set: it is another kind of "mythology" dispersed in time, a sequence of temporal fragments not joined together but disseminated through repetitions and different modes of enjoyment, in memories and successive knowledges.

Another model: the subtle art whose theory was elaborated by medieval poets and romancers who insinuate innovation into the text itself, into the terms of a tradition. Highly refined procedures allow countless differences to filter into the authorized writing that serves them as a framework, but whose law does not determine their operation. These poetic ruses, which are not linked to the creation of a proper (written) place of their own, are maintained over the centuries right up to contemporary reading, and the latter is just as agile in practicing diversions and metaphorizations that sometimes are hardly even indicated by a "pooh!" interjected by the reader.

The studies carried out in Bochum elaborating a *Rezeptionsästhetik* (an esthetics of reception) and a *Handlungstheorie* (a theory of action) also provide different models based on the relations between textual tactics and the "expectations" and successive hypotheses of the receiver who considers a drama or a novel as a premeditated action.[26] This play of textual productions in relation to what the reader's expectations make him produce in the course of his progress through the story is presented, to be sure, with a weighty conceptual apparatus; but it introduces dances between readers and texts in a place where, on a depressing stage, an orthodox doctrine had erected the statue of "the work" surrounded by consumers who were either conformers or ignorant people.

Through these investigations and many others, we are directed toward a reading no longer characterized merely by an "impertinent absence," but by advances and retreats, tactics and games played with the text. This process comes and goes, alternately captivated (but by what? what is it which arises both in the reader and in the text?), playful, protesting, fugitive.

We should try to rediscover the movements of this reading within the body itself, which seems to stay docile and silent but mines the reading in its own way: from the nooks of all sorts of "reading rooms" (including lavatories) emerge subconscious gestures, grumblings, tics, stretchings, rustlings, unexpected noises, in short a wild orchestration of the body.[27] But elsewhere, at its most elementary level, reading has become, over the past three centuries, a visual poem. It is no longer accompanied, as it used to be, by the murmur of a vocal articulation nor by the movement of a muscular manducation. To read without uttering the words aloud or at least mumbling them is a "modern" experience, unknown for millennia. In earlier times, the reader interiorized the text; he made his voice the body of the other; he was its actor. Today, the text no longer imposes its own rhythm on the subject, it no longer manifests itself through the reader's voice. This withdrawal of the body, which is the condition of its autonomy, is a distancing of the text. It is the reader's *habeas corpus.*

Because the body withdraws itself from the text in order henceforth to come into contact with it only through the mobility of the eye,[28] the geographical configuration of the text organizes the activity of the reader less and less. Reading frees itself from the soil that determined it. It detaches itself from that soil. The autonomy of the eye suspends the body's complicities with the text; it unmoors it from the scriptural place; it makes the written text an ob-ject and it increases the reader's possibilities of moving about. One index of this: the methods of speed reading.[29] Just as the airplane makes possible a growing independence with respect to the constraints imposed by geographical organization, the techniques of speed reading obtain, through the rarefaction of the eye's stopping points, an acceleration of its movements across the page, an autonomy in relation to the determinations of the text and a multiplication of the spaces covered. Emancipated from places, the reading body is freer in its movements. It thus transcribes in its attitudes every subject's ability to convert the text through reading and to "run it" the way one runs traffic lights.

In justifying the reader's impertinence, I have neglected many aspects. Barthes distinguished three types of reading: the one that stops at the pleasure afforded by words, the one that rushes on to the end and "faints with expectation," and the one that cultivates the desire to write:[30] erotic, hunting, and initiatory modes of reading. There are others, in dreams, battle, autodidacticism, etc., that we cannot consider here. In any event, the reader's increased autonomy does not project him, for the media extend their power over his imagination, that is, over everything he lets emerge from himself into the nets of the text—his fears, his dreams, his fantasized and lacking authorities. This is what the powers work on that make out of "facts" and "figures" a rhetoric whose target is precisely this surrendered intimacy.

But whereas the scientific apparatus (ours) is led to share the illusion of the powers it necessarily supports, that is, to assume that the masses are transformed by the conquests and victories of expansionist production, it is always good to remind ourselves that we mustn't take people for fools.

Part V
Ways of Believing

Chapter XIII Believing and Making People Believe

> I like the word *believe*. In general,
> when one says "I know," one doesn't
> know, one believes.
>
> Marcel Duchamp, *Duchamp du signe*
> (Paris, Flammarion, 1975, p. 185)

JEWS, Léon Poliakov once said, are French people who, instead of no longer going to church, no longer go to synagogue. In the comic tradition of the *Hagadah*, this joke referred to past beliefs that no longer organize practices. Political convictions seem today to be following the same path. One is a socialist because one *used to be* one, no longer going to demonstrations, attending meetings, sending in one's dues, in short, without paying. More reverential than identifying, membership is marked only by what is called a *voice*, (*voix*: a voice, a vote) this vestige of speech, one vote per year. Living off a semblance of "belief," the party carefully collects the relics of former convictions and, given this fiction of legitimacy, succeeds quite well in managing its affairs. It has only to multiply the citation of these phantom witnesses by surveys and statistics, to re-cite their litany.

A rather simple technique keeps the pretense of this belief going. All that is required is that the surveys ask not about what directly attaches its "members" to the party, but about what does not attract them elsewhere—not about the energy of convictions, but their inertia: "If it is false that you believe in something else, then it must be true that you are still on our side." The results of the operation thus count (on) vestiges of

177

membership. They bet on the *erosion* itself of every conviction, since these vestiges indicate both the *ebbing-away* of what those questioned formerly believed and the *absence* of a stronger credibility that draws them elsewhere: "voices" do not go away; they remain there; they lie inertly where they were, but nevertheless make up the same total. The toting up becomes a tale. This fiction might very well be an appendix to Borges's *Esse est percipi.*[1] It is the fable of a slippage which figures cannot register but which affects beliefs nonetheless.

As a first approximation, I define "belief" not as the object of believing (a dogma, a program, etc.) but as the subject's investment in a proposition, the *act* of saying it and considering it as true[2]—in other words, a "modality" of the assertion and not its content.[3] The capacity for believing seems to be receding everywhere in the field of politics. That capacity once supported the functioning of "authority." Since Hobbes, political philosophy, especially in the English tradition, has considered this articulation as fundamental.[4] Through this link, politics made its relationship of difference and continuity with religion explicit. But the will to "make people believe" ("*faire-croire*") that gives life to institutions, provided in both cases a counterpart for a search for love and/or identity.[5] It is thus important to investigate the ups and downs of believing in our societies and the practices that have their source in these displacements.

The devaluation of beliefs

For a long time people assumed that the reserves of belief were limitless. All one had to do was to create islands of rationality in the ocean of credulity, isolate and secure the fragile conquests made by critical thinking. The rest, considered inexhaustible, was supposed to be transportable toward other objects and other ends, just as waterfalls are harnessed by hydroelectric plants. People tried to "capture" this force by moving it from one place to another: from the so-called pagan societies they led it toward the Christianity it was supposed to support; later it was diverted from the Churches in the direction of political monarchy; and later still from a traditional religiousness to the institutions of the Republic, the national organization of schools and its educational ideology, or various forms of socialism. These "conversions" consisted in capturing the energy of belief by moving it about. What was not transportable, or not yet transported, into the new areas of progress appeared as "superstition";

what could be used by the reigning order was accorded the status of a "conviction." The fund was so rich that in exploiting it people forgot the necessity of analyzing it. Campaigns and crusades consisted in conveying and investing the energy of believing in good places and on good objects (to be believed).

Little by little, belief became polluted, like the air and the water. The motive energy, always resistant but manipulable, finally begins to run out. People notice at the same time that no one knows what it is. It is strange paradox that so many polemics and meditations on both ideological content and the institutional frameworks provided for it have not been (except in English philosophy, from Hume to Wittgenstein, H. H. Price, Hintikka or Quine) accompanied by a clarification of the nature of the act of believing. Today, it is no longer enough to manipulate, transport, and refine belief; its composition must be analyzed because people want to produce it artificially; commercial and political marketing studies are still making partial efforts in this direction.[6] There are now too many things to believe and not enough credibility to go around.

An inversion is produced. The old powers cleverly managed their "authority" and thus compensated for the inadequacy of their technical or administrative apparatus: they were systems of clienteles, allegiances, "legitimacies," etc. They sought, however, to make themselves more independent of the fluctuations of these fidelities through rationalization, the control and organization of space. As the result of this labor, the powers in our developed societies have at their disposal rather subtle and closely-knit procedures for the control of all social networks: these are the administrative and "panoptic" systems of the police, the schools, health services, security, etc.[7] But they are slowly losing all credibility. They have more power and less authority.

Technicians are often not concerned with this problem, since they are preoccupied with extending and making more complex the mechanisms for maintenance and control. An illusory confidence. The sophistication of the discipline does not compensate for the fact that subjects no longer invest and commit themselves in believing. In businesses, the demobilization of workers is growing faster than the surveillance network of which it is the target, pretext, and effect. Wasting of products, diversion of time, "*la perruque*," turn-over or inactivity of employees, etc., undermine from within a system which, as in the Toyota factories, tends to become a form of imprisonment in order to prevent any sort of escape.[8] In administrations, offices, and even in political and religious groups a cancerous growth of the apparatus is the consequence of the evaporation of convictions, and this cancer becomes in turn the cause of a new evaporation of believing. Looking out for one's own interests is no substitute for belief.[9]

Believing is being exhausted. Or at least it takes refuge in the areas of the media and leisure activities. It goes on vacation; but even then it does not cease to be an object captured and processed by advertising, commerce, and fashion. In order to bring back some of these beliefs that are retreating and disappearing, businesses have begun to fabricate their own simulacra of credibility. Shell oil produces the Credo of "values" that "inspire" its top administrators and that its managers and employees must adopt as well. The same sort of thing is found in countless other businesses, even if they are slow in getting in motion and still count on the fictive capital of an earlier family, house, or regional "spirit."

Where is the material to be found which can be used to inject credibility into these mechanisms? There are two traditional sources, the one political, and the other religious: in the first, the mobility or ebbing away of conviction among militants is compensated for by an over-development of administrative institutions and managerial staff; in the second, on the contrary, institutions that are disintegrating or closing in on themselves allow the beliefs that they long promoted, maintained, and controlled be scattered in every direction.

An archeology: the transits of believing

The relations between these two funds of credibility are strange and ancient.

1. *Religiousness* seems easier to exploit. Marketing agencies avidly make use of the remains of beliefs that were formerly violently opposed as superstitions. Advertising is becoming evangelical. Many managers in the economic and social sphere are disturbed by the slow breaking up of the Churches in which lie the remains of "values" which the managers want to recuperate and make use of by rebaptizing them as "up-to-date." Before these beliefs go down with the ships that carried them, they are hurriedly taken off and put in businesses and administrations. The people who use these relics no longer believe in them. They nevertheless form, along with all sorts of "fundamentalists," ideological and financial associations in order to refit these shipwrecks of history and

make Churches museums of beliefs without believers, put there in reserve so that they can be exploited by laissez-faire capitalism.

This recuperation functions on the basis of two tactical hypotheses that are probably erroneous. The first postulates that belief remains attached to its objects and that by preserving the latter one also preserves the former. In reality (as both history and semiotics demonstrate), the investment of believing passes from one myth to another, from one ideology to another, or from statement to statement.[10] Thus belief withdraws from a myth and leaves it almost intact, but without any role, transformed into a document.[11] In the course of these transitions, a conviction that is still attached to the areas it is gradually abandoning is not strong enough to combat the movements that would transport it elsewhere. There is no equivalence between the objects that still hang on to it and those that mobilize it somewhere else.

The other tactical hypothesis does suppose that belief still remains tied to its first objects, but on the contrary that it can be artificially detached from them; that its escape into the stories purveyed by the media, the "paradises" of leisure activities, or the various retreats of intimacy or travel, etc., could be halted or diverted; that one could thus bring it back into the fold, into the disciplinary order, that it has left behind. But conviction cannot be so easily planted in the fields from which it is disappearing. It cannot be so easily directed back to administrations or businesses that have become "incredible." The liturgies that claim to "provide motivation" or "set great store by" workplaces do not transform their functioning. Therefore they do not produce believers. The public is not so credulous. It is amused by these celebrations and simulacra. But it is not taken in by them.

2. *Political* organizations have slowly substituted themselves for the Churches as the places of believing practices, but for this very reason, they seem to have been haunted by the return of a very ancient (pre-Christian) and very "pagan" alliance between power and religion. It is as though now that religion has ceased to be an autonomous power (the "power of religion," people used to say), politics has once again become religious. Christianity had opened a gap in the interconnection of the visible objects of belief (the political authorities) and its invisible objects (the gods, spirits, etc.). But it maintained that distinction only by constituting a clerical, dogmatic, and sacramental power in the place left open by the temporary deterioration of the political order at the end of antiquity. It was in the eleventh and twelfth centuries that, under the

sign of "The Peace of God," ecclesiastical powers imposed their "order" on civil powers in conflict.[12] The following centuries show the deterioration of that order to the advantage of secular sovereigns. In the seventeenth century, the Churches receive their models and their rights from the monarchies, even if they still represent a "religiousness" that legitimizes the temporal powers and that temporal powers gradually transfer to their own account. With the breakdown of ecclesiastical power over the past three centuries, beliefs have flowed back toward the political, but without bringing with them the divine or celestial values that the Churches had set aside, regulated, and taken up.

This complex ebb and flow, which has made the transition from the political to Christian religiousness and from the latter to a new politics[13] has had as its effect an individualization of beliefs (the common frame of reference being fragmented into social "opinions" or individual "convictions") and of movements among beliefs across an increasingly diversified network of possible objects. The idea of democracy corresponded to the will to manage this multiplication of convictions which had replaced the faith that had founded an order. What is striking is that by breaking up the ancient system, that is, the religious credibility of the political order, Christianity finally compromised the believability of the religiousness that it detached from the political; thus it contributed to the discrediting of what it had appropriated to itself in order to make itself autonomous, and made possible the ebbing away of these beliefs in the direction of political authorities henceforth deprived of (or liberated from?) the spiritual authorities that had formerly been a relativizing as well as a legitimizing principle. The return of a "pagan" repressed was thus affected by this decline of the "spiritual." The erosion of Christianity left an indelible mark on the modern age: the "incarnation" or historicization that in the eighteenth century Rousseau already calls a "civil religion."[14] To the pagan State, which "made no distinction between its gods and its laws," Rousseau opposes a "religion" of the citizen, "whose articles of faith it is for the sovereign to determine." "If anyone, after having publicly recognized these very dogmas, conducts himself as if he did not believe in them, let him be put to death." This civil religion of the *citizen* was distinguished from a spiritual religion of *man*, the individual, asocial, and universal religion of *The Creed of a Priest of Savoy*. This prophetic view, far less incoherent than it has been said to be, already articulates the development of a "civil" and political dogmatics on the radicalization of an individual conscience *free from* any dogma and deprived of any powers. Since then, sociological analysis has verified the accuracy of this foresight.[15]

From the time of the Enlightenment on, belief is reinvested in the political system alone, in proportion as the "spiritual powers" which had guaranteed the civil powers in Antiquity and had entered into competition with them in the Christian West lost their previous positions, and became scattered or miniaturized.

From "spiritual" power to leftist opposition

The distinction—today archeological—between the temporal and the spiritual as two jurisdictions, nevertheless remains structurally inscribed in French society, but it is now *within* the political system. The place that was formerly occupied by the Church or Churches vis-à-vis the established powers remains recognizable, over the past two centuries, in the functioning of the opposition known as leftist. In political life as well, a mutation of ideological content can leave a social "form" intact.[16] One index of these transitions that displace beliefs but preserve the same structural schema, would be the history of Jansenism: a prophetic opposition (the Port-Royal of the seventeenth century) is transformed into the political opposition of an "enlightened" and parliamentary milieu in the eighteenth century. There one can already see that an intelligentsia of intellectuals (*clercs*) or notables replaces the opposition that a "spiritual" power supported against (or on the margins of) political or "civil" authorities.

Whatever may have been the case in the past, we can see, if we leave aside excessively facile (and apolitical) remarks about the psychosociological traits characteristic of all militancy,[17] that there is vis-à-vis the established order, a relationship between the Churches that defended an *other world* and the parties of the left which, since the nineteenth century, have promoted a *different future*. In both cases, similar functional characteristics can be discerned: ideology and doctrine have an importance that is not given them by those in power; the project of another society results in discourse (reformist, revolutionary, socialist, etc.) being given the primary role over against the fatality or normality of facts; legitimization by means of ethical values, by a theoretical truth, or by appealing to a roll call of martyrs has to compensate for the legitimacy that can be claimed by every power through the mere fact of its existence; the techniques of "making people believe" play a more decisive role when it is a matter of something that does not yet exist;[18] intransigencies and doctrinal vetoes are thus stronger than in places where the established power permits and often requires compromises; and finally, by an apparently contradictory logic, every reformist power is tempted to acquire political advantages, to transform itself into an ecclesiastical administration in order to support its project, to thus lose its primitive "purity" or change it into a mere decoration of the apparatus, and to transform its militants into officials or conquerors.

This analogy has structural grounds; they do not directly involve a psychology of militancy or a critical sociology of ideologies; but rather they involve first of all the logic of a "place" that produces and reproduces, as its effects, militant mobilizations, tactics of "making people believe," and ecclesiastical institutions in a relationship of distance, competition, and future transformations with respect to the established powers.

The transition from various forms of Christianity to various forms of socialism through the mediation of "heresies" or sects has been the object of many studies,[19] which themselves operate the very passages they analyze. But if these transitions transport vestiges of religious belief in the direction of new political formations, one cannot draw the conclusion that these vestiges of abandoned beliefs make it legitimate to see anything religious in these movements. One is forced to draw that conclusion only if one makes the unjustified assumption that the objects *believed* are the same as the act of *believing*, and that, as a corollary, there is something religious about every group in which elements that *have been* religious are still working.

Another analytical model seems to be more in tune with the realities of history and anthropology: Churches, indeed religions themselves, would be not so much referential unities as social variants of the possible relations between the act of believing and the objects believed; they would be, on this view, particular historical configurations (and manipulations) of relationships linking the (formal) modalities of *believing* and knowing with the (quasi-lexical) series of available *contents*. Today, the acts of believing and knowing are distributed otherwise than in the religions of earlier times; believing no longer modalizes what is believed according to the same rules; in short, the objects to be believed or known, their mode of definition, their status and their inventory have been largely changed and renewed. Thus one cannot isolate and inscribe in a continuity two constellations of "beliefs" by merely noting that they have in common an act of believing, an element that is assumed to be invariable.

In order to analyze the relations between speaking and believing in the new, political and militant variant presented by leftist parties in a place still historically determined by the role earlier played by the Churches, the archeological perspective must be given up. We must locate the modes in which believing, knowing, and their contents reciprocally define each other today, and in that way try to grasp a few of the ways believing and making people believe function in the political formations in which, within this system, the tactics made possible by the exigencies of a position and the constraints of a history are deployed. This approach to the current situation can discern in it two mechanisms through which a body of dogma has always made itself believed: on the one hand, the claim to be *speaking in the name of a reality* which, assumed to be inaccessible, is the principle of both what is believed (a totalization) and the act of believing (something that is always unavailable, unverifiable, lacking); and on the other, the ability of a discourse authorized by a "reality" to distribute itself in the form of *elements that organize practices*, that is, of "articles of faith." These two traditional resources are found again today in the system that combines the narrativity of the media—an establishment of the real—with the discourse of products to be consumed—a distribution of this reality in the form of "articles" that are to be believed and bought. It is the first that needs to be stressed, the second being already quite well known.

The establishment of the real

The media transform the great silence of things into its opposite. Formerly constituting a secret, the real now talks constantly. News reports, information, statistics, and surveys are everywhere. No story has ever spoken so much or shown so much. Not even the ministers of the gods ever *made them talk* in such a continuous, detailed, and imperative way as the producers of revelations and rules do these days *in the name of* current reality. Narrations about what's-going-on constitute our orthodoxy. Debates about figures are our theological wars. The combatants no longer bear the arms of any offensive or defensive idea. They move forward camouflaged as facts, data, and events. They present themselves as messengers from a "reality." Their uniform takes on the color of the economic and social ground they move into. When they advance, the terrain itself seems to advance. But in fact they fabricate the terrain, simulate it, use it as a mask, accredit themselves by it, and thus create the scene of their law.

European anti-nuclear demonstrations, German or Italian terrorism, ghetto riots, Khomeini, Carter, etc.: these fragments of history are organized into articles of doctrine. "Be quiet," says the TV anchorman or the political representative, "These are the facts. Here are the data, the circumstances, etc. Therefore you must. . . ." Narrated reality constantly tells us what must be believed and what must be done. What can you oppose to the facts? You can only give in, and obey what they "signify," like an oracle, like the oracle of Delphi.[20] The fabrication of simulacra thus provides the means of producing believers and hence people practicing their faiths. This establishment of the real is the most visible form of our contemporary dogmas. It is thus also the one most disputed among the parties.

This institution of the real no longer has its own proper place, neither seat nor *ex cathedra* authority. An anonymous code, information innervates and saturates the body politic. From morning to night, narrations constantly haunt streets and buildings. They articulate our existences by teaching us what they must be. They "cover the event," that is to say, they *make* our legends (*legenda*, what is to be read and said) out of it. Captured by the radio (the voice is the law) as soon as he awakens, the listener walks all day long through the forest of narrativities from journalism, advertising, and television, narrativities that still find time, as he is getting ready for bed, to slip a few final messages under the portals of sleep. Even more than the God told about by the theologians of earlier days, these stories have a providential and predestining function: they organize in advance our work, our celebrations, and even our dreams. Social life multiplies the gestures and modes of behavior *(im)printed* by narrative models; it ceasely reproduces and accumulates "copies" of stories. Our society has become a recited society, in three senses: it is defined by *stories* (*récits*, the fables constituted by our advertising and informational media), by *citations* of stories, and by the interminable *recitation* of stories.

These narrations have the twofold and strange power of transforming seeing into believing, and of fabricating realities out of appearances. A double reversal. On the one hand, the modern age, which first arose out of a methodic effort of observation and accuracy that struggled against credulity and based itself on a contract between the seen and the real, now transforms this relation and offers to *sight* precisely what must be *believed.* Fiction defines the field, the status, and the objects of vision. The media, advertising, and political representation all function in this way.

To be sure, there was already fiction in earlier ages, but it was in circumscribed, esthetic, and theatrical places: it pointed to itself (for example, by means of perspective, an art of illusion); it provided, along with the rules of its game and the conditions of its production, its own metalanguage.[21] It spoke only in the name of language. It narrativized a symbolic order, leaving the truth of things in suspension and virtually secret. Today, fiction claims to make the real present, to speak in the name of the facts and thus to cause the semblance it produces to be taken as a referential reality. Hence those to whom these legends are directed (and who pay for them) are not obliged to believe what they don't see (a traditional position), but rather to believe what they see (a contemporary position).

This reversal of the terrain on which beliefs develop results from a mutation in the paradigms of knowledge: the ancient postulate of the invisibility of the real has been replaced by the postulation of its visibility. The modern socio-cultural scene refers to a "myth." This scene defines the social referent by its visibility (and thus by its scientific or political representativeness); it articulates on this new postulate (the belief that the real is visible) the possibility of our knowledge, observations, proofs, and practices. On this new stage, an indefinitely extensible field of optical investigations and of a scopic drive, the strange collusion between believing and the question of the real still remains. But now it is a question of what is *seen, observed,* or *shown.* The contemporary "simulacrum"[22] is in short the latest localization of belief in vision, the identification of the *seen* with what is to be *believed*—once the hypothesis has been given up that claimed that the waters of an invisible ocean (the Real) came back to haunt the shores of the visible and to make them the results, decodable signs or deceptive reflections, of its presence. The simulacrum is what the relationship of the visible to the real becomes when the assumption crumbles that an invisible immensity of Being (or of beings) lies hidden behind appearances.

The recited society

Vis-à-vis the stories of images, which are now no more than "fictions," visible and legible productions, the spectator-observer *knows* that they are merely "semblances," the results of manipulations—"*I know perfectly well that it's so much hogwash"*—*but all the same* he assumes that these simulations have the status of the real:[23] a belief survives the refutation that everything we know about their fabrication makes available to him. As a television viewer put it, "If it were false, people would have the information." He thus postulated *other* social places that can guarantee the validity of what he knows to be fictive, and that postulation permitted him to believe in it "all the same." It is as if belief could no longer be expressed in direct convictions, but only through the detour of what others are thought to believe. Belief no longer rests on an invisible alterity hidden behind signs, but on what other groups, other fields, or other disciplines are supposed to be. The "real" is what, in a given place, reference to another place makes people believe in. The same is true even in scientific disciplines. For example, the relationships between data processing and history function on the basis of an astonishing quid pro quo: from computerizing, historians seek an accreditation by a "scientific" power that can give a technical and real weight to their discourse; from history, computer specialists seek a validation of their work by the "reality" provided by the "concreteness" of historical erudition. Each expects from the other a guarantee that will give weight to his own simulacrum.[24]

And the same is true in politics. Each party derives its credibility from what it believes and makes others believe about its referent (the revolutionary "wonders" achieved in the East?) or about its adversary (the vices and misfortunes of the bad guys on the other side). Every political discourse gains effects of reality from what it assumes, and makes others assume, regarding the economic analysis that supports it (an analysis that is itself validated by this reference to the political). Within each party, the professional discourses of the "leaders" stand up because of the credulity that they assume on the part of simple militants or on that of voters; reciprocally, the "I know perfectly well that it's so much hogwash" of many voters has as its counterpoint their assumption that the managers of the political apparatus are moved by convictions and knowledge. Belief thus functions on the basis of the reality-value that one assumes "all the same" in the other, even when one "knows perfectly well," all too well, to what extent "It's a pile of crap" in the place where one is oneself.

Citation thus appears to be the ultimate weapon for making people believe. Because it plays on what the other is assumed to believe, it is the means by which the "real" is instituted. To cite the other on their behalf is hence to make credible the simulacra produced in a particular place. Opinion "surveys" have become the most elementary and passive procedure of this citation. The perpetual self-citation—the multiplication of surveys—is the fiction by which the country is led to believe what it *is*. Every citizen assumes about all the others what, without believing it himself, he learns about the belief of others. Replacing doctrines that have become unbelievable, citation allows the technocratic mechanisms to make themselves credible for each individual *in the name of the others*. To cite is thus to give reality to the simulacrum produced by a power, by making people believe that others believe in it, but without providing any believable object. But it is also to designate the "anarchists" or "deviants" (to cite them before the tribunal of public opinion); it is to condemn to the aggressivity of the public those who, asserting through their acts that they do not believe in it, demolish the fictive "reality" that each individual can preserve "all the same" only by reference to the convictions of others.

To the extent that this instrument that "creates opinion" is manipulable by those that have it at their disposition, it is legitimate to inquire into the opportunities it offers for changing "belief" into "mistrust," into "suspicion," and indeed into denunciation, as well as into the opportunity for citizens to manipulate politically what serves as a circular and objectless credibility for political life itself.

Chapter XIV   The Unnamable

THE STAFF of a hospital withdraws from the dying man: "the syndrome of withdrawal on the part of doctors and nurses."[1] This distancing is accompanied by orders in a vocabulary that treats the patient as though he were already dead: "He needs to *rest.* . . . Let him *sleep.*" It is *necessary* that the dying man remain *calm* and *rest.* Beyond the care and the sedatives required by the sick man, this order appeals to the staff's inability to *bear* the uttering of anguish, despair, or pain: it must not be *said.*

The dying are outcasts because they are deviants in an institution organized by and for the conservation of life. An "anticipated mourning," a phenomenon of institutional rejection, puts them away in advance in "the dead man's room"; it surrounds them with silence or, worse yet, with lies that protect the living against the voice that would break out of this enclosure to cry: "I am going to die." This cry would produce an embarrassingly graceless dying. The lie ("Of course not; you're going to get better") is a way of assuring that communication will not occur.

If the forbidden word were to be pronounced, it would betray the struggle that mobilizes the hospital staff and that, assuming that *to care for* means *to cure,* does not want to recognize failure; and that would be blasphemy.

An unthinkable practice

More than that, as a dead man on reprieve, the dying man *falls* outside the *thinkable,* which is identified with what one can *do.* In leaving the field circumscribed by the possibilities of treatment, it enters a region of meaninglessness. Nothing can be said in a place where nothing more can be done. Along with the lazy man, and more than he, the dying man is the immoral man: the former, a subject that does not work; the latter, an object that no longer even makes itself available to be worked on by others; both are intolerable in a society in which the disappearance of

subjects is everywhere compensated for and camouflaged by the multiplication of the tasks to be performed. It took Nazism, which was logical
in its technocratic totalitarianism, to treat the dead and make available
to the procedures of exploitation the limit that usually opposes them:
the inert, the cadaver.

In this combination between subjects without action and operations
without author, between the anguish of individuals and the administration of practices, the dying man raises once again the question of the
subject at the extreme frontier of inaction, at the very point where it is
the most impertinent and the least bearable. In our society, the absence
of work is non-sense; it is necessary to eliminate it in order for the
discourse that tirelessly articulates tasks and constructs the Occidental
story of "There's always something to do" to continue. The dying man is
the lapse of this discourse. He is, and can only be, ob-scene. And hence
censured, deprived of language, wrapped up in a shroud of silence: the
unnamable.

The family has nothing to say about it either. The sick man is taken
away by the institution that takes charge not of the individual, but of his
illness, an isolated object transformed or eliminated by technicians
devoted to the defense of health the way others are attached to the
defense of law and order or tidiness. Driven out of a society which, in
conformity with the utopias of earlier ages, cleans out of its streets and
houses everything that is parasitic on the rationality of work—waste
products, delinquency, infirmity, old age—the sick man must follow his
illness to the place where it is treated, in the specialized enterprises
where it is immediately transformed into a scientific and linguistic object
foreign to everyday life and language. He is set aside in one of the
technical and secret zones (hospitals, prisons, refuse dumps) which relieve
the living of everything that might hinder the chain of production and
consumption, and which, in the darkness where no one wants to pene-
trate, repair and select what can be sent back up to the surface of
progress. Captured at that point, he becomes an unknown to his own
people. He no longer lives in their homes or in their speech. Perhaps the
exile will return from the foreign land whose language his people do not
know, a land which can only be forgotten. If he does not return, he will
remain a distant, non-signifiable object of a labor and failure impossible
to trace out in space and in the familiar language.

Considered on the one hand as a failure or a provisional halt in the
medical struggle, and on the other, removed from common experience

and thus arriving at the limit of scientific power and beyond familiar practices, death is an elsewhere. In a society that officially recognizes "rest" only in the forms of inertia or waste, death is given over, for example, to religious languages that are no longer current, returned to rites that are now empty of the beliefs that once resided in them. It is stuck away in these antiquated spaces that are also "displaced" by scientific productivity, but that provide at least a few signs (now undecipherable) to spell out this object that has been deprived of any sense. An exemplary, national spectacle: the pomp that surrounded De Gaulle's death had long been considered "superstitious" by most of the notables that committed their dead leader to it. What they could not name, they entrusted to a language they couldn't believe in. In religious, diabolical, magical or fantastic repertoires, those marginalized vocabularies, what is secretly laid to rest or what can re-emerge in disguise is the death that has become unthinkable and unnamable.[2]

Saying and believing

When it is repressed, death returns in an exotic language (that of a past, of ancient religions or distant traditions); it has to be invoked in foreign dialects; it is as difficult to speak about it in one's own language as it is for someone to die "at home": these are the marks that define an excluded element, one that can return only in disguise. It is a paradoxical symptom of this death without words that a whole literature designates the point where relations with the meaningless are focused. Texts proliferate around this wound on reason. Once again, it supports itself on what cannot be mentioned. Death is the problem of the subject.

One index of this: analytical cures show to what extent experience is articulated on the position of the subject with respect to his death. The melancholic says: "I can't die;[3] the obsessive says: "I cannot not die" ("Above all," says Freud, "the obsessed need the possibility of dying in order to resolve their conflicts").[4] But before appearing in the field of psychoanalytic exchange, this position of the subject is connected with the Oedipal question: "Is it when I am no longer anything at all that I really become a man?". Jacques Lacan comments: "That is where the rest of the story begins: beyond the pleasure principle." But it is precisely there that a third silence is added to those of the institution concerned and of common language: the silence of the subject himself. The subject especially seeks to *say* death. Boris Vian:

> I don't want to kick off
> No sir, no way,
> before I've tasted
> the taste that tortures me
> the strongest taste of all.
> I don't want to kick off
> before I've tasted
> the savor of death.

The difference between kicking off (*crever*) on a trash heap—a haunting fear that underlies the struggle for life that is becoming general in the West—and dying (*mourir*) is a *speech* that articulates, on the collapse of possessions and representations, the question: "What does it mean to *be*?" An "idle" question. This is a speech that no longer says *anything*, that *has* nothing other than the loss out of which saying is formed. Between the machine that stops or kicks off, and the act of dying, there is the *possibility* of saying. The *possibility of dying* functions in this in-between space.

Stopped at the threshold of the difference between kicking off and dying, the dying person is prevented from saying this nothing that he is becoming, unable to do the act that would only produce his question. It would even be sufficient for him to have as his place the one he would receive in the language of the other, at this moment when he no longer has property or papers to present. To be simply *called*: "Lazarus!"—and traced by his proper name in the language of another desire, without anything proper to him, in his death as at his birth, gives him the right to it: this would be a kind of communication beyond mere exchange. In it the necessary connection of desire with what it cannot have, with a loss, could be acknowledged. To be called in that way would be to "symbolize" death, to find words (that convey no informative content) for it, to open within the language of interlocution a resurrection that does not restore to life.

But this place is refused the isolated person. The loss of his powers and social roles also prevents him from having what this loss seemed to allow: access to the interpersonal relation whose lexicon tells only: "I miss you."

There is nevertheless a first and last coincidence of dying, believing, and speaking. In fact, all through my life, I can ultimately only *believe* in my death, if "believing" designates a relation to *the other* that precedes me and is constantly occurring. There is nothing so "other" as my death, the index of all alterity. But there is also nothing that makes clearer the place from which I can say my desire for the other; nothing that makes clearer my gratitude for being received—without having any guarantee or goods to offer—into the powerless language of my expectation of the other; nothing therefore defines more exactly than my death what *speaking* is.

Writing

The "last moment" is only the ultimate point in which the desire to say takes refuge, exacerbates and destroys itself. No doubt the part of death that takes the form of expectation has previously penetrated into social life, but it always has to mask its obscenity. Its message is seen in the faces that are slowly decaying, but they have only lies with which to say what they presage (be quiet, you stories of getting old told by my eyes, my wrinkles, and so many forms of dullness), and we are careful not to let them speak (don't tell us, faces, what we don't want to know).

The *immoral* secret of death is deposited in the protected caverns reserved for it by psychoanalysis and religion. It resides in the vast metaphors of astrology, necromancy, or sorcery, languages that are tolerated so long as they constitute areas of obscurantism from which societies of progress "distinguish" themselves. Thus the impossibility of saying goes much further back than the moment when the speaker's efforts are cancelled along with the speaker himself. It is inscribed in all the procedures that quarantine death or drive it beyond the limits of the city, outside of time, work, and language, in order to protect a place.

But in producing an image of the dying man, I proceed in the same way. I am participating in the illusion that localizes death elsewhere, in the hospital or in the last moments: I am transmogrifying it into an image of the other; by identifying this image with the dying person, I make it *the place where I am not*. Through the representation, I exorcise death, which is shut up next door, relegated to a moment that I assume is not mine. I protect my place. The dying person whom I speak about remains ob-scene if he is not myself.

The reversal begins in the very work of writing, whose representations are only its result and/or waste product. I ask myself what I am constructing, since "meaning" is hidden there in the gesture, in the act of writing. Why write, if not in the name of an impossible speech? At the beginning of writing, there is a loss. What cannot be said—an impossible adequation between presence and the sign—is the postulate of the labor that is constantly beginning anew and that has as its principle a nowhere of identity and a sacrifice of the thing. Joyce's injunction, "Write it, damn you, write it!," arises from a presence taken away from the sign.[5] Writing repeats this lack in each of its graphs, the relics of a walk through language. It spells out an absence that is its precondition and its goal. It proceeds by successive abandonments of occupied places, and it articulates itself on an exteriority that eludes it, on its addressee come from abroad, a visitor who is expected but never heard on the scriptural paths that the travels of a desire have traced on the page.

As a practice of the loss of speech, writing has no meaning except outside itself, in a different place, that of the reader, which it produces as its own necessity by moving toward this presence it cannot reach. It goes toward a speech that will never be given it and which, for that very reason, constructs the movement of being indefinitely linked to an untethered, ab-solute response, that of the other. From this loss writing is formed. It is the gesture of a dying man, a defection of possession (*avoir*) while crossing the field of a knowledge (*savoir*), a modest apprenticeship in "giving a sign."

In this way, the death that cannot be said can be written and find a language, even though, in this work of expenditure, the need constantly returns, the need to possess through the voice, to deny the limit imposed by the uncrossable space articulating two different presences, to be blinded by knowledge to the fragility that every place's relation with others establishes.

Therapeutic power and its double

We can distinguish from this "literary" writing that is constructed in relation to death the "scientific" system (which is also a scriptural system) that starts out from a break between life and death, and faces death as a defeat, a fall, or a threat. Since the seventeenth century, this division between life and death has been necessary in order to make possible ambitious scientific discourses capable of capitalizing progress without suffering from the lack of the other. But their mutation into institutions of power alone has allowed them to constitute themselves.

Thus the break that opposed to death a conquering labor and the will to occupy the immense empty space of the countryside in the eighteenth

century—an area of misery, the new land of the living dead—by means
of an economic and therapeutic administration, this break organized
knowledge in relationship to poverty and suffering. An institutionaliza-
tion of medical knowledge produced the great utopia of a *therapeutic
politics* embracing all the means of struggling against death's operations
within the social space, from schools to hospitals. Its general transformation into a power gave a "medical" appearance to an administrative
apparatus charged with *healing* and, still more, with organizing *order* as
a means of *prevention*.

This prophylactic campaign was supposed to caulk up all the cracks
through which the enemy slipped in. It inscribed the schools themselves
as a particular sector of a "medical police"; it invaded the realms of
private life in order to fill up, by means of prophylactic measures, all the
secret and intimate passageways that were available to illness; it established hygiene as a national problem in the struggle against biological
woes. This medical model of politics was simultaneously related to the
Occidental ambition to produce an indefinite *progress* of the *body* (in an
economy of challenge for which sports became the public stage) and to
the obsession with a secret and permanent degeneration (which compromised the biological capital on which the colonizing expansion of the
country was based).

Writing, a possibility of composing a space in conformity with one's
will, was articulated on *the body* as on a mobile, opaque, and fleeting
page.[6] From this articulation the book became the laboratory experi-
ment, in the field of an economic, demographic or pedagogical space.
The book is, in the scientific sense of the term, a "fiction" of the scriptible
body; it is a "scenario" constructed by a vision of the future that seeks to
make the body what a society can write. From that point on, one no
longer writes *on* the body. It is the body that must transform itself into
writing. This body-book, the relationship of life to what is written, has
gradually taken on, from demography to biology, a scientific form whose
postulate is in every case the struggle against aging considered sometimes
as an inevitable fate, sometimes as a set of manipulable factors. This
science is the body changed into a blank page on which a scriptural
operation can produce indefinitely the advancement of a will-to-do, a
progress.

But like writing paper, this body-support wears out. What is produced as a management of life, as a mastery or writing of the body
constantly bespeaks death at work. What escapes or returns into scientific discourse betrays the obsessive adversary it claims to exorcize. And

on all sides, a literature proliferates around political and therapeutic institutions. It brings this devil back to the surface and narrates the disturbing proximity of what has been exiled. From Nietzsche to Bataille, from Sade to Lacan, the "literature," which ever since the eighteenth century the establishment of "scientific" discourse has driven out of its "own" field and constituted as other, marks in language the return of the eliminated. Today, it is also the area of *fiction*. It acknowleges that part of knowledge of which knowledge does not speak. It is "different" only insofar as, no longer dealing with the objects produced by scriptural operation, it takes as its subject this operation itself; it speaks about writing itself, the working of the book in the field of death; it is the return of the scriptural myth on itself; it is "fiction" in the sense that, within the space of the book, it allows the reappearance of the indiscreet other whose place the *social* text wanted to take; it dramatizes, in the very place where it was eliminated, the inseparable excluded element whose question is raised repeatedly by sexuality or death. Answering science with a derisiveness still marked by the fantastic vision science has created or in terms of a poetics of alteration and dispossession, scriptural space becomes erotic. In the form of the myth of progress—the Book— the dangerous game of reconstruction develops. The body itself finally *writes* itself therein, but as an ecstasy arising from a wound inflicted by the other, as the "expenditure" of a pleasure that is indissociable from the ephemeral, as the elusive vanishing point that links "excess" to the mortal.

   In a scriptural problematics tied to the ability not to miss any part of time going by, to count it and accumulate it, to profit from what has been acquired so as to make capital substitute for immortality, the body returns as the *instant*, the simultaneity of life and death: both of them in the same place.

The mortal

It remains that death is not named. But it is written in the discourse of life, without its being possible to assign it a particular place. Biology finds "death imposed from within." François Jacob: "In reproduction through sexuality, individuals have to die."[7] Death is the necessary condition of evolution. The law of the species is that individuals must lose their place. The transmission of capital and its progress are guaranteed by a testament that always has to be signed by a dead man.

Beyond the signs that, from all sides, bring the connection of both sexuality and death to writing *into* writing, one can ask whether the historical movement that displaces the repressed figures—"In Freud's time, it was sexuality and moralism; now, it's an unlimited technological violence and an absurd death"[8]—is not rather the progressive revelation of the model that articulated social practices and that comes to representation as its efficacity diminishes. The decadence of a civilization constructed on the power of writing against death is shown by the possibility of writing what organized it. Only the end of an age makes it possible to say what made it live, as if it had to die in order to become a book.

To write (this book), then, is to be forced to march through enemy territory, in the very area where loss prevails, beyond the protected domain that had been delimited by the act of localizing death elsewhere. It is to produce sentences with the lexicon of the mortal, in proximity to and even within the space of death. It is to *practice* the relation between enjoying and manipulating, in the in-between space where a loss (a lapse) of the production of goods creates the possibility of an expectation (a belief) without appropriation but already grateful. Since Mallarmé, scriptural experience has deployed itself in the relation between the act of moving forward and the death-dealing soil on which its wandering leaves its track. In this respect, the writer is also a dying man who is trying to speak. But in the death that his footsteps inscribe on a black (and not blank) page, he knows and he can express the desire that expects from the other the marvellous and ephemeral excess of surviving through an attention that it alters.

Indeterminate

"The anarchy of the chiaroscuro of
the everyday."

Lukacs

*T*HEORY FAVORS a pluralist epistemology composed of a "multiplicity of points of view, each of them having roughly an equal
power of generality." It is an art of "circulating along paths or
fibers," an art of transportation and intersection; for theory progress is
an "interlacing." Depending on individual physiology, it is supposed to
lead to "a philosophy of communication without substance, that is, with
neither fixity nor reference."[1]

But rational *technics* liquidates dogmatism in a less light-hearted way.
It resists the interferences that create opacity and ambiguity in planning
projects or reductions to two dimensions. It has its own mode of operation, that of *legibility* and *distinguishing* between functions, on the page
where it can *write* them side by side, one after the other, in such a way
as to be able to transfer this image onto the ground or onto the façade,
in cities or in machines.

The *legibility* of the functional relations between elements and the
reproduction of the model by enlargements and reliefs—these are the
two operational principles of technics. To be sure, they have taken a
road of an unlimited sophistication, responding to the diversification of
demand, itself moreover included within the system, put on cards, and
analytically distributed over a space whose essence (even inside the computer)[2] is to be a readable artifact, an object open from end to end to the
survey of an immobile eye. A strange chiasm: theory moves in the direction of the indeterminate, while technology moves toward the functionalist distinction and in that way transforms everything and transforms
itself as well. As if the one sets out lucidly on the twisting paths of the
aleatory and the metaphoric,[3] while the other tries desperately to suppose that the utilitarian and *functionalist* law of its own mechanism is
"natural."

199

It is that which happens beneath technology and disturbs its operation which interests us here. This is technology's limit, which has long since been noticed but to which we must give a significance other than the delimitation of a no man's land. This is a matter of actual practices. Conceptual engineers are familiar with this sort of movement, which they call "resistance" and which disturbs functionalist calculations (an elitist form of bureaucratic structure). They cannot not perceive the fictive character instilled in an order by its relationship to everyday reality.[4] But they must *not* acknowledge this relationship. It would be a sort of *lèse-majesté* to talk ironically about this subject in offices, and the guilty person would be cashiered.[5] Do not touch: this is a work of art. Leaving this functionalist rationality to the proliferation of its elegant euphemisms (euphemisms that persist everywhere in the discourse of administration and power), let us then return to the murmuring of everyday practices.

They do not form pockets in economic society. They have nothing in common with these marginalities that technical organization quickly integrates in order to turn them into signifiers and objects of exchange. On the contrary, it is through them that an uncodeable difference insinuates itself into the happy relation the system would like to have with the operations it claims to administer. Far from being a local, and thus classifiable, revolt, it is a common and silent, almost sheeplike subversion—our own. I will point out only two symptoms: a "ubiquity" of the place, and gaps in time. This will suggest that social spaces, which are stratified, cannot be reduced to their unregulatable and constructable surface and that avatars reintroduce the unthought element of the circumstantial into calculated time. There are illegibilities of the layered depths in a single place, of ruses in action and of historical accidents. The writing of these evocations is sketched out, ironically and fleetingly, in graffiti, as if the bicycle painted on a wall, the insignia of a common transit, detached itself and made itself available for indeterminate tours.[6]

Stratified places

The kind of difference that defines every place is not on the order of a juxta-position but rather takes the form of imbricated strata. The elements spread out on the same surface can be enumerated; they are available for analysis; they form a manageable surface. Every urban "renovation" nonetheless prefers a *tabula rasa* on which to write in cement the composition created in the laboratory on the basis of discrete "needs" to which functional responses are to be made. The system also produces need, the primary "substance" of this composition, by isolating it. This unit is as neat and clean (*propre*) as digits are. Moreover, the lack of satisfaction that defines each need calls for and justifies in advance the construction that combines it with other needs. This is the logic of production: ever since the eighteenth century, it has engendered its own discursive and practical space, on the basis of points of concentration— the office, the factory, the city. It rejects the relevance of places it does not create.

However, beneath the fabricating and universal writing of technology, opaque and stubborn places remain. The revolutions of history, economic mutations, demographic mixtures lie in layers within it, and remain there, hidden in customs, rites, and spatial practices. The legible discourses that formerly articulated them have disappeared, or left only fragments in language. This place, on its surface, seems to be a collage. In reality, in its depth it is ubiquitous. A piling up of hetereogeneous places. Each one, like a deteriorating page of a book, refers to a different mode of territorial unity, of socioeconomic distribution, of political conflicts and of identifying symbolism.

The whole, made up of pieces that are not contemporary and still linked to totalities that have fallen into ruins, is managed by subtle and compensatory equilibria that silently guarantee complementarities. These infinitesimal movements, multiform activities, are homologous to that "boiling mass of electrons, protons, photons, . . . all entities whose properties are ill-defined and in perpetual interaction" by means of which, according to René Thom, physical theory represents the universe. These movements give the illusion, in a neighborhood or village, of "immobility." An illusory inertia. This operation first became visible from that point at which, from the distance of a class that has "distinguished" itself from the rest, observation grasps only the relation between what it wants to produce and what resists it. The village, the neighborhood, the block are moreover not the only things that make the fragments of heterogeneous strata function together. The smallest sentence in common language works (*marche*) in the same way. Its semantic unity plays on compensatory equilibria that are just as subtle, on which syntactical or lexical analysis imposes a superficial framework, that of an "elite" that takes its models for reality. It would be more appropriate to appeal to the oneiric (but theoretical because it articulates practice) model evoked by Freud in discussing the city of Rome, whose epochs *all* survive in the *same* place, intact and mutually interacting.[7]

The place is a palimpsest. Scientific analysis knows only its most recent text; and even then the latter is for science no more than the result of its epistemological decisions, its criteria and its goals. Why should it then be surprising that operations conceived in relation to this reconstitution have a "fictive" character and owe their (provisional?) success less to their perspicacity than to their power of breaking down the complexion of these interrelations between disparate forces and times.

Casual time

Another figure of the transportation of planning projects in the direction of what they do not determine is the unforeseen. The time that passes, interrupts or connects (and which has no doubt never been thought) is not programmed time. This would be a truism if it were not put in parentheses by prospective planning projects, even when they construct multiple hypotheses. Casual time appears only as the darkness that causes an "accident" and a lacuna in production. It is a lapse in the system, and its diabolic adversary; it is what historiography is supposed to exorcize by substituting for these incongruities of the other the transparent organicity of a scientific intelligibility (correlations, "causes" and effects, serial continuities, etc.). What prospective studies do not do, historiography takes care of, responding to the same (fundamental) requirement of covering up the obscenity of indeterminacy with the production of a (fictive) "reason."

These times constructed by discourse appear, in reality, as broken and jerky. Subjected to "servitudes" and dependencies,[8] theoretical time is in fact a time *linked* to the improbable, to failures, to diversions, and thus displaced by its other. It is the equivalent of what circulates in language as a "temporal metaphorics."[9] And, strangely, the relation of the manipulable to gaps is precisely what constitutes symbolization, which is a putting-together of what coheres without being coherent, of what makes connection without being thinkable.

The gap or failure of *reason* is precisely the blind spot that makes it accede to *another* dimension, the dimension of *thinking*, which articulates itself on the different as its indeterminable necessity. The symbolic is inseparable from gaps. Everyday practices, based on their relation to an occasion, that is, on casual time, are thus, scattered all along duration, in the situation of *acts* of thought. Permanent practices of thought.

Thus to eliminate the unforeseen or expel it from calculation as an illegitimate accident and an obstacle to rationality is to interdict the possibility of a living and "mythical" practice of the city. It is to leave its inhabitants only the scraps of a programming produced by the power of the other and altered by the event. Casual time is what is narrated in the actual discourse of the city: an indeterminate fable, better articulated on the metaphorical practices and stratified places than on the empire of the evident in functionalist technocracy.

Notes

"Introduction"

1. See M. de Certeau, *La Prise de parole* (Paris: DDB, 1968); *La Possession de Loudun* (Paris: Julliard-Gallimard, 1970); *L'Absent de l'histoire* (Paris: Mame, 1973); *La Culture au pluriel* (Paris: UGE 10/18, 1974); *Une Politique de la langue* (with D. Julia and J. Revel) (Paris: Gallimard, 1975); etc.

2. From the Greek *poiein* "to create, invent, generate."

3. See Emile Benveniste, *Problèmes de linguistique générale* (Paris: Gallimard, 1966), I, 251–266.

4. Michel Foucault, *Surveiller et punir* (Paris: Gallimard, 1975); *Discipline and Punish*, trans. A. Sheridan (New York: Pantheon, 1977).

5. From this point of view as well, the works of Henri Lefebvre on everyday life constitute a fundamental source.

6. On art, from the *Encyclopédie* to Durkheim, see below pp. 66–68.

7. For this literature, see the booklets mentioned in *Le Livre dans la vie quotidienne* (Paris: Bibliothèque Nationale, 1975) and in Geneviève Bollème, *La Bible bleue, Anthologie d'une littérature "populaire"* (Paris: Flammarion, 1975), 141–379.

8. The first of these two monographs was written by Pierre Mayol, the second by Luce Giard (on the basis of interviews made by Marie Ferrier). See *L'Invention du quotidien*, II, Luce Giard and Pierre Mayol, *Habiter, cuisiner* (Paris: UGE 10/18, 1980).

9. By Erving Goffman, see especially *Interaction Rituals* (Garden City, N.Y.: Anchor Books, 1976); *The Presentation of Self in Everyday Life* (Woodstock, N.Y.: The Overlook Press, 1973); *Frame Analysis* (New York: Harper & Row, 1974). By Pierre Bourdieu, see *Esquisse d'une théorie de la pratique. Précédée de trois études d'ethnologie kabyle* (Genève: Droz, 1972); "Les Stratégies matrimoniales," *Annales: économies, sociétés, civilisations* 27 (1972), 1105–1127; "Le Langage autorisé," *Actes de la recherche en sciences sociales*, No. 5–6 (November 1975), 184–190; "Le Sens pratique," *Actes de la recherche en sciences sociales*, No. 1 (February 1976), 43–86. By Marcel Mauss, see especially "Techniques du corps," in *Sociologie et anthropologie* (Paris: PUF, 1950). By Marcel Détienne and Jean-Pierre Vernant, *Les Ruses de l'intelligence. La mètis des Grecs* (Paris: Flammarion, 1974). By Jeremy Boissevain, *Friends of Friends. Networks, Manipulators and Coalitions* (Oxford: Blackwell, 1974). By Edward O. Laumann, *Bonds of Pluralism. The Form and Substance of Urban Social Networks* (New York: John Wiley, 1973).

10. Joshua A. Fishman, *The Sociology of Language* (Rowley, Mass.: New-bury, 1972). See also the essays in *Studies in Social Interaction*, ed. David Sudnow (New York: The Free Press, 1972); William Labov, *Sociolinguistic Patterns* (Philadelphia: University of Pennsylvania Press, 1973); etc.

11. Oswald Ducrot, *Dire et ne pas dire* (Paris: Hermann, 1972); and David K. Lewis, *Convention: a Philosophical Study* (Cambridge, Mass.: Harvard University Press, 1974), and *Counterfactuals* (Cambridge, Mass.: Harvard University Press, 1973).

12. Georg H. von Wright, *Norm and Action* (London: Routledge & Kegan Paul, 1963); *Essay in Deontic Logic and the General Theory of Action* (Amsterdam: North Holland, 1968); *Explanation and Understanding* (Ithaca, N.Y.: Cornell University Press, 1971). And A. C. Danto, *Analytical Philosophy of Action* (Cambridge: Cambridge University Press, 1973); Richard J. Bernstein, *Praxis and Action* (London: Duckworth, 1972); and *La Sémantique de l'action*, ed. Paul Ricoeur and Doriane Tiffeneau (Paris: CNRS, 1977).

13. A. N. Prior, *Past, Present and Future: a Study of "Tense Logic"* (Oxford: Oxford University Press, 1967) and *Papers on Tense and Time* (Oxford: Oxford University Press, 1968). N. Rescher and A. Urquhart, *Temporal Logic* (Oxford: Oxford University Press, 1975).

14. Alan R. White, *Modal Thinking* (Ithaca, N.Y.: Cornell University Press, 1975); G. E. Hughes and M. J. Cresswell, *An Introduction to Modal Logic* (Oxford: Oxford University Press, 1973); I. R. Zeeman, *Modal Logic* (Oxford: Oxford University Press, 1975); S. Haacker, *Deviant Logic* (Cambridge: Cambridge University Press, 1976); *Discussing Language with Chomsky, Halliday, etc.*, ed. H. Parret (The Hague: Mouton, 1975).

15. As it is more technical, the study concerning the logics of action and time, as well as modalization, will be published elsewhere.

16. Jacques Sojcher, *La Démarche poétique* (Paris: UGE 10/18, 1976), 145.

17. See Fernand Deligny, *Les Vagabonds efficaces* (Paris: Maspero, 1970); *Nous et l'innocent* (Paris: Maspero, 1977); etc.

18. See M. de Certeau, *La Culture au pluriel*, 283–308; and "Actions culturelles et stratégies politiques," *La Revue nouvelle*, April 1974, 351–360.

19. The analysis of the principles of isolation allows us to make this criticism both more nuanced and more precise. See *Pour une histoire de la statistique* (Paris: INSEE, 1978), I, in particular Alain Desrosières, "Eléments pour l'histoire des nomenclatures socio-professionnelles," 155–231.

20. The works of P. Bourdieu and those of M. Détienne and J.-P. Vernant make possible the notion of "tactic" more precise, but the socio-linguistic investigations of H. Garfinkel, H. Sacks, et al. also contribute to this clarification. See notes 9 and 10.

21. M. Détienne and J.-P. Vernant, *Les Ruses de l'intelligence*.

22. See S. Toulmin, *The Uses of Argument* (Cambridge: Cambridge University Press, 1958); Ch. Perelman and L. Ollbrechts-Tyteca, *Traité de l'argumentation* (Bruxelles: Université libre, 1970); J. Dubois, et al., *Rhétorique générale* (Paris: Larousse, 1970); etc.

23. The works of Corax, said to be the author of the earliest Greek text on rhetoric, are lost; on this point, see Aristotle, *Rhetoric*, II, 24, 1402a. See W. K. C. Guthrie, *The Sophists* (Cambridge: Cambridge University Press, 1971), 178–179.

24. Sun Tzu, *The Art of War*, trans. S. B. Griffith (Oxford: The Clarendon Press, 1963). Sun Tzu (Sun Zi) should not be confused with the later military theorist Hsün Tzu (Xun Zi).

25. *Le Livre des ruses. La Stratégie politique des Arabes*, ed. R. K. Khawam (Paris: Phébus, 1976).

26. See Jean Baudrillard, *Le Système des objets* (Paris: Gallimard, 1968); *La Société de consommation* (Paris: Denoël, 1970); *Pour une critique de l'économie politique du signe* (Paris: Gallimard, 1972).

27. Guy Debord, *La Société du spectacle* (Paris: Buchet-Chastel, 1967).

28. Roland Barthes, *Le Plaisir du texte* (Paris: Seuil, 1973), 58; *The Pleasure of the Text*, trans. R. Miller (New York: Hill and Wang, 1975).

29. See Gérard Mordillat and Nicolas Philibert, *Ces Patrons éclairés qui craignent la lumière* (Paris: Albatros, 1979).

30. See the essays of H. Sacks, E. A. Schegloff, etc., quoted above. This analysis, entitled *Arts de dire*, will be published separately.

31. See below, Part III, Chapters VII to IX.

32. We have devoted monographs to these practices in which the proliferating and disseminated bibliography on the subject will be found (see *L'Invention du quotidien*, II, *Habiter, cuisiner*, by Luce Giard and Pierre Mayol).

33. See, for example, A. Lipietz, "Structuration de l'espace foncier et aménagement du territoire," *Environment and Planning*, A, 7 (1975), 415–425, and "Approche théorique des transformations de l'espace français," *Espaces et Sociétés*, No. 16 (1975), 3–14.

34. The analyses found in *Travaux et recherches de prospective* published by the Documentation Française, in particular in volumes 14, 59, 65 and 66, and notably the studies by Yves Barel and Jacques Durand have served as the basis for this investigation into futurology. It will be published separately.

35. W. Gombrowicz, *Cosmos* (Paris: Gallimard Folio, 1971), 165–168; originally *Kosmos* (1965); *Cosmos*, trans. E. Mosbacker (London: Macgibbon and Kee, 1967).

1. *"A Common Place: Ordinary Language"*

1. Robert Musil, *L'Homme sans qualités* (Paris: Gallimard Folio, 1978), I, 21; originally *Der Mann ohne Eigenschaften* (1930); *The Man Without Qualities*, trans. E. Wilkins and E. Kaiser (London: Secker and Warburg, 1953–65).

2. Robert Klein, *La Forme et l'intelligible* (Paris: Gallimard, 1970), 436–444. See also Enrico Castelli-Gattinara, "Quelques considérations sur le niemand et . . . personne," in *Folie et déraison à la Renaissance*, Proceedings of a Conference in Bruxelles, 1973 (Bruxelles: Université Libre, 1976), 109–118.

3. S. Freud, *Gesammelte Werke* (henceforth cited as G. W.), XIV, 431–432. In this text from *Civilization and its Discontents*, trans. J. Riviere (Garden City: Doubleday, 1958), § 1, he refers to *The Future of an Illusion*, trans. J. Strachey (New York: Norton, 1961), which also starts out in § 1 from the opposition between a "minority" and the "majority" (the "masses") which motivates his analysis.

4. *The Future of an Illusion*, § 7.

5. G. W., XIV, 431.

6. See M. de Certeau, *L'Ecriture de l'histoire* (Paris: Gallimard, 1978), 7–8.

7. G. W., XIV, 431.

8. Freud, letter to Lou Andréas-Salomé, 28 July 1929, in Lou Andréas-Salomé, *Correspondance avec Sigmund Freud* (Paris: Gallimard, 1970), 225; *Sigmund Freud and Lou Andréas-Salomé: Letters*, ed. E. Pfeiffer (New York: Harcourt, Brace Janovich, 1972).

9. Ibid.

10. G. W., XIV, 506.

11. See *L'Ecriture de l'histoire*, 312–358.

12. See the analysis of the expert in *Abus de savoir* (Paris: DDB, 1977).

13. See below, Part IV, Uses of Language.

14. See II, *Habiter, cuisiner*, by Luce Giard and Pierre Mayol.

15. L. Wittgenstein, *Philosophical Investigations* (Oxford: Blackwell, 1976), § 116, 48.

16. L. Wittgenstein, *Tractatus Logico-Philosophicus* (London: Routledge & Kegan Paul, 1961), § 6.53, 150–151.

17. *Philosophical Investigations*, § 494, 138.

18. See the letter to Ficker concerning the *Tractatus*: "My book draws limits to the sphere of the ethical from the inside as it were, and I am convinced that this is the ONLY rigorous way of drawing those limits"—quoted in Allan Janik and Stephen Toulmin, *Wittgenstein's Vienna* (New York: Simon & Schuster, 1973), 192. Thus, Wittgenstein says, the *Tractatus* has two parts, the one, the written book, and the other, the essential one, which is not and cannot be written, on ethics itself.

19. *Philosophical Investigations*, § 122, 49. See Jacques Bouveresse, *La Parole malheureuse* (Paris: Minuit, 1971), 299–348.

20. On this aspect of history, see M. de Certeau, *L'Ecriture de l'histoire*, 63–122, and "Ecriture et histoire," *Politique aujourd'hui*, November–December 1975, 65–77. I shall not consider here the philosophical debates concerning Marx and Wittgenstein (the latter tried to go to work in the USSR). See the studies by F. Rossi-Landi ("Per un Uso Marxiano di W."), Tony Manser ("The End of Philosophy: Marx and W.") or Ted Benton ("Winch, W. and Marxism," *Radical Philosophy*, No. 13, 1976). A historical materialism that is proper to this "bourgeois" can be recognized in Wittgenstein but no "science" (in the Marxist sense) of history.

21. See L. Wittgenstein, "A Lecture on Ethics," *The Philosophical Review*, 74 (1965), 3–12, especially the last two pages. See also the remarks quoted by

Norman Malcolm, *Ludwig Wittgenstein, a Memoir* (London: Oxford University Press, 1959).

22. *Philosophical Investigations*, § 109: " . . . looking into the workings of our language."

23. Quoted by Norman Malcolm, *Ludwig Wittgenstein, a Memoir*, pp. 49–50.

24. This word, of Viennese origin, designates "all the possible human styles of thought, character and language" (Janik and Toulmin, p. 231) or, more generally, the *factual* (historical) structurations of our existence.

25. See for example J. L. Austin, *Philosophical Papers*, ed. J. O. Urmson and G. J. Warnock (Oxford: Oxford University Press, 1969), 181–182.

26. On this English tradition, see G. J. Warnock, *English Philosophy since 1900*, 2nd ed. (Oxford: Oxford University Press, 1969), 19–20, 100–102, etc.; and especially *Philosophy and Ordinary Language*, ed. Charles E. Caton (Urbana, Ill.: 1963) and *Ordinary Language*, ed. V. C. Chapel (Englewood Cliffs, N.J.: Prentice Hall, 1964).

27. See Adolf Loos' text translated in *Traverses*, No. 7 (1976), 15–20.

28. Musil, *L'Homme sans qualités*.

29. The word "execrate" characterizes his allergy to a style of thought. See, for example, *Lectures and Conversations on Aesthetics, Psychology and Religious Belief*, ed. C. Barrett (Berkeley: University of California Press, 1966), 27–28; and J. Bouveresse, "Les derniers jours de l'humanité," *Critique*, August–September 1975, 753–805.

30. See the preface to *Philosophical Remarks*, ed. R. Rhees (Oxford: Blackwell, 1975).

31. *L'Homme sans qualités*, I, 74–75.

32. Ibid., 75.

33. *Philosophical Investigations*, § 194, 79.

2. *"Popular Cultures"*

1. This analysis formed the basis for a seminar undertaken on the basis of an investigation carried out as early as 1971 and of a preliminary report, *Frei Damião: Sim ou Não? E os Impasses da Religião Popular* (Recife: mimeographed); all the documents collected were not made available. An analysis of the same kind bore on an investigation made of the very popular pilgrimage of Senhor do Bonfim (Salvador, Brazil). See Fernando Silveira Massote, "Esplosione Sociale del Sertao Brasiliano," (Diss. Urbino (Italy), 1978), 74–183, on religion.

2. "My beloved is an idea (egalitarian society) to which I have devoted my arms and my heart," extract from the anarchist song *Amore Ribelle*, quoted in Jean-Louis Comolli, *La Cecilia* (Paris: Daniel & Cie, 1976), 99.

3. "Hurry and come up, O Sun of the future. We want to live a free life. We no longer want to serve others," extract from *Canto dei Malfatorri*, quoted in ibid., 103. On the film, see also M. de Certeau, J. Revel, et al., *Ça Cinéma*,

No. 10–11 (1976), 38–44.

4. See Willy Apollon, *Le Vaudou. Un Espace pour les "voix"* (Paris: Galilée, 1976).

5. See, for example, Tomé Cabral, *Dicionario de Těrmos e Expressões Populares* (Fortaleza: Universidade Federal do Ceará, 1972).

6. See M. de Certeau, *La Culture au pluriel* (Paris: UGE 10/18, 1974), 283–308; and "Actions culturelles et stratégies politiques," *La Revue nouvelle*, April 1974, 351–360.

7. Marcel Détienne and Jean-Pierre Vernant, *Les Ruses de l'intelligence. La Mètis des Grecs* (Paris: Flammarion, 1974).

8. Pierre Bourdieu, *Esquisse d'une théorie de la pratique* (Genève: Droz, 1972) and especially "Le Sens pratique," *Actes de la recherche en sciences sociales*, No. 1 (February 1976), 43–86.

9. See below, Part IV, Uses of Language.

10. Thus the research of A. Charraud, F. Loux, Ph. Richard and M. de Virville at the Centre d'Ethnologie Française: see their report "Analyse de contenu de proverbes médicaux," Paris, MSH, 1972, or the article by F. Loux, *Ethnologie française*, No. 3–4 (1971), 121–126. The same methods had earlier been applied to an "Essai de description des contes populaires," Paris, MSH, 1970.

11. See, for example, Alberto Mario Cirese, *I Proverbi: Struttura delle Definizioni* (Urbino: Centro di Semiotica, 1972), on Sardinian proverbs.

12. These units have been variously termed "types" (Aarne), "motifs" (Thompson), "functions" (Propp), "tests" (Meletinsky), etc.

13. D.-P. Schreber, *Mémoires d'un névropathe* (Paris: Seuil, 1975), 60.

14. To analyze "the imprint of the process of enunciation on the utterance" is, as is well known, strictly speaking the object of a linguistics of enunciation. See O. Ducrot and T. Todorov, *Dictionnaire encyclopédique des sciences du langage* (Paris: Seuil, 1972), 405.

15. On modality, by which the locutor assigns a status (concerning existence, certitude, obligation, etc.) to his utterance (*dictum* or *lexis*), see, for example, *Langages*, No. 43 (September 1976).

16. Sun Tzu, *The Art of War*, trans. S. B. Griffith (Oxford: The Clarendon Press, 1963), a work dating from the 4th century B.C.

17. *Le Livre des ruses. La Stratégie politique des Arabes*, ed. R. K. Khawam (Paris: Phébus, 1976).

18. In this respect, science would be the generalization of a ruse: the artifice is no longer located in the use of ordinary language (with its countless rhetorical "turns"), but in the production of proper languages (artificial languages guaranteeing the univocal and transparent use of constructed terms).

19. Lévi-Strauss opposes *play*, which is "disjunctive," producing differences between camps that were initially equal, to the *rite*, which is "conjunctive," establishing or re-establishing union. See *La Pensée sauvage* (Paris: Plon, 1962), 44–47; *The Savage Mind* (Chicago: University of Chicago Press, 1966).

20. See Roger J. Girault, *Traité du jeu de go* (Paris: Flammarion, 1977), 2 vol.

21. See R. Jaulin, *La Géomancie. Analyse formelle* (Paris: Plon, 1966);

A. Ader and A. Zempleni, *Le Bâton de l'aveugle* (Paris: Hermann, 1972); J.-P. Vernant et al., *Divination et rationalité* (Paris: Seuil, 1974); etc.

22. One could analyze the reciprocity between games and tales in the light of Nicole Belmont's research on the relations between popular "observances" and "beliefs"; see "Les croyances populaires comme récit mythologique," *L'Homme*, 10 (1970), No. 2, 94–108.

23. Vladimir Propp, *Morphologie du conte* (1928) (Paris: Gallimard-Seuil, 1970); *Morphology of the Folktale*, trans. L. Scott (Austin: University of Texas Press, 1968); to which we must add: *Le Radici Storiche dei Raconti di Fate* (Torino: Einaudi, 1949). On Propp, see especially A. Dundes, *The Morphology of North-American Indian Folktales* (Helsinki: Academia Scientiarum Fennica, 1964); A. J. Greimas, *Sémantique structurale* (Paris: Larousse, 1966), 172–213; C. Lévi-Strauss, *Anthropologie structurale deux* (Paris: Plon, 1973), 139–173; A. Régnier, "La Morphologie selon V. J. Propp," in *La Crise du langage scientifique* (Paris: Anthropos, 1974), and "De la morphologie selon V. I. Propp à la notion de système préinterprétafif," *L'Homme et la société*, No. 12, 171–189.

24. The expression is Régnier's in *L'Homme et la société*, 172.

25. *Morphologie du conte*, 31.

26. Thus in gypsy tales, the hero never lies, but he has the advantage of knowing how to make the orders he receives *mean something different* from what the master or the powerful thought they were telling him. See D. Paulme and C. Bremond, *Typologie des contes africains du décepteur. Principes d'un index des ruses* (Urbino: Centro di Semiotica, 1976); or, from a theoretical point of view, Louis Marin, *Sémiotique de la Passion* (Paris: Aubier-DDB, 1971), 97–186.

27. For R. Jakobsen, even the mutations and relations of phonemes in glossolalia and "prophecies in tongues"—discourses deprived of meaning and constituting an "abstract popular art"—obey rules so rigorous that one can, on that basis, seek out the more complex "compositional principles" of stratified specimens (both audible and signifying) in the oral tradition; see *Selected Writings* (The Hague: Mouton, 1966), IV, 642. The combining of letters, in these meaningless formulas (of the type *Am stram gram . . .*), would thus have the value of algebraic formulas indicating the formal possibilities of producing texts. Is there a formalization thus inscribed in this "abstract" literature, and does it furnish logical models for practices fabricating popular "expressions"?

28. See P. Bourdieu's critical analyses in his *Le Métier de sociologue*, 2nd ed. (La Haye: Mouton, 1973), preface; and M. Godelier, *Horizon. Trajets marxistes en anthropologie* (Paris: Maspero, 1973), etc.

29. See M. de Certeau, *La Culture au pluriel*, 55–94.

30. Miklos Haraszti, *Salaire aux pièces* (Paris: Seuil, 1976), 136–145. On "bousillés" (glassware produced by glassworkers for their own ends), see Louis Mériaux, "Retrouvailles chez les verriers," *Le Monde*, 22–23 October 1978. And see also M.-J. and J.-R. Hissard, "Henri H. perruquiste," *Autrement*, No. 16, November 1978, 75–83.

31. Marcel Mauss, "Essai sur le Don," in *Sociologie et anthropologie* (Paris: PUF, 1966), 145–279; *The Gift*, trans. I. Cunnison (New York: Norton, 1967).

3. "'Making Do': Uses and Tactics"

1. See in particular A. Huet et al., *La Marchandise culturelle* (Paris: CNRS, 1977), which is not satisfied merely with analyzing products (photos, records, prints), but also studies a system of commercial repetition and ideological reproduction.

2. See, for example, *Pratiques culturelles des Français* (Paris: Secrétariat d'Etat à la Culture - SER, 1974), 2 vol. Alvin Toffler, *The Culture Consumers* (Baltimore: Penguin, 1965), remains fundamental and pioneering, although it is not statistically based and is limited to mass culture.

3. On the premonitory theme of the "celibate machine" in the art (M. Duchamp, et al.) or the literature (from Jules Verne to Raymond Roussel) of the early twentieth century, see J. Clair et al., *Les Machines célibataires* (Venice: Alfieri, 1975).

4. See, for example, on the subject of the Aymaras of Peru and Bolivia, J.-E. Monast, *On les croyait Chrétiens: les Aymaras* (Paris: Cerf, 1969).

5. See M. de Certeau, "La Longue marche indienne," in *Le Réveil indien en Amérique latine*, ed. Yves Materne and DIAL (Paris: Cerf, 1976), 119-135.

6. G. Ryle, "Use, Usage and Meaning," in *The Theory of Meaning*, ed. G. H. R. Parkinson (Oxford: Oxford University Press, 1968), 109-116. A large part of the volume is devoted to use.

7. Richard Montague, "Pragmatics," in *La Philosophie contemporaine*, ed. Raymond Klibansky (Firenze: La Nuova Italia, 1968), I, 102-122. Y. Bar-Hillel thus adopts a term of C. S. Peirce, of which the equivalents are, in B. Russell, "ego-centric particulars"; in H. Reichenbach, "token-reflexive expressions"; in N. Goodman, "indicator words"; in W. V. Quine, "non-eternal sentences"; etc. A whole tradition is inscribed in this perspective. Wittgenstein belongs to it as well, the Wittgenstein whose slogan was "Don't ask for the meaning; ask for the use" in reference to normal use, regulated by the institution that is language.

8. See "The Proverbial Enunciation," above, p. 18.

9. See Emile Benveniste, *Problèmes de linguistique générale* (Paris: Gallimard, 1974), II, 79-88.

10. Fernand Deligny, *Les Vagabonds efficaces* (Paris: Maspero, 1970), uses this word to describe the trajectories of young autistic people with whom he lives, writings that move through forests, wanderings that can no longer make a path through the space of language.

11. See "Indeterminate," below, p. 199.

12. Ibid.

13. According to John von Neumann and Oskar Morgenstern, *Theory of Games and Economic Behaviour*, 3rd ed. (New York: John Wiley, 1964), "there is only strategy when the other's strategy is included."

14. "Strategy is the science of military movements outside of the enemy's field of vision; tactics, within it" (von Bülow).

15. Karl von Clausewitz, *Vom Kriege*; see *De la guerre* (Paris: Minuit, 1955),

212–213; *On War*, trans. M. Howard and P. Paret (Princeton: Princeton University Press, 1976). This analysis can be found moreover in many other theoreticians, ever since Machiavelli. See Y. Delahaye, "Simulation et dissimulation," *La Ruse (Cause Commune* 1977/1) (Paris: UGE 10/18, 1977), 55–74.

16. Clausewitz, *De La guerre*, 212.

17. Freud, *Jokes and their Relation to the Unconscious*, trans. J. Strachey (London: The Hogarth Press and the Institute of Psychoanalysis, 1960).

18. Aristotle, *Rhetoric*, II, 24, 1402a: "by making the worse argument seem the better"; trans. W. Rhys Roberts (New York: The Modern Library, 1954). The same "discovery" is attributed to Tisias by Plato (*Phaedrus*, 273b–c). See also W. K. C. Guthrie, *The Sophists* (Cambridge: Cambridge University Press, 1971), 178–179. On Corax's *technē* mentioned by Aristotle in relation to the "loci of apparent enthymemes," see Ch. Perelman and L. Ollbrechts-Tyteca, *Traité de l'argumentation* (Bruxelles: Université Libre, 1970), 607–609.

19. Freud, *Jokes and their Relation to the Unconscious*, on the techniques of wit.

20. See S. Toulmin, *The Uses of Argument* (Cambridge: Cambridge University Press, 1958); Perelman and Ollbrechts-Tyteca, *Traité de l'argumentation*; J. Dubois et al., *Rhétorique générale* (Paris: Larousse, 1970); etc.

21. See *I-Ching*, the *Book of Changes*, which represents all the possible situations of beings in the course of the universe's mutations by means of 64 hexagrams formed by 6 interrupted or full lines.

22. M. Détienne and J.-P. Vernant, *Les Ruses de l'intelligence. La Mètis des Grecs* (Paris: Flammarion, 1974).

23. See M. Rodinson, *Islam et capitalisme* (Paris: Seuil, 1972); *Islam and Capitalism*, trans. B. Pearce (New York: Pantheon, 1973).

4. *"Foucault and Bourdieu"*

1. See above, Chapter II, p. 22, on the tactics of which "panoplies" are made available by popular legends and ways of speaking, but situated in a hidden place.

2. Michel Foucault, *Surveiller et punir* (Paris: Gallimard, 1975); *Discipline and Punish*, trans. A. Sheridan (New York: Pantheon, 1977). On Foucault's earlier work, see M. de Certeau, *L'Absent de l'histoire* (Paris: Mame, 1974), 115–132.

3. Foucault, *Surveiller et punir*, 28, 96–102, 106–116, 143–151, 159–161, 185, 189–194, 211–217, 238–251, 274–275, 276, etc.: a series of theoretical "tableaux" marks the development of the book; it isolates an historical object and invents a discourse adequate to it.

4. See especially Gilles Deleuze, "Ecrivain, non: un nouveau cartographe," *Critique*, No. 343 (December 1975), 1207–1227.

5. Serge Moscovici, *Essai sur l'histoire humaine de la nature* (Paris: Flammarion, 1968).

6. Pierre Legendre, *L'Amour du censeur. Essai sur l'ordre dogmatique* (Paris: Seuil, 1974).

7. Claude Lévi-Strauss, *Tristes tropiques* (Paris: Plon, 1958); *Tristes Tropiques*, trans. J. Russell (New York: Criterion, 1962); especially the pages on "the return," a meditation on the journey that is inverted and changed into an investigation of memory.

8. Pierre Bourdieu, *Esquisse d'une théorie de la pratique. Précédée de trois études d'ethnologie kabyle* (Genève: Droz, 1972). The title of the book is that of the second part, which is theoretical. French critiques of Pierre Bourdieu are not very numerous in contrast to the activity focused on Foucault. Is this a result of the fears and the admiration simultaneously inspired by a Béarnian empire? The "ideological" character of Bourdieu's positions is criticized by Raymond Boudon, *L'Inégalité des chances* (Paris: Armand Colin, 1973) and *Effets pervers et ordre social* (Paris: PUF, 1977). From a Marxist perspective; see Christian Baudelot and Roger Establet, *L'École capitaliste en France* (Paris: Maspero, 1974); Jacques Bidet, "Questions à P. Bourdieu," *Dialectiques*, No. 2; Louis Pinto, "La Théorie de la pratique," *La Pensée*, April 1975; etc. From an epistemological point of view, see Louis Marin, "Champ théorique et pratique symbolique," *Critique*, No. 321 (February 1974). W. Paul Vogt has presented Bourdieu's theses in "The Inheritance and Reproduction of Cultural Capital," *The Review of Education*, Summer 1978, 219-228. See J.-M. Geng, *L'Illustre inconnu* (Paris: UGE 10/18, 1978), pp. 53-63, on "sociological totalization" in Bourdieu's work and the production of a "sociological faith," a criticism to which Bourdieu quickly replied with "Sur l'objectivation participante," *Actes de la recherche en sciences sociales*, No. 23 (September 1978), 67-69.

9. P. Bourdieu, "Les Stratégies matrimoniales dans le système de reproduction," *Annales: économies, sociétés, civilisations*, 27 (1972), 1105-1127; "Le Langage autorisé," *Actes de la recherche en sciences sociales*, No. 5-6 (November 1975), 183-190; "Le Sens pratique," ibid., No. 1 (February 1976), 43-86. And that social epic of "taste" constituted by *La Distinction. Critique sociale du jugement* (Paris: Minuit, 1979), in particular chapters II and III, 9-188.

10. *Revue française de sociologie*, 15 (1974), 3-42.

11. See "Les Stratégies matrimoniales."

12. It is this confrontation that P. Bourdieu, J.-C. Passeron and J.-C. Chamboredon urged in *Le Métier de sociologue*, 2nd ed. (La Haye: Mouton, 1973), 108-109.

13. *Esquisse d'une théorie de la pratique*, 11.

14. See Jacques Derrida, *Marges de la philosophie* (Paris: Minuit, 1972), 247-324; *Margins of Philosophy*, trans. A. Bass (Chicago: University of Chicago Press, 1982).

15. See Bourdieu's analysis in *Esquisse d'une théorie de la pratique*, 45-69.

16. See P. Bourdieu and J.-C. Passeron, *Les Héritiers* (Paris: Minuit, 1964) *La Reproduction* (Paris: Minuit, 1970); etc.

17. See Bourdieu's criticisms of this study, when he republishes it in 1972, in *Esquisse d'une théorie de la pratique*, p. 11.

18. See "Avenir de classe," *Revue française de sociologie*, 15 (1974), 22, 33–34, 42, etc.

19. *Esquisse*, 211–227; "Les Stratégies matrimoniales," 1107–1108; "Le sens pratique," 51–52; etc.

20. "Les Stratégies matrimoniales," 1109; etc.

21. Ibid.

22. See particularly "Le Sens pratique," 54–75.

23. *Le Métier de sociologue*, 257–264.

24. It is well known that in traditional societies, the "home" designates both the house (the property) and the family (the genealogical body).

25. "Avenir de classe," 11–12. Cf. above, note 18. Bourdieu does not in any case take into consideration studies on the individual strategies of consumers in our societies. See, concerning A. O. Hirschmann, *Exit, Voice and Loyalty* (Cambridge, Mass.: Harvard University Press, 1970), ibid., p. 8, note 11.

26. *Esquisse*, 175–177, 182; "Avenir de classe," 28–29; etc.

27. *Esquisse*, 202.

28. Ibid., 177–179.

29. The idea and the term of *exis* (*habitus*) come from Marcel Mauss, *Sociologie et anthropologie* (Paris: PUF, 1966), 368–369; and Panofsky had also stressed, in famous texts cited by Bourdieu, the theoretical and practical importance of *habitus* in medieval society (see *Le Métier de sociologue*, 253–256). In Bourdieu's work, the idea goes way back: see *Le Métier de sociologue*, 16, 84, etc., on the sociologist's "schemes," or *L'Amour de l'art* (Paris: Minuit, 1969), 163, on "taste." Today the idea is asserted through an impressive array of scholastic terms and axioms, very interesting indices for a possible reading, in contemporary technocracy, of a return to the medieval order.

30. *Esquisse*, 175, 178–179; "Avenir de classe," 28–29; *La Distinction*, 189–195.

31. See the praise of the hero, in "Avenir de classe," 28. Thus one can henceforth study "the strategies of *habitus*" (ibid., 30; my italics).

5. *"The Arts of Theory"*

1. Kant already pointed this out in his *Kritik der Reinen Vernunft*: the scientist is a "judge who forces the witnesses to answer questions that he has formulated himself."

2. Emile Durkheim, *Les Formes elémentaires de la vie religieuse* (Paris: PUF, 1968); *The Elementary Forms of the Religious Life*, trans. J. W. Swain (New York: Free Press, 1962). See also W. S. F. Pickering, *Durkheim on Religion* (London: Routledge & Kegan Paul, 1975).

3. Sigmund Freud, *Totem and Taboo* (London: The Hogarth Press and the Institute of Psychoanalysis, 1955).

4. See Fritz Raddatz, *Karl Marx, une biographie politique* (Paris: Fayard, 1978).

5. See *Le Livre dans la vie quotidienne* (Paris: Bibliothèque Nationale, 1975).

6. Louis-François Jouffret founded the *Société des observateurs de l'homme* in 1799.

7. Plato, *Gorgias*, 465a. See Giuseppe Cambiano, *Platone e la tecniche* (Torino: 1971).

8. J. Guillerme and J. Sebestik, "Les Commencements de la technologie," *Thalès*, 12 (1966), 1–72, give a series of examples of this intermediary status: the arts are the objects of *Descriptions* (2, 4, 32, 37, 41, 46–47, etc.) and, assumed to be incomplete, they must be *perfected* (8, 14, 29, 33, etc.).

9. "Art," *Encyclopédie* (Genève: Pellet, 1773), III, 450–455.

10. "Catalogue," ibid. It was written by David, on the basis of a manuscript by Girard. See, on this subject, "Les Commencements de la technologie," 2–3.

11. Fontenelle, "Préface," in *Histoire de l'Académie royale pour 1699*, where *Sur la description des arts* is published. Quoted in "Les Commencements de la technologie," 33, note 1.

12. Emile Durkheim, *Education et sociologie* (Paris: Alcan, 1922), 87. See P. Bourdieu, *Esquisse d'une théorie de la pratique* (Genève: Droz, 1972), 211, who recognizes therein a "perfect description" of *docta ignorantia*.

13. Durkheim, *Les Formes elémentaires de la vie religieuse*, 495.

14. Christian Wolff, "Preface" for the German translation of Belidor, *Architecture hydraulique* (1740). Quoted in "Les Commencements de la technologie," 23, note 2.

15. H. de Villeneuve, "Sur quelques préjugés des industriels," (1832), quoted ibid., 24.

16. In many respects, the position of the Expert is a variant of this one. See above, Chapter 1, p. 6.

17. See above, Chapter II, p. 21.

18. A constant theme in Freud, even though the status of this "knowledge" remains theoretically indeterminate.

19. On this evolution, from the plan for a *Critique of Taste* (1787) to the composition of the *Critique of Judgment* (1790), see Victor Delbos, *La Philosophie pratique de Kant* (Paris: PUF, 1969), 416–422. Kant's text is found in *Kritik der Urteilskraft*, § 43, in *Werke*, ed. W. Weischedel (n.p.: Insel, 1957), V, 401–402. Bourdieu's critique of Kantian esthetics, which is fundamental ("a social relation that is denied") but carried out with a sociological knife, is situated in a perspective different from my own, even though it concerns the Kantian distinction between "free art" and "necessary art" (*La Distinction. Critique sociale du jugement* (Paris: Minuit, 1979), 565–583).

20. See A. Philonenko, *Théorie et praxis dans la pensée morale et politique de Kant et de Fichte en 1793* (Paris: Vrin, 1968), 19–24; Jurgen Heinrichs, *Das Problem der Zeit in der Praktischen Philosophie Kants* (Bonn: H. Bouvier, 1968), 34–43; Paul Guyer, *Kant and the Claims of Taste* (Cambridge, Mass.: Harvard University Press, 1979), 120–165, 331–350.

21. Quoted in Philonenko, *Théorie et praxis*, 22, note 17.

22. Kant, *Kritik der Urteilskraft*, § 43.

23. Freud, *Gesammelte Werke*, XIII, 330; XIV, 66, 250, etc.

24. Kant, *Kritik des Reiner Vernunft*, quoted in Philonenko, *Théorie et praxis*, 21.

25. See above, Chapter II, p. 24.

26. *Das Mag in der Theorie Richtig Sein, Taugt aber nicht für die Praxis*. The text (see Kant, *Werke*, ed. W. Weischedel, 1964, VI, 127) has been republished and introduced by Dieter Heinrich with the whole debate from the end of 1793 to the beginning of 1794 concerning the relation between theory and practice: I. Kant, F. Gentz, and A. W. Rehberg, *Über Theorie und Praxis* (Frankfurt/Main: Suhrkamp, 1967). I shall quote this remarkable collection. See also the valuable English translation of Kant's text in a volume published separately and justifiably: Kant, *On the Old Saw: That May Be Right in Theory but it Won't Work in Practice*, intr. G. Miller, trans. E. B. Ashton (Philadelphia: University of Pennsylvania, 1974).

27. On Kant and the Revolution, see L. W. Beck, "Kant and the Right of Revolution," *Journal of the History of Ideas*, 32 (1971), 411–422; and especially the collection *Kant on History*, ed. L. W. Beck (New York: Library of Liberal Arts, 1963).

28. Luke 2:41–50, on the child Jesus, "sitting in the midst of the doctors, both hearing them, and asking them questions." The theme reappears in chapbook literature in *L'Enfant sage à trois ans*; on this text, see Charles Nisard, *Histoire des livres populaires* (Paris: Amyot, 1854, II, 16–19) and quoted in Geneviève Bollème, *La Bible bleue* (Paris: Flammarion, 1975), 222–227.

29. Kant et al., *Über Theorie und Praxis*, 41. The italics are Kant's.

6. *"Story Time"*

1. See above, Chapter I, p. 8.

2. Jack Goody, "Mémoire et apprentissage dans les sociétés avec ou sans ecriture: la transmission du Bagre," *L'Homme*, 17 (1977), 29–52. See also the same author's *The Domestication of the Savage Mind* (Cambridge: Cambridge University Press, 1977).

3. Marcel Détienne, *Les Jardins d'Adonis* (Paris: Gallimard, 1972); *The Gardens of Adonis*, trans. J. Lloyd (Atlantic Highlands, New Jersey: Humanities Press, 1977); *Dionysos mis à mort* (Paris: Gallimard, 1977); *Dionysos Slain* (Baltimore: Johns Hopkins Press, 1979); cf. Détienne, Vernant et al., *La Cuisine du sacrifice* (Paris: Gallimard, 1979).

4. See *Explorations in the Ethnography of Speaking*, ed. Richard Bauman and Joel Sherzer (Cambridge: Cambridge University Press, 1974); *Studies in Social Interaction*, ed. David Sudnow (London: Collier-Macmillan; New York: The Free Press, 1972).

5. Marcel Détienne and Jean-Pierre Vernant, *Les Ruses de l'intelligence. La Mètis des Grecs* (Paris: Flammarion, 1974).

6. Ibid., 9–10.

7. "Memory," in the ancient sense of the term, which designates a presence to the plurality of times and is thus not limited to the past.

8. Expressions in quotation marks in this section are from Détienne and Vernant, *Les Ruses de l'intelligence*, 23–25.

9. See M. de Certeau, "L'Etrange secret. Manière d'écrire pascalienne," *Rivista di Storia e Letteratura Religiosa*, 13 (1977), 104–126.

10. See Maurice Halbwachs, *Les Cadres sociaux de la mémoire* (La Haye: Mouton, 1975).

11. See Frances A. Yates, *The Art of Memory* (London: Routledge and Kegan Paul, 1966).

12. See below, Part IV, Uses of Language.

13. See below, and also above in Chapter II, p. 22.

14. Françoise Frontisi-Ducroux, *Dédale. Mythologie de l'artisan en Grèce ancienne* (Paris: Maspero, 1975).

15. Aristotle, *Fragmenta*, ed. V. Rose (Stuttgart: Teubner, 1967) fragment 668.

16. Aristotle, *Metaphysics*, A, 2, 982 b18.

7. *"Walking in the City"*

1. See Alain Médam's admirable "New York City," *Les Temps modernes*, August–September 1976, 15–33; and the same author's *New York Terminal* (Paris: Galilée, 1977).

2. See H. Lavedan, *Les Représentations des villes dans l'art du Moyen Age* (Paris: Van Oest, 1942); R. Wittkower, *Architectural Principles in the Age of Humanism* (New York: Norton, 1962); L. Marin, *Utopiques: Jeux d'espaces* (Paris: Minuit, 1973); etc.

3. M. Foucault, "L'Oeil du pouvoir," in J. Bentham, *Le Panoptique* (Paris: Belfond, 1977), 16.

4. D. P. Schreber, *Mémoires d'un névropathe* (Paris: Seuil, 1975), 41, 60, etc.

5. Descartes, in his *Regulae*, had already made the blind man the guarantor of the knowledge of things and places against the illusions and deceptions of vision.

6. M. Merleau-Ponty, *Phénoménologie de la perception* (Paris: Gallimard Tel, 1976), 332–333.

7. See F. Choay, "Figures d'un discours inconnu," *Critique*, April 1973, 293–317.

8. Urbanistic techniques, which classify things spatially, can be related to the tradition of the "art of memory": see Frances A. Yates, *The Art of Memory* (London: Routledge and Kegan Paul, 1966). The ability to produce a spatial organization of knowledge (with "places" assigned to each type of "figure" or "function") develops its procedures on the basis of this "art." It determines utopias and can be recognized even in Bentham's *Panopticon*. Such a form remains stable in spite of the diversity of its contents (past, future, present) and its projects (conserving or creating) relative to changes in the status of knowledge.

9. See André Glucksmann, "Le Totalitarisme en effet," *Traverses*, No. 9, 1977, 34–40.

10. M. Foucault, *Surveiller et punir* (Paris: Gallimard, 1975); *Discipline and Punish*, trans. A. Sheridan (New York: Pantheon, 1977).

11. Ch. Alexander, "La Cité semi-treillis, mais non arbre," *Architecture, Mouvement, Continuité*, 1967.

12. See R. Barthes's remarks in *Architecture d'aujourd'hui*, No. 153, December 1970—January 1971, 11–13: "We speak our city . . . merely by inhabiting it, walking through it, looking at it." Cf. C. Soucy, *L'Image du centre dans quatre romans contemporains* (Paris: CSU, 1971), 6–15.

13. See the numerous studies devoted to the subject since J. Searle's "What is a Speech Act?" in *Philosophy in America*, ed. Max Black (London: Allen & Unwin; Ithaca, N.Y.: Cornell University Press, 1965), 221–239.

14. E. Benveniste, *Problèmes de linguistique générale* (Paris: Gallimard, 1974), II, 79–88, etc.

15. R. Barthes, quoted in C. Soucy, *L'Image du centre*, 10.

16. "*Here* and *now* delimit the spatial and temporal instance coextensive and contemporary with the present instance of discourse containing I": E. Benveniste, *Problèmes de linguistique générale* (Paris: Gallimard, 1966), I, p. 253.

17. R. Jakobson, *Essais de linguistique générale* (Paris: Seuil Points, 1970), p. 217.

18. On modalities, see H. Parret, *La Pragmatique des modalités* (Urbino: Centro di Semiotica, 1975); A. R. White, *Modal Thinking* (Ithaca, N.Y.: Cornell University Press, 1975).

19. See Paul Lemaire's analyses, *Les Signes sauvages. Une Philosophie du langage ordinaire* (Ottawa: Université d'Ottawa et Université Saint-Paul, 1981), in particular the introduction.

20. A. J. Greimas, "Linguistique statistique et linguistique structurale," *Le Français moderne*, October 1962, 245.

21. In a neighboring field, rhetoric and poetics in the gestural language of mute people, I am grateful to E. S. Klima of the University of California, San Diego and U. Bellugi, "Poetry and Song in a Language without Sound," an unpublished paper; see also Klima, "The Linguistic Symbol with and without Sound," in *The Role of Speech in Language*, ed. J. Kavanagh and J. E. Cuttings (Cambridge, Mass.: MIT, 1975).

22. *Conscience de la ville* (Paris: Anthropos, 1977).

23. See Ostrowetsky, "Logiques du lieu," in *Sémiotique de l'espace* (Paris: Denoël-Gonthier Médiations, 1979), 155–173.

24. *Pas à pas. Essai sur le cheminement quotidien en milieu urbain* (Paris: Seuil, 1979).

25. In his analysis of culinary practices, P. Bourdieu regards as decisive not the ingredients but the way in which they are prepared and used: "Le Sens pratique," *Actes de la recherche en sciences sociales*, February 1976, 77.

26. J. Sumpf, *Introduction à la stylistique du français* (Paris: Larousse, 1971), 87.

27. On the "theory of the proper," see J. Derrida, *Marges de la philosophie*

(Paris: Minuit, 1972), 247–324; *Margins of Philosophy*, trans. A. Bass (Chicago: University of Chicago Press, 1982).

28. Augoyard, *Pas à pas*.

29. T. Todorov, "Synecdoques," *Communications*, No. 16 (1970), 30. See also P. Fontanier, *Les Figures du discours* (Paris: Flammarion, 1968), 87–97; J. Dubois et al., *Rhétorique générale* (Paris: Larousse, 1970), 102–112.

30. On this space that practices organize into "islands," see P. Bourdieu, *Esquisse d'une théorie de la pratique* (Genève: Droz, 1972), 215, etc.; "Le Sens pratique," 51–52.

31. See Anne Baldassari and Michel Joubert, *Pratiques relationnelles des enfants à l'espace et institution* (Paris: CRECELE-CORDES, 1976); and by the same authors, "Ce qui se trame," *Parallèles*, No. 1, June 1976.

32. Derrida, *Marges*, 287, on metaphor.

33. Benveniste, *Problèmes*, I, 86–87.

34. For Benveniste, "discourse is language considered as assumed by the person who is speaking and in the condition of intersubjectivity" (ibid., 266).

35. See for example S. Freud, *The Interpretation of Dreams*, trans. J. Strachey (New York: Basic Books, 1955), Chapter VI, § 1–4, on condensation and displacement, "processes of figuration" that are proper to "dreamwork."

36. Ph. Dard, F. Desbons et al., *La Ville, symbolique en souffrance* (Paris: CEP, 1975), 200.

37. See also, for example, the epigraph in Patrick Modiano, *Place de l'Étoile* (Paris: Gallimard, 1968).

38. Joachim du Bellay, *Regrets*, 189.

39. For example, *Sarcelles*, the name of a great urbanistic ambition (near Paris), has taken on a symbolic value for the inhabitants of the town by becoming in the eyes of France as a whole the example of a total failure. This extreme avatar provides its citizens with the "prestige" of an exceptional identity.

40. *Superstare*: "to be above," as something in addition or superfluous.

41. See F. Lugassy, *Contribution à une psychosociologie de l'espace urbain. L'Habitat et la forêt* (Paris: Recherche urbaine, 1970).

42. Dard, Desbons et al., *La Ville, symbolique en souffrance*.

43. Ibid., 174, 206.

44. C. Lévi-Strauss, *Tristes tropiques* (Paris: Plon, 1955), 434–436; *Tristes tropiques*, trans. J. Russell (New York: Criterion, 1962).

45. One could say the same about the photos brought back from trips, substituted for and turned into legends about the starting place.

46. Terms whose relationships are not thought but postulated as necessary can be said to be symbolic. On this definition of symbolism as a cognitive mechanism characterized by a "deficit" of thinking, see Dan Sperber, *Le Symbolisme en général* (Paris: Hermann, 1974); *Rethinking Symbolism*, trans. A. L. Morton (Cambridge: Cambridge University Press, 1975).

47. F. Ponge, *La Promenade dans nos serres* (Paris: Gallimard, 1967).

48. A woman living in the Croix-Rousse quarter in Lyon (interview by Pierre Mayol): see *L'Invention du quotidien*, II, *Habiter, cuisiner* (Paris: UGE 10/18, 1980).

49. See *Le Monde* for May 4, 1977.

50. See note 48.

51. See the two analyses provided by Freud in *The Interpretation of Dreams* and *Beyond the Pleasure Principle*, trans. J. Strachey (New York: Liveright, 1980); and also Sami-Ali, *L'Espace imaginaire* (Paris: Gallimard, 1974), 42-64.

52. J. Lacan, "Le Stade du miroir," *Écrits* (Paris: Seuil, 1966), 93-100; "The Mirror Stage," in *Écrits: A Selection*, trans. A. Sheridan (New York: Norton, 1977).

53. S. Freud, *Inhibitions, Symptoms and Anxiety* (New York: Norton, 1977).

54. V. Kandinsky, *Du spirituel dans l'art* (Paris: Denoël, 1969), 57.

9. *"Spatial Stories"*

1. John Lyons, *Semantics* (Cambridge: Cambridge University Press, 1977), II, 475-481, 690-703.

2. George A. Miller and Philip N. Johnson-Laird, *Language and Perception* (Cambridge, Mass.: Harvard University Press, 1976).

3. See below, p. 118.

4. Albert E. Scheflen and Norman Ashcraft, *Human Territories. How we Behave in Space-Time* (Englewood Cliffs, N.J.: Prentice-Hall, 1976).

5. E. A. Schegloff, "Notes on a Conversational Practice: Formulating Place," in *Studies in Social Interaction*, ed. David Sudnow (New York: The Free Press, 1972), pp. 75-119.

6. See, for example, École de Tartu, *Travaux sur les systèmes de signes*, ed. Y. M. Lotman and B. A. Ouspenski (Paris: PUF; Bruxelles: Complexe, 1976), 18-39, 77-93, etc.; Iouri Lotman, *La Structure du texte artistique* (Paris: Gallimard, 1973), 309, etc; Jüri Lotman, *The Structure of the Artistic Text*, trans. R. Vroon (Ann Arbor: Department of Slavic Languages and Literatures, The University of Michigan, 1977); B. A. Uspenskii, *A Poetics of Composition*, trans. V. Zavarin and S. Witting (Berkeley: University of California Press, 1973).

7. M. Merleau-Ponty, *Phénoménologie de la perception* (Paris: Gallimard Tel, 1976), 324-344.

8. Charlotte Linde and William Labov, "Spatial Networks as a Site for the Study of Language and Thought," *Language*, 51 (1975), 924-939. On the relation between practice (*le faire*) and space, see also Groupe 107 (M. Hammad et al.), *Sémiotique de l'espace* (Paris: DGRST, 1973), 28.

9. See, for example, Catherine Bidou and Francis Ho Tham Kouie, *Le Vécu des habitants dans leur logement à travers soixante entretiens libres* (Paris: CEREBE, 1974); Alain Médam and Jean-François Augoyard, *Situations d'habitat et façons d'habiter* (Paris: ESA, 1976); etc.

10. See George H. T. Kimble, *Geography in the Middle Ages* (London: Methuen, 1938); etc.

11. Roland Barthes, *L'Empire des signes* (Genève: Skira, 1970), pp. 47-51.

12. The map is reproduced and analyzed by Pierre Janet, *L'Evolution de la mémoire et la notion du temps* (Paris: Chahine, 1928), 284-287. The original is

in Cuauhtinchan (Puebla, Mexico).

13. See, for example, Louis Marin, *Utopiques: Jeux d'espaces* (Paris: Minuit, 1973), 257–290, on the relation between figures (a "discourse-tour") and the map (a "system-text") in three representations of the city in the seventeenth century: a relation between a "narrative" and a "geometric."

14. Quoted in Bidou and Ho Tham Kouie, *Le Vécu des habitants*, 55.

15. Ibid., 57 and 59.

16. Janet, *L'Evolution de la mémoire*, particularly the lectures on "the procedures of narrative" and "fabrication" (249–294). Médam and Augoyard have used this unit to define the subject matter of their investigation (*Situations d'habitat*, 90–95).

17. Lotman, in École de Tartu, *Travaux sur les systèmes de signes*, 89.

18. Georges Dumézil, *Idées romaines* (Paris: Gallimard, 1969), 61–78, on "Ius fetiale."

19. Ibid.

20. Ibid., 31–45.

21. Miller and Johnson-Laird, *Language and Perception*, 57–66, 385–390, 564, etc.

22. Christian Morgenstern, "Der Lattenzaun" (the picket fence), in *Gesammelte Werke* (München: Piper, 1965), 229.

23. See Nicole Brunet, "Un Pont vers l'acculturation. Ile de Noirmoutiers," Diss. (DEA Ethnologie) Université de Paris VII, 1979.

24. See M. de Certeau, "Délires et délices de Jérôme Bosch," *Traverses*, No. 5–6 (1976), 37–54.

25. See Françoise Frontisi-Ducroux, *Dédale. Mythologie de l'artisan en Grèce ancienne* (Paris: Maspero, 1975), 104, 100–101, 117, etc., on the mobility of these rigid statues.

26. Jules Michelet, *La Sorcière* (Paris: Calmann-Lévy, n.d.), 23–24.

27. See, for example, on the subject of this ambiguity, Emmanuel Le Roy Ladurie, *Le Carnaval de Romans* (Paris: Gallimard, 1979); *The Carnival at Romans*, trans. M. Fenney (New York: George Braziller, 1979).

28. See Paolo Fabbri, "Considérations sur la proxémique," *Langages*, No. 10 (June 1968), 65–75. E. T. Hall defined proxemics as "the study of how man unconsciously structures spaces—the distance between men in the conduct of daily transactions, the organization of space in his houses and buildings, and ultimately the lay out of his towns" ("Proxemics: the Study of Man's Spatial Relations," in *Man's Image in Medicine and Anthropology*, ed. I. Gladston (New York: International Universities Press, 1963)).

10. *"The Scriptural Economy"*

1. Translated from Grundtvig, *Budstikke i Høinorden* (1864), 31 X 527; text quoted by Erica Simon, *Réveil national et culture populaire en Scandinavie. La genèse de la Højskole nordique, 1844–1878* (Copenhague, 1960), 59.

2. Simon, *Réveil national et culture populaire*, 54–59.

3. J. Derrida, *Positions* (Paris: Minuit, 1972), p. 41; *Positions*, trans. A. Bass (Chicago: University of Chicago Press, 1981).

4. Karl Marx, "1844 Manuscripts," in Marx and Engels, *Werke* (Berlin: Dietz, 1961), I, 542–544.

5. See M. de Certeau et al., *Une Politique de la langue* (Paris: Gallimard, 1975).

6. Shakespeare, *The Comedy of Errors*, III, i, 13.

7. See Lucette Finas, *La Crue* (Paris: Gallimard, 1972), preface, on the reading that is an inscription of the text on the body.

8. On this history, A. Macfarlane, *The Origins of English Individualism* (Oxford: Blackwell, 1978); and earlier, C. B. Macpherson, *The Political Theory of Possessive Individualism. Hobbes to Locke* (Oxford: Oxford University Press, 1964).

9. See especially Charles Webster, *The Great Instauration. Science, Medicine and Reform, 1626–1660* (New York: Holmes & Meier, 1975), 246–323.

10. Jean-Pierre Peter, "Le Corps du délit," *Nouvelle revue de psychanalyse*, No. 3 (1971), 71–108: the three successive figures of the body distinguished by Peter could be related to the three paradigms from physics of which they are variants and applications, namely, the physics of impacts (seventeenth century), the physics of action at a distance (eighteenth century) and thermodynamics (nineteenth century).

11. Webster, *The Great Instauration*, especially his "Conclusions," 484–520.

12. On this new power of writing over history, see M. de Certeau, *L'Ecriture de l'histoire*, 2nd ed. (Paris: Gallimard, 1978).

13. See Jean Baudrillard, *L'Echange symbolique et la mort* (Paris: Gallimard, 1976), 75–95; and the essays in *Traverses*, No. 10, February 1978, a special issue entitled *Le Simulacre*.

14. They oscillate in this way, displayed on glossy paper, in the excellent book by André Velter and Marie-José Lamothe, *Les Outils du corps*, photos by Jean Marquis (Paris: Hier et Demain, 1978). But they are also found in technical catalogs, for instance *Chirurgie orthopédique* (Paris: Chevalier Frères, 5–7, place de l'Odéon).

15. A reference to Michel Foucault, *Surveiller et punir* (Paris: Gallimard, 1975), *Discipline and Punish*, trans. A. Sheridan (New York: Pantheon, 1977), whose analyses open a vast field to be explored and inventoried, extending even beyond the panoptical mechanisms.

16. It was one of Durkheim's ideas that the social code inscribes itself on an individual nature and so mutilates it. The first form of writing would thus be *mutilation*, which gives it an emblematic value. See Emile Durkheim, *Les Formes elémentaires de la vie religieuse* (Paris: PUF, 1968); *The Elementary Forms of the Religious Life*, trans. J. W. Swain (New York: Free Press, 1972).

17. See Pierre Legendre, *L'Amour du censeur* (Paris: Seuil, 1974).

18. Michel Carrouges, *Les Machines célibataires* (Arcanes, 1954) and the revised and augmented edition (1975); and *Junggesellen Maschinen/ Les Machines célibataires*, ed. Jean Clair and Harold Szeemann (Venice: Alfieri, 1975).

19. See *The Interpretation of Dreams* (*Die Traumdeutung*), Chapter VII, on

the "psychischen Apparat." The expression "theoretische Fiktion" refers particularly to "the fiction of a primitive psychical apparatus."

20. See Katherine S. Dreier and Matta Echaurren, "Duchamp's Glass 'La Mariée mise à nu par ses célibataires, même'. An Analytical Reflection," (1944) in *Selected Publications*, III: *Monographs and Brochure* (New York: Arno Press, 1972).

21. Alfred Jarry, *Les Jours et les nuits* (1897).

22. Jean-Claude Milner, *L'Amour de la langue* (Paris: Seuil, 1978), 98–112.

23. Michel Sanouillet, in Marcel Duchamp, *Duchamp du signe. Ecrits*, ed. M. Sanouillet (Paris: Flammarion, 1975), 16.

24. See Jean-François Lyotard, *Les Transformateurs Duchamp* (Paris: Galilée, 1977), 33–40.

11. *"Quotations of Voices"*

1. "Vox" (in praise of the voice) in the collecion of poems entitled *Ingenii Familia*, which includes "Ingenium," "Liber," "Vox," "Memoria," and "Oblivio," in Gabriel Cossart, *Orationes et Carmina* (Paris: Cramoisy, 1675), 234.

2. Daniel Defoe, *Robinson Crusoe* (Harmondsworth: Penguin, 1975), 162.

3. On this aspect of myth, see Claude Rabant, "Le Mythe à l'avenir (re)commence," *Esprit*, April 1971, 631–643.

4. See above, Chapter X, p. 133.

5. See Michel de Certeau, *L'Ecriture de l'histoire*, 2nd ed. (Paris: Gallimard, 1978), 197–203.

6. See M. de Certeau et al., *Une politique de la langue* (Paris: Gallimard, 1975), 82–98, 110–121.

7. F. de Saussure, *Cours de linguistique générale*, ed. Tullio de Mauro (Paris: Payot, 1974), 30.

8. Tullio de Mauro's note, ibid., 420.

9. Ibid., p. 138–139; and also Cl. Haroche et al., "La Sémantique et la coupure saussurienne: Langue, langage, discours," *Langages*, No. 24 (1971), 93–106.

10. See D. Bertaux, *Histoires de vies ou récits des pratiques? Méthodologies de l'approche biographique en sociologie* (Paris: CORDES, 1976).

11. Louis Hjelmslev, *Prolégomènes à une théorie du langage* (Paris: Minuit, 1968), 139–142; *Prolegomena to a Theory of Language*, trans. F. J. Whitfield (Madison: University of Wisconsin Press, 1968).

12. Marguerite Duras, *Nathalie Granger* (Paris: Gallimard, 1973), 105; and the interview by Benoît Jacquot, in *Art Press*, October 1973.

13. Pierre Jakez Helias, *Le Cheval d'orgueil* (Paris: Plon, 1975), 41 and 27.

14. Ibid., 54.

15. Ibid., 55.

16. Ibid., 69–75.

12. *"Reading as Poaching"*

1. Alvin Toffler, *The Culture Consumers* (Baltimore: Penguin, 1965), 33–52, on the basis of Emanuel Demby's research.

2. *Pratiques culturelles des Français* (Paris: Secrétariat d'Etat à la Culture, S. E. R., 1974, 2 vols.

3. According to a survey by Louis–Harris (September–October 1978), the number of readers in France grew 17% over the past twenty years: there is the same percentage of people who read a great deal (22%), but the percentage of people who read a little or a moderate amount has increased. See Janick Jossin, in *L'Express* for 11 November 1978, 151–162.

4. See Jean Ehrard, *L'Idée de nature en France pendant la première moitié du XVIIIe siècle* (Paris: SEPVEN, 1963), 753–767.

5. François Furet and Jacques Ozouf, *Lire et écrire. L'Alphabétisation des Français de Calvin à Jules Ferry* (Paris: Minuit, 1977), I, 349–369, 199–228.

6. See for example J. Mehler and G. Noizet, *Textes pour une psycholinguistique* (La Haye: Mouton, 1974); and also Jean Hébrard, "Ecole et alphabétisation au XIXe siècle," Colloque "Lire et écrire," MSH, Paris, June 1979.

7. Furet and Ozouf, *Lire et écrire*, 213.

8. Michel Charles, *Rhétorique de la lecture* (Paris: Seuil, 1977), 83.

9. Jorge Luis Borges, quoted by Gérard Genette, *Figures* (Paris: Seuil, 1966), 123.

10. Charles, *Rhétorique de la lecture*, 61.

11. As is well known, "lector" was, in the Middle Ages, the title of a kind of University Professor.

12. See especially *Recherches actuelles sur l'enseignement de la lecture*, ed. Alain Bentolila (Paris: Retz CEPL, 1976); Jean Foucambert and J. André, *La Manière d'être lecteur. Apprentissage et enseignement de la lecture, de la maternelle au CM2* (Paris: SERMAP OCDL, 1976); Laurence Lentin, *Du parler au lire. Interaction entre l'adulte et l'enfant* (Paris: ESF, 1977); etc. To these should be added at least a portion of the abundant American literature: Jeanne Sternlicht Chall, *Learning to Read, the Great Debate . . . 1910–1965* (New York: McGraw-Hill, 1967); Dolores Durkin, *Teaching Them to Read* (Boston: Allyn & Bacon, 1970); Eleanor Jack Gibson and Harry Levin, *The Psychology of Reading* (Cambridge, Mass.: MIT, 1975); Milfred Robeck and John A. R. Wilson, *Psychology of Reading: Foundations of Instruction* (New York: John Wiley, 1973); *Reading Disabilities. An International Perspective*, ed. Lester and Muriel Tarnopol (Baltimore: University Park Press, 1976); etc., along with three important journals: *Journal of Reading*, since 1957 (Purdue University, Department of English), *The Reading Teacher*, since 1953 (Chicago International Reading Association), *Reading Research Quarterly*, since 1965 (Newark, Delaware, International Reading Association).

13. See the bibliography in Furet and Ozouf, *Lire et écrire*, II, 358–372, to which we can add Mitford McLeod Mathews, *Teaching to Read, Historically Considered* (Chicago: University of Chicago Press, 1966). Jack Goody's studies

(*Literacy in a Traditional Society* [Cambridge: Cambridge University Press, 1968] and *The Domestication of the Savage Mind* [Cambridge: Cambridge University Press, 1977], etc.) open several paths toward an ethnohistorical analysis.

14. In addition to statistical investigations, see J. Charpentreau et al., *Le Livre et la lecture en France* (Paris: Editions ouvrières, 1968).

15. Roland Barthes, of course: *Le Plaisir du texte* (Paris: Seuil, 1973), *The Pleasure of Text*, trans. R. Miller (New York: Hill and Wang, 1975), and "Sur la Lecture," *Le Français aujourd'hui*, No. 32 (January 1976), pp. 11–18. See, somewhat at random, in addition to the works already cited, Tony Duvert, "La Lecture introuvable," *Minuit*, No. 1 (November 1972), 2–21; O. Mannoni, *Clefs pour l'imaginaire* (Paris: Seuil, 1969), 202–217; Michel Mougenot, "Lecture/écriture," *Le Français aujourd'hui*, No. 30 (May 1975); Victor N. Smirnoff, "L'Oeuvre lue," *Nouvelle revue de psychanalyse*, No. 1 (1970), 49–57; Tzvetan Todorov, *Poétique de la prose* (Paris: Seuil, 1971), 241 et seq.; Jean Verrier, "La Ficelle," *Poétique*, No. 30 (April 1977); *Littérature*, No. 7 (October 1972); *Esprit*, December 1974, and January 1976; etc.

16. See, for example, Michel Charles' "propositions" in his *Rhétorique de la lecture*.

17. Descartes, *Principia*, IV, 205.

18. Pierre Kuentz, "Le tête à texte," *Esprit*, December 1974, 946–962, and "L'Envers du texte," *Littérature*, No. 7 (October 1972).

19. Some documents, unfortunately all too rare, shed light on the autonomy of the trajectories, inerpretations, and convictions of Catholic readers of the Bible. See, on the subject of his "farmer" father, Rétif de la Bretonne, *La Vie de mon père* (1778) (Paris: Garnier, 1970), 29, 131–132, etc.

20. Guy Rosolato, *Essais sur le symbolique* (Paris: Gallimard, 1969), 288.

21. Theresa de Avila considered reading to be a form of prayer, the discovery of another space in which desire could be articulated. Countless other authors of spiritual works think the same, and so do children.

22. Marguerite Duras, *Le Camion* (Paris: Minuit, 1977), and "Entretien à Michèle Porte," quoted in *Sorcières*, No. 11 (January 1978), 47.

23. Jacques Sojcher, "Le Professeur de philosophie," *Revue de l'Université de Bruxelles*, No. 3–4 (1976), 428–429.

24. Barthes, *Le Plaisir du texte*, 58.

25. Claude Lévi-Strauss, *La Pensée sauvage* (Paris: Plon, 1962), 3–47; *The Savage Mind* (Chicago: University of Chicago Press, 1966). In the reader's "*bricolage*," the elements that are re-employed, all being drawn from official and accepted bodies of material, can cause one to believe that there is nothing new in reading.

26. See in particular the works of Hans Ulrich Gumbrecht ("Die Dramenschliessende Sprachhandlung im Aristotelischen Theater und ihre Problematisierung bei Marivaux") and of Karlheinz Stierle ("Das Liebesgeständnis in Racines *Phèdre* und das Verhältnis von (Sprach-)Handlung und Tat"), in *Poetica* (Bochum), 1976; etc.

27. Georges Perec had discussed this very well in "Lire: Esquisse sociophysiologique," *Esprit*, January 1976, 9–20.

28. It is nonetheless known that the muscles that contract the vocal cords and constrict the glottis remain active in reading.

29. See François Richaudeau, *La Lisibilité* (Paris: Retz CEPL, 1969); or Georges Rémond, "Apprendre la lecture silencieuse à l'ecole primaire," in Bentolila, *La manière d'être lecteur*, 147–161.

30. Barthes, "Sur la lecture," 15–16.

13. *"Believing and Making People Believe"*

1. Jorge Luis Borges and Adolfo Bioy Casares, *Crónicas de Bustos Domecq; Chronicles of Bustos Domecq*, trans N. T. di Giovanni (New York: Dutton, 1976), in particular the chapter "Esse est percipi" ("To exist is to be seen").

2. See W. V. Quine and J. S. Ullian's remarks in *The Web of Belief* (New York: Random House, 1970), 4–6.

3. On this subject, see Jaakko Hintikka, *Knowledge and Belief. An Introduction to the Logic of the Two Notions* (Ithaca, N.Y.: Cornell University Press, 1969); Rodney Needham, *Belief, Language and Experience* (Oxford: Blackwell, 1972); Ernest Gellner, *Legitimation of Belief* (Cambridge: Cambridge University Press, 1974); John M. Vickers, *Belief and Probability* (Dordrecht: Reidel, 1976); *Languages*, No. 43 (September 1976); etc.

4. See, for example, R. S. Peters and Peter Winch, "Authority," in *Political Philosophy*, ed. Anthony Quinton (Oxford: Oxford University Press, 1973), 83–111.

5. Pierre Legendre, *L'Amour du censeur* (Paris: Seuil, 1974), 28.

6. See, for example, Dale Carnegie, *Public Speaking and Influencing Men in Business* (New York: Association Press, 1931), and especially Martin Fishbein and Icek Ajzen, *Belief, Attitude, Intention and Behavior* (Reading, Mass.: Addison-Wesley, 1975).

7. See Michel Foucault, *Surveiller et punir* (Paris:Gallimard, 1975); *Discipline and Punish*, trans. A. Sheridan (New York: Pantheon, 1977); etc.

8. Kamata Satoshi, *Toyota, l'usine du désespoir* (Paris: Editions ouvrières, 1976): a still "paleotechnical" system in which it is a question of regulating all activities, and not yet of attaching them by means of values whose goal is to produce believers. See Miklos Haraszti, *Salaire aux pièces* (Paris: Seuil, 1976).

9. In local administration and especially in the urban sub-system, as Pierre Grémion stated it, there is no longer any legitimating mechanism: *Le Pouvoir périphérique. Bureaucrates et notables dans le système politique français* (Paris: Seuil, 1976), 416 et seq.

10. See M. de Certeau, *La Culture au pluriel* (Paris: UGE 10/18, 1974), 11–34. From a logical point of view, it is precisely to these displacements of belief from statement to statement that Quine and Ullian devote their first analyses (*The Web of Belief*, 8–9).

11. To the analysis of journeys that transport a myth from one tribe to another and "extenuate" it gradually into a legendary tradition, an epic elaboration or a political ideology (see Lévi-Strauss, *Anthropologie structurale deux* [Paris: Plon, 1973], pp. 301–315), we must thus add the analysis of these slow disinvestments, through which belief withdraws from a myth.

12. See Georges Duby, *Guerriers et paysans* (Paris: Gallimard, 1976), 184 et seq.; *The Early Growth of the European Economy: Warriors and Peasants*, trans. H. S. Clarke (Ithaca: Cornell University Press, 1974).

13. See M. de Certeau, *L'Ecriture de l'histoire*, 152–212.

14. Jean-Jacques Rousseau, *Le Contrat social*, IV, 8.

15. See Robert N. Bellah, *Beyond Belief. Essays on Religion in a Post-traditional World* (New York: Harper & Row, 1970), 168–189, on the "civil religion" in the United States.

16. Maurice Agulhon has demonstrated this by analyzing the persistence of a "form" of Southern French sociality in spite of the variability of its contents, successively devout (sixteenth-seventeenth centuries), Masonic (eighteenth century) and socialist (nineteenth century): *Pénitents et Francs-Maçons de l'ancienne Provence* (Paris: PUF, 1968).

17. A reproach that could be addressed to Yvon Bourdet's subtle analyses, which are excessively centered on the psychology or the ethics of militancy, a figure isolated from the historical place in which it occurs: *Qu'est-ce qui fait courir les militants?* (Paris: Stock, 1976).

18. Daniel Mothé correctly notes that the militant is pessimistic about the present and optimistic about the future: *Le Métier de militant* (Paris: Seuil, 1973).

19. See particularly the numerous studies by Henri Desroche.

20. "Signify," in the sense of the Heraclitean fragment: "The oracle at Delphi does not speak, it does not dissimulate, it signifies" (Diels, fragment 93).

21. See Erwin Panofsky, *La Perspective comme forme symbolique* (Paris: Minuit, 1975); E. H. Gombrich, *Art and Illusion*, 4th ed. (London: Phaidon, 1972); R. Klein, *La Forme et l'Intelligible* (Paris: Gallimard, 1970).

22. On simulacrum, see references in Chapter X, note 13, p. 223.

23. See O. Mannoni, *Clefs pour l'imaginaire ou l'autre scène* (Paris: Seuil, 1969), 9–33: "Je sais bien mais quand même" (on belief).

24. M. de Certeau, "History: Science and Fiction," in *Social Science as Moral Inquiry*, ed. N. Haan et al. (New York: Columbia University Press, 1983), 125–152.

14. *"The Unnamable"*

1. Maurice Berger and Françoise Hortala, *Mourir à l'hôpital* (Paris: Centurion, 1974), 155.

2. See M. de Certeau, *L'Absent de l'histoire* (Paris: Mame, 1973).

3. See Guy Le Gaufey, "La Douleur mélancolique, la mort impossible et le réel," *Lettres de l'école freudienne*, No. 13 (December 1974), 38–49.

4. See Serge Leclaire, *Démasquer le réel* (Paris: Seuil, 1971), 121–146.

5. James Joyce, *Giacomo Joyce* (New York: Viking, 1959), XIV.

6. On this topological structure of "*two* in the *same* place," the structure of the split subject, see M. de Certeau, *L'Ecriture de l'histoire*, 2nd ed. (Paris: Gallimard, 1978), 337–352.

7. François Jacob, *La Logique du vivant* (Paris: Gallimard, 1970), 331–332.

8. Robert Jay Lifton, *Death in Life. The Survivors of Hiroshima* (New York, 1968), quoted by A. Alvarez, *Le Dieu sauvage. Essai sur le suicide* (Paris: Mercure de France, 1972), 281; *The Savage God* (New York: Random House, 1972).

Indeterminate

1. Michel Serres, *Hermès II. L'Interférence* (Paris: Minuit, 1972), 12–13.

2. Manuel Janco and Daniel Furjot, *Informatique et capitalisme* (Paris: Maspero, 1972), 117–127.

3. Gerald Holton, *Thematic Origins of Scientific Thought. Kepler to Einstein* (Cambridge, Mass.: Harvard University Press, 1974), especially 91–161, on the imaginary presuppositions of science and the "complementarity" that articulates logical rigor on imaginary structures. See also, on the role of metaphor in scientific reasoning, Mary Hesse, *The Structure of Scientific Interference* (London: Macmillan, 1974), the first and last chapters.

4. For example, on the actual itineraries that bring a project to a decision, one would have to have many edifying (!) "stories" similar to those that Lucien Sfez published as an addendum, unfortunately in summary form, in his *Critique de la décision* (Paris: Armand Colin, 1973), 353–356. But can that be admitted?

5. To "blasphemy" (which "lets out" the secret and "betrays" more than it reveals), Benveniste opposes "euphemism" ("Jiminy Christmas" for "Jesus Christ") which "makes allusion to a linguistic profanation without actually carrying it out" (*Problèmes de linguistique générale* (Paris: Gallimard, 1974), II, 254–257). A welcome concept.

6. See Ernest Berringer's graffiti in New York.

7. See M. de Certeau, *L'Ecriture de l'histoire*, 2nd ed. (Paris: Gallimard, 1978), 312–358.

8. Terms employed by Jean-Claude Perrot in his masterful study *Genèse d'une ville moderne. Caen au XVIIIe siècle* (Paris: Mouton, 1975), 54–98, to designate the relation of "theories" about urban evolution to the actual development.

9. See Harald Weinrich, *Le Temps* (Paris: Seuil, 1973), 225–258; *Tempus, Besprochene und erzählte Welt* (Stuttgart: Kohlhammer, 1971).